The Rise of Blockchains

Disrupting Economies and Transforming Societies

Nir Kshetri

Professor of Business, University of North Carolina-Greensboro, USA

Edward Elgar
PUBLISHING

Cheltenham, UK • Northampton, MA, USA

Published by
Edward Elgar Publishing Limited
The Lypiatts
15 Lansdown Road
Cheltenham
Glos GL50 2JA
UK

Edward Elgar Publishing, Inc.
William Pratt House
9 Dewey Court
Northampton
Massachusetts 01060
USA

Paperback edition 2023

A catalogue record for this book
is available from the British Library

Library of Congress Control Number: 2022941188

This book is available electronically in the **Elgar**online
Business subject collection
http://dx.doi.org/10.4337/9781802208177

Printed on elemental chlorine free (ECF)
recycled paper containing 30% Post-Consumer Waste

ISBN 978 1 80220 816 0 (cased)
ISBN 978 1 80220 817 7 (eBook)
ISBN 978 1 0353 2528 3 (paperback)

Printed and bound in the USA

Contents

Figures

Tables

In Focus boxes

Acronyms and abbreviations

4IR	Fourth Industrial Revolution
4R	Fourth Revolution
AAIS	American Association of Insurance Services
ACORD	Association for Cooperative Operations Research and Development
ADB	Asian Development Bank
Agtech	Agriculture Technology
AI	Artificial Intelligence
AIA	Agro Industria Associades
AML	Anti-money Laundering
AP	Associated Press
API	Application Programming Interface
AR	Augmented Reality
ASCAP	American Society of Composers, Authors, and Publishers
ASM	Artisanal and Small-Scale Mining
AWS	Amazon Web Services
AXS	Axie Infinity Shards
B$	Bahamian Dollar
B2B	Business-to-Business
B2C	Business-to-Customer
BaaS	Blockchain-As-A-Service
BIS	Bank for International Settlements
BSN	Blockchain Service Network
CBB	Central Bank of the Bahamas
CBDC	Central Bank Digital Currency
CCAF	Cambridge Centre for Alternative Finance
CFT	Combating the Financing of Terrorism

CNES	Centre National d'Études Spatiales
COVID-19	Coronavirus Disease 2019
CQL	Carrefour Quality Line
CSAIL	Computer Science and Artificial Intelligence Laboratory
CSP	Cloud Services Provider
DAO	Decentralized Autonomous Organization
DApps	Decentralized Applications
DAU	Daily Active Users
DCEP	Digital Currency Electronic Payment
DDoS	Distributed Denial of Service
DeFi	Decentralized Finance
DLT	Distributed Ledger Technology
DNS	Domain Name System
DRC	Democratic Republic of Congo
DUI	Unique Identity Document
DVR	Digital Video Recorder
EC	European Commission
eCNY	Digital Yuan
EFTG	European Financial Transparency Gateway
EHR	Electronic Health Records
EPA	Environmental Protection Agency
ESAP	European Single Access Point
ESMA	European Securities and Markets Authority
ETH	Ether
EU	European Union
EUMETSAT	European Organization for the Exploitation of Meteorological Satellites
FATF	Financial Action Task Force
FBSC	Food and Beverage Supply Chains
FDA	Food and Drug Administration
FinTech	Financial Technology
GBT	Global Batch Traceability

GCal	Gem Certification & Assurance Lab
GDP	Gross Domestic Product
GDPR	General Data Protection Regulations
GEN	Global Entrepreneurship Network
GIA	Gemological Institute of America
GPM	Global Precipitation Measurement
GPS	Global Positioning System
GPT	General Purpose Technology
GSBN	Global Shipping Business Network
GSER	Global Startup Ecosystem Report
GSOD	Global Surface Summary of the Day
HIPPA	Health Insurance Portability and Accountability Act
ICO	Initial Coin Offering
ICT	Information and Communications Technology
ID4D	Identification for Development
IoT	Internet of Things
IP	Internet Protocol
IPFS	Interplanetary File Storage System
ISRC	International Standard Recording Codes
ISRO	Indian Space Research Organization
ISWC	International Standard Work Codes
IT	Information Technology
JAXA	Japan Aerospace Exploration Agency
KP	Kimberley Process
KSI	Keyless Signature Infrastructure
KYC	Know Your Customer
LC	Letter of Credit
LDCs	Least Developed Countries
LSCM	Logistics and Supply Chain Management
MFI	Microfinance Institution
ML	Machine Learning
MNC	Multi-National Companies

MoreVP	More Viable Plasma
Multisig	Multi-signature
NASA	National Aeronautics and Space Administration
NDIP	National Digital Identity Platform
NFC	Near-Field-Communication
NFT	Non-Fungible Token
NGO	Non-governmental organization
NIFA	China's National Internet Finance Association
NIRS	Near-Infrared Reflectance Spectroscopy
NOAA	National Oceanic and Atmospheric Administration
NUCAFE	National Union of Coffee Agribusinesses and Farm Enterprises
OBP	Oracle's blockchain platform
OEM	Original Equipment Manufacturer
OFW	Filipino overseas worker
OpenIDL	Open Insurance Data Link
OSS	Open Source Software
OTC	Over-the-Counter
P2E	Play-to-Earn
P2P	Peer-To-Peer
PHP	Philippine Peso
PoA	Proof of Authority
PoC	Proof of Concept
PoS	Proof of Stake
PoW	Proof of Work
PPB	Parts Per Billion
PPP	Public–Private Partnership
PRO	Public Rights Organization
PRS	Paul Reed Smith
QR	Quick Response
RFID	Radio Frequency Identification
ROFR	Right of first refusal
ROI	Return on Investment

SaaS	Software-as-a-Service
SACEM	Société des auteurs, compositeurs et éditeurs de musique
SAP	Systems, Applications & Products in Data Processing
SCF	Supply Chain Finance
SCM	Supply Chain Management
SDK	Software Development Kits
SLA	Service Level Agreement
SLP	Smooth Love Potion
SMBC	Sumitomo Mitsui Financial Group
SMEs	Small and Medium-Sized Enterprises
TaaS	Traceability-as-a-Service
TCR	Token Curated Registry
TF	Trade Finance
TPS	Transactions Per Second
TQM	Total Quality Management
TVL	total value locked
TWh	Terawatt-hours
UAW	Unique Active Wallets
UNCDF	U.N. Capital Development Fund
UNDF	United Nations Development Fund
UNODC	United Nations Office on Drugs and Crime
UCP	Universal Product Code
USPTO	US Patent and Trademark Office
VC	Venture Capital
VoIP	Voice over Internet Protocol
WFP	World Food Programme
WHO	World Health Organization
WSSC	Washington Suburban Sanitary Commission
XLM	Stellar Lumens

PART I

Blockchain and organizational transformation

1. Blockchain basic: Definitions, key concepts and characteristics

1.1   INTRODUCTION

Blockchain has been among the most talked-about technologies over the last several years. This technology is viewed as 'the biggest disruptor to industries since the introduction of the Internet'[1] and a computing mega-trend with a potential to shape the world in the near future.[2]

The demand for blockchain–related products is growing rapidly. The global blockchain market was estimated at US$ 5.3 billion in 2021, which is expected to reach US$ 34 billion by 2026.[3]

Investments in blockchain projects have also been increasing rapidly. From 2012 to 2020, over 3,000 blockchain venture capital (VC) deals were closed worldwide. More than US$ 16 billion was invested by 928 different angel investors, venture capitalists, business incubators and corporates.[4] In the first 11 months of 2021, global VC funding in blockchain reached US$ 30 billion across 1,278 deals[5] compared to US$ 3.1 billion in the full year 2020.[6]

---

[1]   PWCHK.com 2016 'Blockchain the Biggest Disruptor to Industries Since the Introduction of the Internet – PwC' http://www.pwchk.com/home/eng/pr_070716 .html.

[2]   WEF [World Economic Forum] 2015 'Deep Shift Technology Tipping Points and Societal Impact Survey Report' http://www3.weforum.org/docs/WEF_GAC15 _Technological_Tipping_Points_report_2015.pdf.

[3]   L Wood (2021) *The Worldwide Blockchain Industry Is Expected to Reach $34 Billion by 2026 – ResearchAndMarkets.com.* [online] Available at: https:// www.businesswire.com/news/home/20211014005790/en/The-Worldwide-Blockchain -Industry-is-Expected-to-Reach-34-Billion-by-2026---ResearchAndMarkets.com.

[4]   Cointelegraph (April 6, 2021) *Venture Capitalists Invest over $16B in Blockchain Equity since 2012.* [online] Available at: https://cointelegraph.com/news/venture -capitalists-invest-over-16b-in-blockchain-equity-since-2012.

[5]   Rahul Rai (Jan 2, 2022) 'An Overview of Web3 Venture Capital Activity in 2021' https://www.forbes.com/sites/rahulrai/2022/01/02/an-overview-of-web3 -venture-capital-activity-in-2021/?sh=631611601f16.

[6]   M Bellusci (2021) *VCs Invested Record $6.5B in Crypto, Blockchain in Q3: CB Insights.* [online] www.coindesk.com. Available at: https://www.coindesk.com/ business/2021/11/02/vcs-invested-record-65b-in-crypto-blockchain-in-q3-cb-insights/.

According to the Global Startup Ecosystem Report (GSER) 2021 from Startup Genome and the Global Entrepreneurship Network (GEN), blockchain-based businesses account for 10 per cent of start-ups worldwide.[7] The report also found that blockchain was the second-fastest-growing sub-sector in terms of early-stage funding from 2014 to 2020. There was a 121 per cent growth in funding in blockchain during this period. Agriculture technology (Agtech) and new food, which consist of technologies that increase the efficiency of agriculture-related practices, was the only sub-sector that grew faster than blockchain with a 128 per cent increase in such funding.[8]

Cryptocurrencies that use blockchain to record and secure transactions have become increasingly popular (Figure 1.1 below). As of November 18, 2021, online cryptocurrency site CoinMarketCap had listed 7,551 different cryptocurrencies with the total market value of over US$ 2.59 trillion (https:// coinmarketcap.com/). According to Crypto.com, as of mid-2021, 220 million people used cryptocurrencies worldwide. In November 2021, there were more than 75 million users of Bitcoin compared to three million in 2014. Cryptocurrency start-ups have started offering credit cards and loans and individuals and businesses are rapidly embracing digital currencies. Some governments are also involved.[9]

One of the most popular applications of blockchain has been in the creation of non-fungible tokens (NFTs). In economics, a non-fungible asset has unique properties, which means that it cannot be interchanged with something else. Examples include a house, or a painting such as the *Mona Lisa*. In the digital world, NFTs are 'one-of-a-kind' assets that can be bought and sold but have no tangible form of their own. Sales volumes of NFTs reached US$ 10.7 billion in the third quarter (Q3) of 2021 compared to US 1.3 billion in 2021Q2 and US$ 1.2 billion in 2021Q1.[10] A study of Lithuania-based data acquisition and analysis company DappRadar, which tracks decentralized applications (DApps) across multiple blockchains, found that the NFT market exceeded

[7] S Genome (2021) *Startup Genome.* [online] Startup Genome. Available at: https://startupgenome.com/report/gser2021.

[8] G Bienasz (Sept 22, 2021) *Robotics and Blockchain Top Startup Genome's List of Fastest-Growing Industries.* [online] Inc.com. Available at: https://www.inc.com/gabrielle-bienasz/global-startup-ecosystem-report-robotics-artificial-intelligence.html.

[9] E Flitter (Nov 1, 2021) 'Banks Tried to Kill Crypto and Failed. Now They're Embracing It (Slowly)' https://www.nytimes.com/2021/11/01/business/banks-crypto-bitcoin.html.

[10] E Howcroft (Oct 4, 2021) 'NFT sales surge to $10.7 bln in Q3 as crypto asset frenzy hits new highs'. [online] *Reuters.* Available at: https://www.reuters.com/technology/nft-sales-surge-107-bln-q3-crypto-asset-frenzy-hits-new-highs-2021-10-04/.

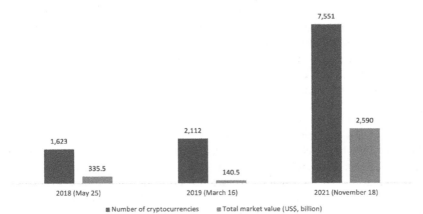

S*ource:*　https://coinmarketcap.com/charts/; https://coinmarketcap.com/all/views/all/.

Figure 1.1　　*Number of cryptocurrencies and their total market value*

US$ 23 billion in 2021 compared to less than US$ 100 million in 2020.[11] According to the US multinational investment bank and financial services company Morgan Stanley, the market for luxury branded NFTs will reach US$ 56 billion by 2030 and NFTs could reach a US$ 240 billion market by then. Among other factors, the metaverse economy will contribute to the growth of the NFT market.[12]

1.2　　WHAT IS BLOCKCHAIN?

Blockchain can be viewed as a decentralized ledger that maintains digital records of a transaction simultaneously on multiple computers or devices. The Chicago-based intellectual property law firm Marshall, Gerstein & Borun LLP[13] suggests that a minimal definition of blockchain should include the following: 'a distributed ledger network using public-key cryptography to cryptographically sign transactions that are stored on a distributed ledger, with

[11]　P Herrera (Dec 17, 2021) 'Dapp Industry Report' https://dappradar.com/blog/2021-dapp-industry-report.

[12]　I Lee (Nov 29, 2021) 'Budweiser is Getting in on the NFT Craze with its "Key to the Budverse" Line of Ethereum-based Collectibles' https://markets.businessinsider.com/news/currencies/budweiser-budverse-nft-1936-gold-rare-core-token-collection-beer-2021-11.

[13]　Marshall, Gerstein & Borun LLP (2017) 'The Emerging Blockchain Patent Landscape.' Lexology http://www.lexology.com/library/detail.aspx?g=cf0c71c5-055a-4d57-92f8-c75d1e282414.

the ledger consisting of cryptographically linked blocks of transactions'. The cryptographically linked blocks of transactions form a blockchain. That is, after a block of records is entered into the ledger, the information in the block is mathematically connected to other blocks. In this way, a chain of immutable records is formed. Note that doing something cryptographically or in a cryptographic manner means that mathematical techniques are used for encrypting and decrypting data. Doing this ensures that data is kept private when it is being transmitted or stored electronically.

Due to this mathematical relationship, the information in a block cannot be changed without changing all blocks. Any change would create a discrepancy which is likely to be noticed by others. Another feature of blockchain is immutability of data, which means that once an object has been created and is recorded in a software code, it cannot be deleted. Blockchain-based transactions are thus indelible and cannot be forged. The immutability feature makes transactions on blockchain auditable, which can improve transparency. Finally, to ensure that only authorized users can access the information, blockchain systems use cryptography-based digital signatures to verify identities of participants. Using complicated algorithms, blockchain systems also create public keys from private keys. Public keys make it possible to share information or for others to send cryptocurrency to your account.

IN FOCUS 1.1 DATA STORAGE IN BLOCKCHAINS

Storing large amount of data on a public blockchain such as Ethereum is expensive. For instance, the cost to store 1 kilobyte of data was 0.00384 ether (ETH) in November 2019. If an average insurance policy document is 1 MB, the cost is 0.00384 ETH x 1024 = US$ 11,466 (based on the price of 1 ETH = 2,916 on January 20, 2022[a]).

Other alternatives include: (a) Centralized storage + blockchain hashes: this approach involves storing content on a traditional server that is rented from a hosting company. When a new document is added to the system, a transaction is recorded on the blockchain. The document also gets its own unique hash: (b) P2P (peer-to-peer) data sharing networks: files are stored on individual users' servers and drives. Each file has a unique hash and the copies can be stored in many devices in the network. Even if some of them malfunction, the data is accessible. Examples include Interplanetary File Storage System (IPFS), Swarm, and Arweave. IPFS is free. However, some argue that it is not reliable for storing sensitive data.

Note: [a] JAXenter (Dec 16, 2019) 'No, You Don't Store Data on the Blockchain – Here's Why.' [online] Available at: https://jaxenter.com/blockchain-data-164727.html.

1.2.1   Blockchain as a Special Type of Distributed Ledger Technology

A distributed ledger technology (DLT) is a decentralized database managed by a number of participants. In such a database, there is no central authority to act as an arbitrator. The distributed nature of the logs of records increases transparency and reduces the chance that the database is manipulated. It is also more challenging to hack or attack the database.

Blockchain is a DLT that has additional features. In a blockchain, the records related to transactions are shared by means of blocks that form a chain. Every block in a blockchain's online ledger has a timestamp. Also a hash pointer to link it to the previous block. Put simply, a hash is a type of cryptographic signature that closes the blocks. The next block starts with that same 'hash', which can be viewed as a type of 'wax seal'.[14]

To sum up, blockchains thus can be viewed as a secure distributed and decentralized digital ledger or database created by a network of computers, which stores continuous blocks containing transaction information in a secure and verifiable manner. The interaction among the computers is facilitated by purposefully designed software in order to get the computers to agree (or achieve consensus) as to what data to add and store on the database.[15]

1.3   KEY CHARACTERISTICS OF BLOCKCHAIN

Three key characteristics of blockchain have been identified – decentralization, immutability and cryptography-based authentication.[16]

1.3.1   Decentralization

Blockchain's value proposition is arguably embedded in decentralization. By supporting decentralized models, blockchain can make sustainability-related activities more transparent and produce trust. Blockchain eliminates the need for a trusted third party in the transfer of value and thus enables faster and less expensive transactions. Even those who are sceptical of the potential of block-

---

[14]   BBVA (2018) 'What Is the Difference between DLT and Blockchain?' [online] NEWS BBVA. Available at: https://www.bbva.com/en/difference-dlt-blockchain/.
[15]   Hummingbot (2018) 'Finance 3.0 WIKI | Ethereum Testnet vs. Mainnet.' *Medium*, Available at: https://medium.com/hummingbot/finance-3-0-wiki-testnet-vs-mainnet-8ab5b78d93.
[16]   N Kshetri (May 29, 2018) 'Blockchain Could Be the Answer to Cybersecurity. Maybe' *Wall Street Journal*, https://www.wsj.com/articles/blockchain-could-be-the-answer-to-cybersecurity-maybe-15276459.

chain in many other fields and applications are optimistic in its trust-producing capabilities.[17]

1.3.2   Immutability

The term immutable comes from object-oriented programming, in which data structure and operations or functions that can be applied are defined by programmers. Immutable means that once an object has been created and is recorded in a software code, it cannot be modified.[18] Blockchain-based transactions are thus indelible and cannot be forged. The immutability feature makes transactions on blockchain auditable, which can improve transparency. A party can be given controlled access to relevant data. For instance, blockchain's distributed ledger model would allow regulators and authorities to access key data and carry out their functions.

1.3.3   Cryptography-based Authentication

To ensure that only authorized users can access the information, blockchain systems use cryptography-based digital signatures to verify identities of participants. Users sign transactions with a private key, which is generated when an account is created. A private key is typically a very long and random alphanumeric code. Using complicated algorithms, blockchain systems also create public keys from private keys. Public keys make it possible to share information. This feature makes it possible to measure and track sustainability-related outcomes. For instance, if a coffee retailer claims that living wages are paid to coffee farmers, the accuracy and truthfulness of such claims can be assessed by checking the payments to digital wallets assigned to the farmers.

1.4   TYPES OF BLOCKCHAIN

There are, broadly speaking, three kinds of blockchains: permissionless (public), permissioned (private) and hybrid.

---

[17]   R Hackett (2017) '7 Reasons Why China Banned ICOs.' Retrieved September 15, 2017, from http://fortune.com/2017/09/05/china-bitcoin-blockchain-ico-ban/*.
[18]   MS Tschantz and MD Ernst (2005) 'Javari: Adding Reference Immutability to Java', Proceedings of the 20th Annual ACM SIGPLAN Conference on Object-oriented Programming, Systems, Languages, and Applications, 211–30.

1.4.1   Public Blockchain

A permissionless blockchain is an open platform. In a way, permissionless blockchains are like a shared database. Anyone can join. Everyone can read everything. However, a user cannot control who can write. Some examples include Bitcoin and Ethereum. The Ethereum network is a public blockchain-based open software platform in which each node can be discovered by and known to other nodes in the network. It has its own cryptocurrency known as Ether.

As another example, the blockchain-based supply chain platform VeChain's VeChainThor is described as a public blockchain.[19] VeChain was started in 2015 as a subsidiary of the Shanghai-based Blockchain-as-a-Service (BaaS) company, BitSE.

1.4.2   Private Blockchains

Private or permissioned blockchains, on the other hand, are restrictive. Access must be granted by some authority.[20] Permissioned blockchains can be designed to restrict access to approved actors such as supply chain partners.

A major drawback of private blockchains is centralization. The creators have control over how it functions. Since there are a small number of nodes to validate transactions, a private blockchain is more susceptible to cyberattacks and abusive behaviour by nodes.[21]

Private blockchains arguably have more promising applications in supply chain management (SCM).[22] Doug Johnson-Poensgen, CEO of Circulor explained that the company originally prototyped its solution on Ethereum but switched to Hyperledger Fabric. The switch was due to Circulor clients' prejudice against public blockchain. Potential users were concerned that maintaining commercial confidentiality could be difficult to configure in a public blockchain.[23]

---

[19]   vechain.org (n.d.) *VeChain Whitepaper | VeChain Builders*. [online] Available at: https://www.vechain.org/whitepaper/#bit_v48i3.

[20]   O Bussmann (2017) 'Bankthink a Public or Private Blockchain? New Ethereum Project Could Mean Both' *American Banker*, https://www.americanbanker.com/opinion/a-public-or-private-blockchain-new-ethereum-project-could-mean-both.

[21]   JAXenter (Dec 19, 2019) 'No, You Don't Store Data on the Blockchain – Here's Why.' [online] Available at: https://jaxenter.com/blockchain-data-164727.html.

[22]   M Staples, S Chen, S Falamaki and A Ponomarev (2017) 'Risks and Opportunities for Systems Using Blockchain and Smart Contracts'. Commonwealth Sci. Ind. Res. Org, Sydney, Australia, Rep. no. EP175103, 2017.

[23]   M Kapilkov (2020) 'Startup Helps Reduce Child Labor in Africa & Aspires to Work with Tesla' Cointelegraph, https://cointelegraph.com/news/startup-helps-reduce-child-labor-in-africa-aspires-to-work-with-tesla.

Hyperledger is a private, permissioned blockchain that has no native crypto-currency. It is an open source collaborative effort, which was created in 2016 by 30 members including IBM, Accenture, BNY Mellon, Intel and Digital Asset Holdings to advance the use of blockchain across various industries. Over half of the companies in the Forbes Blockchain 50 list of February 2020 used Hyperledger.[24]

The Linux Foundation leads the Hyperledger Consortium, which had more than 250 members in July 2018.[25] Hyperledger has three categories of membership: premium, general and associate. Consortium members include IBM, Intel, Accenture, American Express, Daimler, JP Morgan (Premium), Lenovo, SAP, Tencent Cloud (general), Yale University, University of California, Los Angeles (UCLA) and Cambridge University (associate). These members are working together to develop platforms, tools, methodologies, processes, and solutions for enterprise blockchain.

As of August 2020, a premium membership, which comes with benefits such as the right to appoint representatives to the Hyperledger Governing Board, the members-only Premier Legal Committee and to vote representatives to the Marketing Committee, costs US$ 250,000. The fees for general membership varied from US$ 5,000 to US$ 70,000 depending on the size of the company and existing membership in the Linux Foundation. Pre-approved nonprofits, open source projects and government entities are eligible for an associate membership with no charge (https://www.hyperledger.org/about/join).

Hyperledger Fabric is one of the key projects developed under Hyperledger. Its codebase or the collection of source code to build Hyperledger Fabric's system, application or software component comes from three sources:

a. Hyperledger, owned by Digital Asset, formerly called Digital Asset Holdings;
b. IBM's open source blockchain platform, Open Blockchain;
c. Blockchain technology company Blockstream's LibConsensus, derived directly from Bitcoin Core (a descendant of the original Bitcoin software client, that is, distributed to end users of Bitcoin for installation), which

---

[24] Hyperledger (2020) 'Hyperledger Ecosystem Growth Strong as Members Make Headlines & Discuss Production Deployments at Hyperledger Global Forum 2020' Hyperledger, https://www.hyperledger.org/announcements/2020/03/04/hyperledger-ecosystem-growth-strong-as-members-make-headlines-discuss-production-deployments-at-hyperledger-global-forum-2020.
[25] Ibid.

provides the Consensus Layer's part of the code to establish the criteria for a valid block.[26]

Hyperledger Fabric is a modular blockchain system, which allows organizations to develop products, solutions and applications based on blockchain. Key components such as consensus and membership services work on a plug and play basis. It thus allows organizations to conduct confidential transactions without the need of a central authority.

A type of smart contract chaincode is deployed into a network of Hyperledger Fabric nodes to enable interaction with the network's shared ledger. Chaincode handles transactions differently compared to smart contract codes utilized on other blockchain networks, such as Ethereum. In traditional smart contracts, transactions need to be validated, ordered (e.g., by fee cap or the maximum fee that the sender is willing to pay) and broadcasted to nodes before being executed. In chaincode, transactions are executed and then a small number of participants check for 'correctness' based on an 'endorsement policy' designated for the particular type of transaction. The transactions are then ordered, validated in and recorded on the ledger.[27]

Hyperledger Fabric performs better than well-known cryptocurrencies and public blockchains in terms of the speed at which transactions are completed. For instance, as of early 2018, Hyperledger Fabric deployed in a single cloud data centre had a throughput of over 3,500 transactions per second (TPS) with latency rate of less than one second.[28]

1.4.3 Hybrid Blockchains

In hybrid blockchains, businesses use permissioned chains to transact in the background. Using an application programming interface (API), the transactions are connected to a public blockchain, which would allow consumers and others to engage in transactions such as transferring money or accessing information about products in supply chains.[29]

---

[26] MS Paul (2018) *Hyperledger — Chapter 2 | Hyperledger Frameworks & Modules*. [online] *The Startup*. Available at: https://medium.com/swlh/hyperledger -chapter-2-hyperledger-frameworks-modules-cabf50e12105.
[27] coindesk.com (2021) *Hyperledger Fabric*. [online] Available at: https://www .coindesk.com/learn/crypto/hyperledger-fabric/.
[28] IBM Research (2018) 'Behind the Architecture of Hyperledger Fabric' *IBM*, https://www.ibm.com/blogs/research/2018/02/architecture-hyperledger-fabric/.
[29] L Mearian (2020) 'Kadena Launches a Hybrid Platform to Connect Public, Private Blockchains' *Computer World*, https://www.computerworld.com/article/3514711/ kadena-launches-a-hybrid-platform-to-connect-public-private-blockchains.html#:~:

A consortium blockchain can be viewed as a hybrid of public and private blockchains. In such a blockchain, a group governs the network rather than a single entity. Nodes in the network have various types of privileges. Some can control the consensus process. Others participate in transactions. Consortium blockchains are often attractive for entities operating in the same industry. Firms can leverage blockchain to enhance workflow efficiencies, share information and resources, enhance accountability, and promote transparency.[30] One example is R3's open source blockchain platform Corda. As of August 2020, R3 had more than 300 participants from multiple industries (https://www.r3.com/about/).

1.5   ORIGIN, EVOLUTION AND TRAJECTORY OF BLOCKCHAIN

While technologies that were similar to today's blockchain were reported to exist as early as in the late 1970s , its most significant milestone occurred in 2008 when the presumed pseudonymous person or persons Satoshi Nakamoto published the white paper: 'Bitcoin: A Peer-to-Peer Electronic Cash System' (https://bitcoin.org/bitcoin.pdf). The Bitcoin white paper provided a vision for a digital currency that is independent of centralized control, which can be used as a store of value and medium of exchange.[31] In a little over two months after the white paper's publication, the Bitcoin network went live (see Table 1.1).

In order to understand the evolution and development of blockchain, it is critical to have a detailed understanding of the history and context that have shaped this issue. Bitcoin's launch was a response to the economic challenges created by the 2008 global financial crisis. For instance, the text note contained in the genesis block (see Table 1.1) was a reference to an article in *The London Times* about the 2008 global financial crisis, when commercial banks had received trillions of dollars in bailout money from central banks and national governments.[32]

---

text=Brooklyn%2Dbased%20spinoff%20Kadena%20has,transfer%20cryptocurrency %20between%20the%20chains.

[30]   F Blaha and K Katafono (2020) 'Blockchain Application in Seafood Value Chains' *Food And Agriculture Organization of The United Nations*, Rome, http://www .fao.org/3/ca8751en/ca8751en.pdf.

[31]   Cointelegraph (Oct 31, 2021) *Bitcoin White Paper Turns 13 Years Old: The Journey So Far*. [online] Available at: https://cointelegraph.com/news/bitcoin-white -paper-turns-13-years-old-the-journey-so-far.

[32]   SoFi (Dec 20, 2021) 'Bitcoin Price History: Price of Bitcoin 2009–2021.' [online] Available at: https://www.sofi.com/learn/content/bitcoin-price-history/.

Table 1.1   *The evolution of blockchain*

Time	Event	Remarks
October 31, 2008	Publication of a white paper on Bitcoin by Satoshi Nakamoto	Title of the paper: 'Bitcoin: A Peer-to-Peer Electronic Cash System' (https://bitcoin.org/bitcoin.pdf)
January 3, 2009	Bitcoin network went live.[a] The block 0 called the genesis block was mined on this date. It allowed the first group of transactions to begin a blockchain	This block contained a text note that read: 'Chancellor on Brink of Second Bailout for Banks'[b]
February 2011	The price of Bitcoin reached US$ 1.00[c]	It was the first time Bitcoin achieved parity with the US dollar
End-2011	The price of Bitcoin was under US$ 5	Price on December 31, 2011: US$ 4.72[d]
May 3, 2014	Digital artist Kevin McCoy created the non-fungible token 'Quantum'[e]	It was sold for US$ 1.4 million in June 2021[f]
2014	Ethereum was launched	An initial coin offering (ICO) raised US$ 18 million[g]
July 2015	Ethereum's initial version, the Ethereum Frontier network, was launched[h]	The Ethereum Frontier network supported the creation of smart contracts
October 31, 2015	Blockchain was a cover story in *The Economist*	The technology was referred to as 'trust machine'[i]
2017	The first NFT marketplace on Ethereum OpenSea was established[j]	In August 2021, OpenSea accounted for 98 per cent of all Ethereum-based NFTs[k]
December 18, 2017	MakerDAO launched Dai on Ethereum, which was the first fully decentralized stablecoin[l]	MakerDAO was formed in 2014 and was one of the first decentralized autonomous organizations (DAOs) on Ethereum[m] MakerDAO has claimed that Dai is the first DeFi (Decentralized Finance) application to get 'serious adoption'[n]
2018	DeFi started gaining traction	Most of the DeFi tokens with the highest market capitalization were launched after 2018
December 2019	DeFi market reaches US$ 700 million[o]	It reached US$ 13 billion on December 31, 2020
March 2020	About 2 million smart contracts had been deployed on Ethereum, which was a new all-time high[p]	The previous all-time high was in November 2018 (about 1.5 million dropped)

Time	Event	Remarks
March 2021	17.84 million smart contracts had been deployed on Ethereum[q]	The number of ERC-721 contracts, which are used in most NFTs, was around 19,000
October 2021	Facebook announced the change of its name to Meta[r]	Facebook declared that the metaverse is the 'next chapter' for the company as well for the Internet

Notes:

[a] WJ Luther (2016) 'Bitcoin and the Future of Digital Payments' *The Independent Review* Vol 20(3) 397–404, https://www.jstor.org/stable/24562161.

[b] SoFi (2021) 'Bitcoin Price History: Price of Bitcoin 2009–2021' [online] Available at: https://www.sofi.com/learn/content/bitcoin-price-history/.

[c] Ibid.

[d] Blockchain.info (June 17, 2019) 'Bitcoin Prices' accessed November 21, 2021 (https://www.investopedia.com/articles/forex/121815/bitcoins-price-history.asp#citation-12).

[e] Portion (2021) 'The History of NFTs and How They Got Started.' [online] Portion Blog. Available at: https://blog.portion.io/the-history-of-nfts-how-they-got-started/.

[f] VD Liscia (2021) '"First Ever NFT" Sells for $1.4 Million.' [online] *Hyperallergic*. Available at: https://hyperallergic.com/652671/kevin-mccoy-quantum-first-nft-created-sells-at-sothebys-for-over-one-million/.

[g] E Lopatto (2019) 'How Bitcoin Grew Up and Became Big Money.' [online] The Verge. Available at: https://www.theverge.com/2019/1/3/18166096/bitcoin-blockchain-code-currency-money-genesis-block-silk-road-mt-gox.

[h] Blockstuffs (Aug 28, 2020) 'History of Ethereum From Beginning – Blog – Block Stuffs | Complete Stuffs on Blockchain.' [online] www.blockstuffs.com. Available at: https://www.blockstuffs.com/blog/history-of-ethereum-from-beginning.

[i] *The Economist* (Oct 31, 2015) 'The Trust Machine: How the Technology Behind Bitcoin Could Change the World.' [online] Available at: https://www.economist.com/weeklyedition/2015-10-31.

[j] Tonelli (2021) 'NFT Marketplace OpenSea Hits $10B in Total Volume.' [online] Decrypt, Available at: https://decrypt.co/85507/nft-marketplace-opensea-hits-10b-total-volume.

[k] Ibid.

[l] Maker Blog (2017) 'Dai is Now Live!' [online] Available at: https://blog.makerdao.com/dai-is-now-live/.

[m] B Betz (2021) 'MakerDAO's Rune Christensen Joins VC Firm Dragonfly Capital.' [online] Available at: https://www.coindesk.com/business/2021/11/15/makerdaos-rune-christensen-joins-vc-firm-dragonfly-capital/.

[n] John Detrixhe (Oct 13, 2021) 'Everything You Need to Know About DeFi.' Available at: https://qz.com/2065446/everything-you-need-to-know-about-decentralized-finance-defi/.

[o] R Ma (Aug 28, 2020) 'How DeFi Is Reinventing The World's Financial System' *Forbes*, https://www.forbes.com/sites/forbestechcouncil/2020/08/28/how-defi-is-reinventing-the-worlds-financial-system/#509bc4fdbc14.

[p] Cointelegraph (Apr 23, 2020) 'Ethereum Smart Contracts up 75% to Almost 2M in March.' [online] Available at: https://cointelegraph.com/news/ethereum-smart-contracts-up-75-to-almost-2m-in-march.

[q] DL Frost (2021) 'Ethereum ERC-721 Contracts Surge amid NFT Boom.' [online] Decrypt. Available at: https://decrypt.co/62826/ethereum-erc-721-contracts-surge-amid-nft-boom.

[r] NPR.org (2021) 'The Metaverse Is Already Here. The Debate Now Is Over Who Should Own it.' Available at: https://www.npr.org/2021/11/18/1055387297/the-metaverse-is-already-here-the-debate-is-now-over-who-should-own-it.

Bitcoin was created by a community that had libertarian and antiestablishment values and an anticommercial spirit. In many aspects, this movement is similar to the free-software culture. Despite the initial resistance to the open source software (OSS) Linux, this software has been embedded in many commercial applications and services of major technology companies.

Microsoft is a member the Linux Foundation as well as the Linux kernel security mailing list. Microsoft submitted patches to the Linux kernel with a goal to 'create a complete virtualisation stack with Linux and Microsoft hypervisor'.[33] Azure customers get the same benefits for Linux support contracts and Windows Server licences. Several key Microsoft applications are available on Linux.[34]

Some analysts think that this history will repeat itself and blockchain may experience the same diffusion pattern.[35] As predicted by these analysts, key blockchain use cases are becoming normal and routine for big companies, governments, and banks. They are employing blockchain to perform key tasks such as reconciling invoices and verifying product provenance and holding Bitcoin and other cryptocurrency as treasury assets to provide and manage liquidity and to meet legal obligations.[36]

1.6 DEFINITIONS AND EXPLANATIONS OF THE KEY TERMS

1.6.1 Consensus Mechanism

In a shared ledger, it is important to have an efficient, fair, and secure mechanism in order to make sure that only genuine transactions occur and participants agree on the ledger's status. A consensus mechanism performs this task by defining a set of rules to decide the various participants' contributions. The

---

[33] lore.kernel.org (Feb 3, 2021) *[PATCH RFC v1 00/18] Introducing Linux Root Partition Support for Microsoft Hypervisor*. [online] Available at: https://lwn.net/Articles/844957/.

[34] M Branscombe (Dec 2, 2020) 'What Is Microsoft Doing with Linux? Everything You Need to Know About Its Plans for Open Source.' [online] TechRepublic. Available at: https://www.techrepublic.com/article/what-is-microsoft-doing-with-linux-everything-you-need-to-know-about-its-plans-for-open-source/.

[35] J Ito, N Narula and R Ali (2017) 'The Blockchain Will Do to Banks and Law Firms What the Internet Did to Media.' [online] Available at: https://hbr.org/2017/03/the-blockchain-will-do-to-banks-and-law-firms-what-the-internet-did-to-media.

[36] M del Castillo (n.d.) *Blockchain 50 2021*. [online] *Forbes*. Available at: https://www.forbes.com/sites/michaeldelcastillo/2021/02/02/blockchain-50/?sh=561cf2d7231c.

goal is to achieve the necessary agreement on a data value or the network's state.[37]

IN FOCUS 1.2 ETHEREUM SWITCHES TO PROOF OF STAKE

Since 2015, the Ethereum Foundation has been considering a transition from PoW (Proof of Work) to PoS (Proof of Stake), the so-called Casper protocol was designed for this purpose.[a] Initially the Ethereum Foundation expected that the switch would take just one year. It has taken more than six years.[b] The nonprofit organization Ethereum Foundation, which is dedicated to supporting Ethereum and related technologies, has noted that the switch to PoS could reduce Ethereum's energy use by up to 99.95 per cent.[c]

A system chain called the Beacon Chain is at the core of Ethereum's transition to PoS. It serves as the backbone of Ethereum 2.0. The Beacon Chain introduces Proof of Stake to Ethereum and stores and manages the registry of validators.[d] In December 2020, the Beacon Chain for Ethereum 2.0 was deployed, which runs as a 'parallel' chain to the existing Ethereum Mainnet.

The Ethereum 2.0 upgrade would launch 'sharding', which involves splitting up the network into distinct partitions also known as shards. Transaction load will be managed across 64 shard chains, which will improve scalability.[e] Each shard has its own consensus region and ledger. Nodes and validators only process transactions that are local to their shards.[f] Nodes are randomly assigned to each shard. Individual shards, however, share the transaction details with the Beacon Chain.[g]

The Ethereum Arrow Glacier update was released in December 2021, which pushed back the so-called 'difficulty bomb' until June 2022. The term difficulty bomb is used to describe the increasing level of mining difficulty that requires additional computing power to verify transactions entered and increases the amount of time required to mine a new block on the Ethereum blockchain. The purpose of the difficulty bomb is to act as a deterrent for miners, who may continue with PoW even after Ethereum's transitions to PoS.[h]

---

[37] J Frankenfield (2019) *Consensus Mechanism (Cryptocurrency).* [online] Investopedia. Available at: https://www.investopedia.com/terms/c/consensus-mechanism-cryptocurrency.asp.

Notes:
[a] V Zamfir (Aug 1, 2015) 'Introducing Casper "the Friendly Ghost"' https://blog.ethereum.org/2015/08/01/introducing-casper-friendly-ghost/.
[b] C Morris (Dec 8, 2021) 'Ethereum Update Defuses "Difficulty Bomb" That Could Have Stopped Ether Crypto Mining' https://fortune.com/2021/12/08/ethereum-arrow-glacier-update-difficulty-bomb-crypto-mining-proof-of-stake-eth2/.
[c] C Beekhuizen (May 18, 202) 'A Country's Worth of Power, No More!' https://blog.ethereum.org/2021/05/18/country-power-no-more/.
[d] Phase 0 (n.d.) 'The Beacon Chain' https://github.com/ethereum/consensus-specs/blob/dev/specs/phase0/beacon-chain.md.
[e] Samuel Wan (Dec 8, 2021) 'Vitalik Buterin Shares His "Endgame" for Ethereum 2.0' https://cryptoslate.com/vitalik-buterin-shares-his-endgame-for-ethereum-2-0/.
[f] V Chen (2019) 'Kadena's Public Blockchain: 101 and FAQs' *Medium*, https://medium.com/kadena-io/all-about-chainweb-101-and-faqs-6bd88c325b45.
[g] Mark Kolakowski (Dec 9, 2021) 'Ethereum Upgrade Delays "Difficulty Bomb": Potential Mining Halt Pushed to June 2022, Model Shifting to "Proof of Stake"' https://www.investopedia.com/ethereum-upgrade-delays-difficulty-bomb-5212447.
[h] Jake Frankenfield (Apr 16, 2021) 'Difficulty Bomb' https://www.investopedia.com/terms/d/difficulty-bomb.asp.

1.6.1.1 Proof of work

In a Proof of Work (PoW) protocol, all users can compete to verify transactions. Major drawbacks of such protocol include high energy consumption and longer processing time. For instance, the Bitcoin blockchain utilizes a PoW protocol.

1.6.1.2 Proof of stake

In a Proof of Stake (PoS) consensus model, only a small group of nodes can validate transactions. A node's power to validate transactions or responsibility to maintain the public ledger is proportional to the number of virtual currency tokens associated with the node.[38] For instance, a node that owns 10 per cent of the currency available theoretically can validate only 10 per cent of the blocks. It is viewed as a low-cost and low-energy consuming alternative to the PoW algorithm.

To take an example, Vancouver, Canada-based Dapper Labs, which created the CryptoKitties game on Ethereum, developed Flow blockchain, which is specifically built for the high demand of transactions for apps, games, and digital collectibles. Flow uses a PoS model, which requires validators to stake a certain number of Flow tokens in order to participate in the network (See In Focus 1.3: Separation of labour between Flow nodes below)

---

[38] A Gazdecki (2019) 'Proof-Of-Work and Proof-Of-Stake: How Blockchain Reaches Consensus' https://www.forbes.com/sites/forbestechcouncil/2019/01/28/proof-of-work-and-proof-of-stake-how-blockchain-reaches-consensus/#395f865868c8.

(https://momentranks.com/blog/exploring-the-flow-blockchain-the-consumer
-blockchain-nba-top-shot). It is arguably the largest consumer blockchain.[39]

IN FOCUS 1.3 SEPARATION OF LABOR BETWEEN FLOW NODES

Unlike popular blockchains such as Bitcoin and Ethereum, not all Flow
nodes are equal.[a] Labour is separated between nodes vertically (across
the different validation stages for each transaction) rather than horizon-
tally (across different transactions, as with sharding).[b] Note that sharding
involves splitting up the network into distinct partitions also known as
shards. Each shard has its own consensus region and ledger. It thus creates
multiple PoW-based partitions through which multiple parallel chains operate.[c] Nodes and validators only process transactions that are local to their
shards.[d] No sharding means that Flow has a single shared state environment.

A Collection node signs the transaction to indicate two things: (a) the
transaction is well formed. A well formed transaction includes credentials
from the guarantor of the transaction and ensures the legitimacy and integrity of the data (https://www.drchaos.com/post/clark-wilson-security-model);
(b) it will store the transaction text until the Execution nodes finish processing it. Collection nodes are divided into several clusters that cooperate
with each other. Each cluster collects transactions and assembles them into
Collections. A Collection Guarantee is then signed by a supermajority of the
cluster and submitted to the Consensus nodes. In order to be a confirmed as
a node operator, a Collection node is required to stake at least 250,000 Flow.

The main task of Consensus nodes is to form and propose blocks. To do
so, they validate that the signed Collection hashes that are submitted to them
by Collection nodes are signed by the required majority of Collection nodes.
In this way, these nodes function as checkpoints against other Collection
nodes and hold the latter accountable. To be confirmed as a Consensus node
operator, a minimum of 500,000 Flow would be required.

Execution nodes are responsible for executing transactions. They also
maintain the Execution State, which is a 'cryptographically-verifiable data
store for all user accounts and smart contract states'[e]. In addition, they respond to queries related to the Execution State. These nodes compute the
outputs of the blocks that they are provided with. A minimum of 1,250,000
Flow tokens will be required to be staked in order to be a confirmed
Execution node operator.

---

[39]   Brian Kelleher (May 13, 2021) *MomentRanks*. [online] Available at: https://
momentranks.com/blog/exploring-the-flow-blockchain-the-consumer-blockchain-nba
-top-shot.

Verification nodes confirm the correctness of the work of Execution nodes. An individual Verification node checks only a small amount of the total computation. However, collectively Verification nodes check every computation several times parallelly. Verification nodes issue Result Approvals by verifying Execution Receipts provided by Execution nodes. The minimum number of Flow tokens required to be a confirmed Verification node operator is 135,000 (https://docs.onflow.org/node-operation/node-roles/).

Notes:

[a] Flowdocs (n.d.) 'Node Roles' https://docs.onflow.org/node-operation/node-roles/.

[b] onflow.org (n.d.) 'Flow Primer: The Blockchain for Open Worlds.' [online] Available at: https://www.onflow.org/primer.

[c] L Mearian (2020) 'Kadena Launches a Hybrid Platform to Connect Public, Private Blockchains' *Computer World*, https://www.computerworld.com/article/3514711/kadena-launches-a-hybrid-platform-to-connect-public-private-blockchains.html#:~:text=Brooklyn%2Dbased%20spinoff%20Kadena%20has,transfer%20cryptocurrency%20between%20the%20chains.

[d] V Chen (2019) 'Kadena's Public Blockchain: 101 and FAQs' *Medium*, https://medium.com/kadena-io/all-about-chainweb-101-and-faqs-6bd88c325b45.

[e] C Menzel (June 22, 2020) 'Figment's First Look' https://www.figment.io/resources/figments-first-look-flow.

1.6.1.3 Proof of authority

The Proof of Authority (PoA) consensus model relies on a limited number of trustworthy block validators, which are pre-approved. It is viewed as a modified form of PoS, in which a validator's identity rather than the role of stake is important. The nodes responsible for validating transactions are selected based on certain rules.[40]

1.6.2 Smart Contract

Implementing smart contracts is among blockchain's most transformative applications. Smart contracts execute automatically when certain conditions are met. Computerized protocols and user interfaces are used to execute a contract's terms[41] and to 'formalize and secure relationships over public networks'.[42] A smart contract assures a party with certainty that the counterparty will fulfill the promises. In supply chains, for instance, a smart contract system can be established to track products, which automatically determines

---

[40]   POA Network (2017) 'Proof of Authority: Consensus Model with Identity at Stake.' [online] *Medium*. Available at: https://medium.com/poa-network/proof-of-authority-consensus-model-with-identity-at-stake-d5bd15463256.

[41]   N Szabo (1994) Smart Contracts. Unpublished manuscript.

[42]   N Szabo (1997) 'Formalizing and Securing Relationships on Public Networks.' *First Monday* Vol 2(9), https://firstmonday.org/ojs/index.php/fm/article/view/548.

ownership rights. Such a system can also be employed to release payments automatically when products are delivered.[43]

By implementing 'business logic' in supply chains into smart contracts, cost savings can be realized with blockchain. Additional cost savings can be achieved subsequently by removing intermediaries and employees.[44] Computer codes perform the tasks that needed intermediaries before.

The first blockchain to implement smart contracts was Ethereum, which is also the most widely used smart contract platform.[45] [46] Ethereum has a built-in programming language that allows to define smart contracts and provides DApps.

Smart contracts are installed in each node of the Ethereum network. While Bitcoin stores data related to transactions, Ethereum stores diverse types of data such as those related to finance, industry, legal, personal information, community, health, education and governance. These data can be accessed and used by computer programs known as DApps that run on Ethereum. Software developers can choose their own 'rules' for ownership, transactions formats and other aspects (https://www.stateofthedapps.com/whats-a-dapp). Ethereum can thus be customized to offer unique solutions to special needs. It is mainly used to develop B2C (Business-to-Customer) applications. In Ethereum, computers connected in an open and distributed network provide the processing power needed to run a smart contract. The computers in the network also verify and record transactions in the blockchain.

The owners of the computers are awarded with ETH tokens for their contributions. Ethereum can be viewed as the first shared global computer. Bitcoin, on the other hand, is considered to be the first accounting ledger that can be shared globally.[47] Ethereum needs what is referred to as Ethereum Gas in order to execute transactions or smart contracts.

[43]   Binance Academy (n.d.) *Supply Chain.* [online] Available at: https://academy .binance.com/en/glossary/supply-chain.

[44]   J Holbrook (2019) 'Understanding Enterprise Blockchain Cost Modeling Basics' *Medium,* https://medium.com/cryptolinks/enterprise-blockchain-cost-modeling -b7929b2c36a4.

[45]   William M Peaster (May 11, 2020) 'Top 10 Metrics for Understanding the Ethereum Blockchain' https://blockonomi.com/metrics-for-understanding-ethereum -blockchain/.

[46]   V Buterin (2013) 'Ethereum White Paper' https://github.com/ethereum/wiki/ wiki/White-Paper.

[47]   MIT Technology Review (2017) 'Understand Why Ethereum Exists, and You'll Get Why It's A Big Deal' https://medium.com/mit-technology-review/understand-why -ethereum-exists-and-youll-get-why-it-s-a-big-deal-df6765a5805d.

1.6.2.1   Advantages of blockchain-based smart contracts

Regarding how smart contracts are written and executed, three key challenges have been identified in the non-blockchain world. First, there is the lack of transparency. For instance, when smart devices automatically perform actions on a user's behalf, the user may not be able to audit the encrypted information that is sent from the device to the cloud. The user's private data could also be sent. Second, it is possible that a piece of the application is controlled by a single entity. Some infrastructures that support the functioning of the Internet of Things (IoT) devices may not be available when they are needed. For instance, a smart contract may involve charging credit cards after a user refuels. But the credit card information might be stored by a cloud service, which may not be available. For instance, during early 2015–early 2017, cloud downtimes of major cloud services providers AWS (Amazon Web Service), Microsoft and Google were 448 minutes, 1,652 minutes and 506 minutes respectively.[48]

Third, trust is critical in IoT applications involved in the exchange of goods or services. The production of trust may add financial overheads and/or may involve risks related to the violation of trusts. For instance, a vendor may leak credit card information or the credit card company may collude with a party if a dispute arises.[49] Blockchain-based smart contracts can address these shortcomings.

A blockchain-powered smart contract can be executed either 'above' the blockchain or 'on' the blockchain. In the former, the software program runs outside the blockchain and feeds information to the blockchain. In the second case, the software program is coded into blocks.[50]

In many smart contracts that are executed 'above' the blockchain, effective communication between the underlying IoT infrastructure to facilitate reliable and secure processing of IoT data is critical.[51] When blockchain and IoT are integrated into a smart contract framework, the concerned parties need to decide where interactions would take place. Three possibilities can be envis-

---

[48]   K McLaughlin and M Sullivan (2017) 'How AWS Stacks Up against Rivals on Downtime' https://www.theinformation.com/how-aws-stacks-up-against-rivals-on-downtime.

[49]   Y Hanada, L Hsiao and P Levis (2018) 'Smart Contracts for Machine-to-Machine Communication: Possibilities and Limitations.' arXiv preprint arXiv:1605.01987.

[50]   S Farrell, A Griffin, R Hinchliffe and C Warren (2016) '10 Things You Need to Know About Smart Contracts' http://www.kwm.com/en/knowledge/insights/10-things-you-need-to-know-smart-contracts-20160630.

[51]   Ana Reyna, Christian Martín, Jaime Chen, Enrique Soler and M Manuel Díaz (2018) 'On Blockchain and Its Integration with IoT. Challenges and Opportunities' *Future Generation Computer Systems* Vol 88, 173–90, https://doi.org/10.1145/2976749.2978326.

aged: (a) inside the IoT; (b) a design that involves IoT and blockchain; (c) through blockchain. Especially the first approach requires reliable IoT data and low latency in IoT interactions.[52] For instance, in IBM's blockchain trial project involving the transport of fruits from India to the UAE and juice from the UAE to Spain, data related to temperatures and other conditions of fruits and juice are reported by Du's IoT devices are validated by IBM's Watson AI. If these conditions meet those specified in the smart contract, the Spanish bank Santander would release the payments. The Bitcoin blockchain is found to be insufficient to implement smart contracts. In order to address the drawback of Bitcoin, new blockchain platforms have emerged that come with integrated smart contract functionality.[53]

1.6.2.2   The roles of oracles in smart contracts

Access to reliable information about the conditions specified in a contract is a key challenge because the smart contract has no way to know about events that occur outside the blockchain environment. Most smart contracts thus require access to data related to real-world conditions. Such conditions could be temperature, payment completion, price changes, delivery of raw materials at a warehouse or anything that is associated with the smart contract. So-called oracles provide data related to real-world conditions that are needed to enforce smart contracts. Oracles are the only way by which smart contracts interact with data outside the blockchain.[54] Oracles often charge a fee for performing a service.

Oracles thus have a critical role to play in the successful integration of smart contracts in the real world. At the same time, they create complexity. A key challenge is to provide authentication, security and trust in oracles.[55] Among the key requirements, the data sources used by oracles to send to smart contracts must be credible.[56] For instance, if the term of a smart contract involves the temperature of a location, a priori choice needs to be made as to which source to believe when two or more sources provide different temperatures.

---

[52]   Ibid.

[53]   Ibid.

[54]   J Buck (2017) 'Blockchain Oracles, Explained' https://cointelegraph.com/ explained/blockchain-oracles-explained.

[55]   F Zhang, E Cecchetti, K Croman, A Juels and E Shi (2016) 'Town Crier: An Authenticated Data Feed for Smart Contracts' *Proceedings of the 2016 ACM SIGSAC Conference on Computer and Communications Security*, Vienna, Austria, ACM, 270–82.

[56]   B Asolo (2018) 'Blockchain Oracles Explained' https://www.mycryptopedia .com/blockchain-oracles-explained/.

In order to determine whether a given event has occurred, a smart contract may query one or more oracles. Smart contract developers often do not trust a single oracle due to the inherent risk that the oracle may be wrong and/or act unfaithfully.[57] Aggregation of data from multiple oracles is likely to lead to a more accurate view of the data supplied and the real-world conditions specified in the contract.[58]

Oracles often use cryptographic protocols in order to provide evidence that the data they provided have not been altered since they were obtained. Some well-known data sources such as Google or the Yahoo Finance API are not considered to be good to act as oracles because they do not provide cryptographic proof of what was returned to a given query at a point of time in the past.[59]

Oracles that can be utilized in smart contracts come in various forms. Some important forms of these include software oracles and hardware oracles. Software oracles are typically online sources of information such as temperature readings, and the price of various financial assets. The significance of software oracles lies in the fact that they are connected to the Internet, which allows them to supply the up-to-date information required to execute smart contracts.

Hardware oracles, on the other hand, are tasked with sending data to smart contracts when certain events occur in the physical world. Prominent examples of hardware oracles are IoT devices. To take an example, in SCM, if an object that has a sensor attached to it arrives at a warehouse, this data can be sent to a smart contract.[60]

There are several platforms that tack the oracle problem. For instance, blockchain-based middleware Chainlink identifies and authenticates data before a smart contract is triggered. Its on-chain interface has three components: (a) The Reputation Contract stores and tracks metrics related to oracle service providers; (b) The Order-Matching Contract extracts data parameters related to a service level agreement (SLA). It also takes bids from oracle providers; (c) The Aggregating Contract collects responses from oracle providers and calculates the final collective result.[61]

Many potential challenges of oracles need to be considered. As mentioned, oracles may charge a fee for their services. However, when the outcome of

---

[57] L Johnson (2018) 'What Is A Blockchain Oracle?' https://medium.com/lightswap/what-is-a-blockchain-oracle-8d7b94d55bf.

[58] B Curran (2018) 'What Are Oracles? Smart Contracts, Chainlink and "The Oracle Problem"' https://blockonomi.com/oracles-guide/.

[59] Johnson (2018).

[60] Asolo (2018).

[61] Curran, B. (2018) What are Oracles?

a prediction market has a high value, the opportunity cost of collusion may increase. In such a case, an oracle may find an incentive to collude with a bad actor.[62]

Second, the ideal situation would be to rely on multiple oracles. However, this is easier said than done. In niche areas, sufficient number of oracles may not exist. For high-value smart contracts, the probability of the consensus being manipulated could be too high.[63]

Third, the information presented by an oracle could have been hacked. In order to address this, oracles might provide cryptographic proof to ensure that the content of the data is untampered. However, there is also the possibility that a hacker could target the data source feeding the oracle.[64]

Finally, errors can occur with even the most reputable companies. It is thus important to ensure that smart contracts are being executed based on correct information.[65]

1.6.2.3 Hybrid smart contracts

Hybrid smart contracts involve combining codes that run on blockchains (on-chain codes) with data and computation that come from outside the blockchain (off-chain). Decentralized Oracle Networks provide the needed data and computation.[66] One estimate suggested that more than 90 per cent of smart contracts in important areas such as decentralized financial products, lotteries, or decentralized insurance in 2021 involved hybrid smart contracts.[67]

1.6.3   Token and Tokenization

Put simply a cryptographic token (or simply a token) is a digital unit of value that is programmable and recorded on a blockchain or other distributed ledger protocols.[68] Smart contracts are used to manage cryptographic tokens.[69] In

---

[62] Johnson (2018).
[63] Ibid.
[64] Ibid.
[65] Ibid.
[66] Chainlink Blog (2021) *Hybrid Smart Contracts Explained.* [online] Available at: https://blog.chain.link/hybrid-smart-contracts-explained/.
[67] G Anadiotis (2021) 'Chainlink 2.0 Brings Off-chain Compute to Blockchain Oracles, Promotes Adoption of Hybrid Smart Contracts.' [online] *ZDNet.* Available at: https://www.zdnet.com/article/chainlink-2-0-brings-off-chain-compute-to-blockchain-oracles-promotes-adoption-of-hybrid-smart-contracts.
[68] https://gochain.io/what-is-a-token/.
[69] S Voshmgir (2019) *Token Economy: How Blockchains and Smart Contracts Revolutionize the Economy –2019* (Shermin Voshmgir, Blockchainhub Berlin, Germany).

order to access a token, the private key for the address that holds the token is required. The token can only be authorized with the private key.

When a blockchain is used to issue a token, the issuance is recorded on the blockchain ledger. The blockchain also keeps a ledger of all movements of the token.[70] Tokens can be fungible or non-fungible.

1.6.3.1　Fungible token

Fungible tokens are identical. That is, one token cannot be distinguished from another. They are also divisible and interchangeable.[71] Some common examples of a fungible token are payment tokens such as Bitcoin, Monero, ETH and other cryptocurrencies.

Utility tokens, which are often used for fundraising in an Initial Coin Offering (ICO), are also fungible. The tokens that investors buy in an ICO can be used to buy goods or services offered by the token's issuer. It may also represent voting rights in decision-making. Such tokens are also called coins or cryptocurrency assets. The most widely used utility token is the Ethereum-based ERC-20, which is a technical standard used for smart contracts. An ERC-20 token keeps track of token owners at a given point of time.[72] An ERC-20 token can be created with less than 100 lines of codes.[73] Tokens built on Ethereum need to conform to the standard.[74] Before ERC-20 was created, each cryptocurrency had its own system in order to verify account balances and initiate transfers.

1.6.3.2　Non-fungible token

In the beginning blockchain supported only fungible assets such as Bitcoin and other cryptocurrencies. It has evolved to create a special kind of crypto assets known as NFTs.[75]

---

[70] CoreLedger (June 6, 2019) 'What is Tokenization? Everything You Should Know' *Medium*, https://medium.com/coreledger/what-is-tokenization-everything-you-should-know-1b2403a50f0e.

[71] blockchainhub.net (Sept 23, 2018) 'What Is a Fungible Token? What Is a Non-Fungible Token?' *Blockchainhub Berlin*, https://blockchainhub.net/blog/blog/nfts-fungible-tokens-vs-non-fungible-tokens/.

[72] Consensys Media (Aug 24, 2017) 'Making Token Sales Smart' https://media.consensys.net/making-token-sales-smart-28fe2011512f*.

[73] R Wolfson (2017) 'Purchasing Property Online: The Revolutionary Way Ukraine Uses Blockchain for Real Estate' https://www.huffingtonpost.com/entry/purchasing-property-online-the-revolutionary-way-ukraine_us_59933fe7e4b0afd94eb3f565.

[74] RR O'Leary (Sept 11, 2017) 'Ethereum's ERC-20 Token Standard Has Been Formalized' https://www.coindesk.com/ethereums-erc-20-token-standard-formalized.

[75] D Boscovic (March 31, 2021), https://theconversation.com/how-nonfungible-tokens-work-and-where-they-get-their-value-a-cryptocurrency-expert-explains-nfts-157489.

An NFT can be viewed as the digital representation of an asset that is scarce.[76] NFTs that are powered by blockchains can fight counterfeiting. Buyers are likely to be confident that they will actually get what they have paid for. NFTs often have three characteristics[77]: (a) uniqueness: metadata are used to describe factors that make an asset different from other assets. A permanent record which cannot be altered or erased describes the asset represented by an NFT; (b) rarity: NFTs are attractive to represent scarce assets; (c) indivisibility: most NFTs cannot be divided up into smaller denominations. The whole item must be acquired, held and transacted.

In July 2020, the blockchain-based diamond exchange platform Icecap launched a bid/ask trading marketplace for diamond investors. Using the Ethereum ERC-721 standard, Icecap assigns diamonds NFT tokens. Each ERC-721 token is unique and thus is referenced on the blockchain with a unique ID. It is possible to determine the owner of a token with the ID.[78]

Its diamonds are certified by the Gemological Institute of America (GIA) and verified by the Gem Certification & Assurance Lab (GCal).[79] Each diamond is graded based on carat, colour, and clarity. Each token represents the rights to a single specific piece of diamond that is stored in a vault. These tokens can be traded in crypto marketplaces such as OpenSea.io.[80]

The ERC-721 token standard makes it possible for NFT creators to capture information of relevance to their digital artifacts, which can be stored as tokens on the blockchain.

1.6.3.3 Security tokens

Security tokens, which are registered securities in a jurisdiction where they are issued, share characteristics of both fungible tokens and NFTs.[81] Such tokens

---

[76]   blockchainhub.net (2018) What Is a Fungible Token? What Is a Non-Fungible Token? *Blockchainhub Berlin*, https://blockchainhub.net/blog/blog/nfts-fungible -tokens-vs-non-fungible-tokens/.

[77]   Nonfugible Token *Cointelegraph Magazine*, https://cointelegraph.com/ magazine/nonfungible-tokens/#fungible-vs-non-fungible.

[78]   G Nash (2017) 'The Anatomy of ERC721' *Medium*, https://medium.com/crypto -currently/the-anatomy-of-erc721-e9db77abfc24.

[79]   TokenPost (2020) 'Diamonds Have Arrived on the Ethereum Blockchain' *TokenPost*, https://tokenpost.com/Diamonds-have-arrived-on-the-Ethereum-blockchain -5635.

[80]   globenewswire.com (2020) 'Icecap Leverages Tokenization to Launch First Global Investment-Grade Diamond Marketplace' *Icecap*, https://www.globenewswire .com/news-release/2020/07/15/2062623/0/en/Icecap-Leverages-Tokenization-to -Launch-First-Global-Investment-Grade-Diamond-Marketplace.html.

[81]   Adam Dossa, Pablo Ruiz, Stephane Gosselin and Fabian Vogelsteller (2019) *Security Token Standard*. [online] Available at: https://thesecuritytokenstandard.org/.

function as investment contracts and represent complete or fractional legal ownership in an asset such as a real estate asset, a company, and artwork, etc. Security tokens are more heavily regulated by the governments compared to utility tokens.[82]

1.6.4   Mainnet and Testnet

Mainnet is used to describe a blockchain protocol that is fully developed and deployed for actual cryptocurrency transactions with value. That is, such transactions are broadcasted, verified, and recorded on a blockchain.[83]

The term Testnet (Test Network), on the other hand, is used to refer to a blockchain protocol or network in a sandbox environment that is being used by programmers and developers to test smart contracts and DApps in order to create or modify functionalities and monitor network performance.[84] A Testnet is also used to fix bugs and other network failures. In such a network, it is possible for developers to take risks, experiment with new services, and identify the best possible model, which can be implemented in the Mainnet.[85]

Testnets and Mainnets are often operated by different networks. One group of computers agrees to work together to form a Testnet network. Another group agrees to serve as the Mainnet network.[86]

1.6.5   Layer 2

In blockchain, layer 2 refers to solutions that are designed to help scale a blockchain application by handling transactions off the blockchain such as Ethereum Mainnet (layer 1). Layer-2 solutions are built on top of the blockchain and they do not change any rules of the blockchain.[87] Such solutions take advantage of the decentralized security model of Mainnet. Transaction speeds in Ethereum Mainnet are slow when the network is busy, which leads to poor user experience for some types of DApps. Moreover, when the network gets

---

[82]   Ibid.

[83]   O Ifegwu (Aug 16, 2018) 'Mainnet' *Binance Academy*, https://academy.binance .com/glossary/mainnet.

[84]   Hummingbot (2018) 'Finance 3.0 WIKI | Ethereum Testnet vs. Mainnet' *Medium*, https://medium.com/hummingbot/finance-3-0-wiki-testnet-vs-mainnet-8ab5b78d93.

[85]   Ani (July 3, 2020) 'What is Mainnet and Testnet?' https://www.altcoinbuzz.io/ bitcoin-and-crypto-guide/crypto-mainnet-vs-testnet/.

[86]   Hummingbot (2018) 'Finance 3.0 WIKI | Ethereum Testnet vs. Mainnet' *Medium*, https://medium.com/hummingbot/finance-3-0-wiki-testnet-vs-mainnet-8ab5b78d93.

[87]   K Zhang (2018) *The State of Plasma: #1*. [online] *Medium*. Available at: https:// media.consensys.net/the-state-of-plasma-1-6b48c1e4b295.

busier, gas prices increase due to the fact that transaction senders aim to outbid each other. This can make Ethereum use very expensive.[88]

Due partly to the adoption of layer-2 solutions such as Polygon, average gas fees were reported to be decreased by 80 per cent on the Ethereum network in 2021Q2.[89]

IN FOCUS 1.4 POLYGON: A LAYER-2 SCALING SOLUTION

One example of Layer-2 scaling solution is Polygon, which provides tools to create scalable decentralized applications (DApps) that give priority to performance and user experience. Polygon achieves this in large part due to the underlying technical architecture of its PoS Commit Chain. Commit Chains are the generic term used for Plasma. Plasma is a layer-2 scaling solution proposed by Joseph Poon and Vitalik Buterin in the paper 'Plasma: Scalable Autonomous Smart Contracts' for building scalable applications.[a] Plasma uses a combination of smart contracts and cryptographic verification to enable fast and cheap transactions by offloading these transactions from the main Ethereum blockchain into a 'side' chain. These are also referred to as child or Plasma chains, which periodically report back to the main chain and use it to settle any disputes.[b] Commit Chains are transaction networks that operate adjacent to a main blockchain (Ethereum). Batches of transactions are bundled together by the Commit Chains and confirmed before returning data to the main chain. Theoretically, Polygon can have thousands of chains scaling together to increase throughput. Polygon's PoS blockchain serves as a Commit Chain to the Ethereum mainchain, which helps transact without network congestion that is common to Ethereum and other PoW blockchains. As of August 2021, over 80 Ethereum DApps were running on the platform.[c]

Polygon uses More Viable Plasma (MoreVP) scaling solution, which is different from the prototype implementation of Plasma known as Minimal Viable Plasma. In the latter, a transaction is considered to be invalid until it is signed twice. A user signs when they make a transaction to include in the block. When the sender sees that their transaction is mined and reported back to the root chain, the user signs the second time. This is called

[88] ethereum.org (n.d.) *Layer 2 Rollups*. [online] Available at: https://ethereum.org/en/developers/docs/scaling/layer-2-rollups/.
[89] T Ogilvie (n.d.) *Ethereum, the No. 2 Behind Bitcoin, Fights Off Challengers that Offer Cheaper and Faster Blockchains*. [online] *MarketWatch*. Available at: https://www.marketwatch.com/story/ethereum-the-no-2-behind-bitcoin-fights-off-challengers-that-offer-cheaper-and-faster-blockchains-11627058363.

a confirmation signature. This is related to a design involving a concept calledhttps://github.com/omisego/research/blob/master/plasma/plasma -mvp/explore/priority.md_exit-priority. Both signatures need to be sent to the operator as part of the Proof of Authority consensus. Note that a node operator 'runs software that keeps a full copy of the blockchain and broadcasts transactions across the network. Nodes are needed in order to make blockchains work'.[d] A user needs to provide the confirmation signature to withdraw money from the root chain. In MoreVP, no confirmation signatures are needed. In this way, users enjoy faster transaction speeds and a better user experience.[e]

Notes:
[a] J Poon and V Buterin (2017) 'Plasma: Scalable Autonomous Smart Contracts.' [online] Available at: https://plasma.io/plasma.pdf.
[b] docs.ethhub.io (n.d.) 'Plasma – EthHub.' [online] Available at: https://docs.ethhub.io/ethereum-roadmap/layer-2-scaling/plasma/.
[c] Gemini (n.d.) 'Polygon Crypto Layer-2 Scaling (Matic Network).' [online] Available at: https://www.gemini.com/cryptopedia/polygon-crypto-matic-network-dapps-erc20-token#section-polygon-crypto-network-basics.
[d] www.blockchainecosystem.io (n.d.) 'What Does It Mean to Be a Blockchain Node Operator? Are There Any Blockchains Out There that Don't Have Node Operators? – Blockchain ECOsystem.' [online] Available at: https://www.blockchainecosystem.io/ask/what-does-it-mean-to-be-a-blockchain-node-operator-are-there-any-blockchains-out-there-that-don-t-have-node-operators.
[e] omg.network (n.d.) 'The Differences between Minimum Viable Plasma and More Viable Plasma.' [online] Available at: https://omg.network/more-viable-plasma-vs-minimum-viable-plasma/.

1.7   CHAPTER SUMMARY AND CONCLUSION

Blockchain has come a long way since the publication of Satoshi Nakamoto's white paper on Bitcoin in October 2008 and the launch of the live Bitcoin network in January 2009. This technology is not limited to a narrow application of cryptocurrency.

Ethereum's launch in 2014 especially marked a major milestone that opened numerous opportunities for the deployment of blockchain in diverse application areas. Already tens of millions of smart contracts have been written using Ethereum. The Ethereum 2.0 upgrade is especially of great interest. With this upgrade Ethereum can process transactions faster and with lower energy consumption than can the Ethereum 1.0 blockchain network.

Different types of blockchains are already available for different users with varying needs and preferences. The rapid growth of investment by organizations worldwide would lead to further developments in blockchain and is likely to facilitate its rapid diffusion.

1.8   THE ROAD MAP OF THE BOOK

Including this introductory chapter, there are eight chapters in this book organized in three parts. The remaining two chapters in Part I look at organizational transformations that blockchain is likely to create especially in combination with other advanced technologies. Chapter 2 provides an analysis of blockchain's impacts on organizational forms, business models and strategies. In Chapter 3, we examine how many of the trust-related challenges can be overcome by combining blockchain with other advanced technologies.

In the three chapters in Part II, an overview of key application areas of blockchain is provided and some promising use cases are documented. Chapter 4 evaluates blockchain's potential to address various challenges in SCM. This chapter argues that supply chain is a good blockchain use case that yields measurable results of values for companies engaged in economic transactions that cannot be possible with other alternatives. Chapter 5 focuses on blockchain's impacts on security, privacy and compliance issues. It argues that blockchain's deployment would reduce the susceptibility to manipulation and forgery by malicious participants. Chapter 6 delves into blockchain's roles in transforming payment and settlement systems. It offers a detailed description of how blockchain enables new ways of managing money and facilitating payments with ease and in more efficient ways.

In Part III's final two chapters, opportunities, challenges and implications are discussed and the way forward is suggested. In Chapter 7, we highlight the opportunities, barriers, and enablers of blockchain adoption by organizations. Discussion, conclusion and recommendations are provided in Chapter 8.

2. Impacts on organizational forms, business models and strategies

2.1 INTRODUCTION

Blockchain is likely to lead to major disruption in organizational forms and business models. To take an example, the EU describes a future possibility of decentralized autonomous organizations (DAOs) as follows: 'A DAO could own a self-driving car that acts as a taxi 24 hours a day. This would generate income that it would use to pay for its own fuel, repairs and insurance, and save money to replace the vehicle at the end of its useful life.'[1]

The potential of blockchain to transform organizational forms and business models can be better understood by looking at blockchain-led reduction in the cost of verification and the cost of networking.[2] The first component is related to the costs to verify the attributes of a transaction. In the physical world, it is as simple as showing an ID card in order to buy liquor. More complex scenarios include verifying goods moving through a supply chain and the full Know Your Customer (KYC) process in financial transactions with a bank, which involves identifying and verifying a person engaged in a transaction. In an ideal world, a costless verification can be implemented or the cost of verification is nearly zero. In such a world, people know that data have not been tampered with and the cost of knowing that is close to zero and thus integrity and trust can be built easily.

As to blockchain's effect on reducing the cost of networking, various parties can start a self-sustaining process and operate a marketplace. It is not necessary to assign control to a centralized intermediary. This is possible because blockchain can verify the state at a low cost. Economic incentives can be targeted to reward valuable activities from a network perspective. They include contribution of resources needed to operate and scale the network and secure a decen-

---

[1] C Gorey (2017) 'Blockchain 2.0: How It Could Overhaul the Fabric of Democracy and Identity' *SiliconRepublic*, https://www.siliconrepublic.com/enterprise/blockchain-outside-of-fintech.

[2] C Catalini and J Gans (2019) 'Some Simple Economics of the Blockchain.' Rotman School of Management Working Paper 2874598.

tralized stage. The digital marketplaces that result from such collaborations allow the participants to make joint investments to create shared digital assets.[3]

By facilitating the creation of networks and verification of the attributes of a transaction, blockchain can help create and enhance trust among firms and individuals. This is important because trust is at the centre of formalizations, arrangements and institutions, such as contracts. As Bohnet et al., put it: 'Offering the contract is a matter of trust, and performing it, a matter of trust-worthiness'.[4] What makes this observation worthy of comment is blockchain's trustless feature.

In a non-blockchain world, Lynne Zucker (1986) identified three ways to produce trust: (1) institution-based trust is linked to institutions such as government bureaucracies and other formal mechanisms, trade associations and professions; (2) process-based trust is produced from the engagement in trustworthy relationships; and (3) characteristic-based trust is generated by identifiable attributes that are linked with trustworthy behaviour. Blockchain makes it possible to engage in transactions in the absence of any of the mechanisms to produce trust.[5]

Blockchain's trust-producing mechanisms enable a number of new and innovative business models. One way to achieve the objective of a firm's business model is to focus on greater efficiency by designing the activity system to reduce transaction costs.[6] Activities can be designed and engineered to promote greater efficiency.

Blockchain offers special benefits to small- and medium-sized enterprises (SMEs) that often lack the ability to demonstrate attributes that prove their trustworthiness. Especially they are not in a position to produce what Zucker[7] refers to as characteristic-based trust. Note that characteristic-based trust is generated by identifiable attributes that are linked with trustworthy behaviour. Entities that are known to possess certain well-defined attributes (e.g., credit scores) are viewed as trustworthy. Especially most developing economies are characterized by the lack, or poor performance of, credit rating agencies. A national credit bureau would collect and distribute reliable credit information and hence increase transparency and minimize banks' lending risks. This

---

[3]   Ibid., 8.
[4]   Iris Bohnet, Bruno S. Frey and Steffen Huck (2001) 'More Order with Less Law: On Contract Enforcement, Trust, and Crowding' *American Political Science Review* Vol 95(1) 131.
[5]   LG Zucker (1986) 'Production of Trust: Institutional Sources of Economic Structure, 1840–1920' *Research in Organizational Behavior* Vol 8 53–111.
[6]   C Zott and R Amit (2007) 'Business Model Design and the Performance of Entrepreneurial Firms' *Organization Science* Vol 18(2) 181–99.
[7]   Zucker (n 5).

situation puts SMEs in a disadvantaged position in the credit market. This is because SMEs tend to be more informationally opaque than large corporations since the former often lack certified audited financial statements and thus it is difficult for banks to assess or monitor the financial conditions. Thus, an important reason why SMEs face barriers to access financial products concerns informational opacity.[8] Thanks to blockchain, low-cost working capital loans are being provided by B2B (Business-to-Business) partners to finance production activities.

In light of the above observations, this chapter looks at how organizational business models and interorganizational networks are affected by blockchain. It provides insights into the value of evolving and novel business models based on blockchain. It also provides details of blockchain's possible roles in transforming structures and processes at organizational and interorganizational levels that would enable business models that would potentially allow for reduced transactions costs and provide a better value proposition to customers.

2.2   BLOCKCHAIN-BASED BUSINESS MODELS

A business model can be defined as 'a statement of how a firm will make money and sustain its profit stream over time'.[9] Put differently, a business model is a description of a company's intention to create and capture value by linking new technological environments to business strategies.[10] In its simplest form, reducing the costs of offerings and improvements in perceived quality can provide a basis for enhanced value delivery and firm performance. Blockchain offers inherent promises that are relevant to the fulfilment of these goals.

The ideas and concepts that underlie business models build on the value chain structure (value).[11] [12] Most approaches to business models thus centre around value definitions and components of business models encompass a wide range of activities related to creation, delivery and capture of value such

---

[8]   JE Stiglitz and A Weiss (1981) 'Credit Rationing in Markets with Imperfect Information' *American Economic Review* Vol 71(3), 393–410.
[9]   DW Stewart and Q Zhao (2000) 'Internet Marketing, Business Models, and Public Policy' *J. Public Policy Mark.* Vol 19(2) 287–96.
[10]   R Hawkins (2003) 'Looking Beyond the Dot Com Bubble: Exploring the Form and Function of Business Models in the Electronic Marketplace,' in: H Bouwman, B Preissl and C Steinfield (eds), *E-Life after the Dot-com Bust*, (Physica-Varlag, Heidelberg).
[11]   Value chain analysis provides a means to organize and understand the customer value-creating activities and processes in a firm. It focuses on internal activities that add value to a firm's products.
[12]   ME Porter (1985) *Competitive Advantage* (Free Press, New York).

as value proposition, value chain, value offering, customer value, value model, value network, value activity, value interfaces, value ports, value cluster, value exchanges,[13] value systems,[14] target markets, cost and profit model, and competitive strategy.[15]

At the operational level, a business model thus focuses on processes and design that enable the firm to create value. Some of the major decision-related issues include production or delivery of service, administrative processes, resource flows, knowledge management, and logistical streams.[16]

The overall goal of a firm's business model is to exploit a business opportunity by creating value for the various relevant parties and stakeholders. They include fulfilling customers' needs and creating customer surplus, which lead to profitability and growth for the firm as well as its partners.[17] Blockchain is likely to drastically change the way businesses identify, define and carry out various processes and activities to achieve their goals. For some companies, for instance, blockchain may completely redefine their customers, competitors and locations of business operations.

Preliminary evidence from the field indicates that among several mechanisms to reduce costs, blockchain can minimize unnecessary usage of valuable resources. As an illustration of this, consider the Swiss start-up Modum's system to ensure the safe delivery of pharmaceutical drugs. Modum teamed with the University of Zurich to design the system. Most medicines need to be transported under exact temperature, humidity and light conditions in order to ensure usability. Modum's sensors constantly measure these conditions on drugs that are being transported. Under the current system, cargos involve many people and a lot of paperwork, which can be tampered with.[18] Modum's solution aims to address these issues.

A recent regulatory change in the EU, known as Good Distribution Practice of Medicinal Products for Human Use (GDP 2013/C 343/01), requires companies to report any deviations in temperature or other conditions to the distributor as well as the recipient of the affected medicinal products. Currently

---

[13]   JC Linder and CS Cantrell (2001) *Changing Business Models* Institute for Strategic Change, Accenture, Chicago.

[14]   ME Porter (1996) 'What Is Strategy' *Harvard Business Review* Vol 74(6) 61–78.

[15]   H Chesbrough and RS Rosenbaum (2000) 'The Role of the Business Model in Capturing Value from Innovation' (working paper). (Harvard Business School Press, Boston, MA, USA).

[16]   M Morris, M Schindehutte and J Allen (2005) 'The Entrepreneur's Business Model: Toward a Unified Perspective' *Journal of Business Research* Vol 58(6) 726–35.

[17]   Zott and Amit (n 6).

[18]   M Allen (2017) 'How Blockchain Could Soon Affect Everyday Lives' http://www.swissinfo.ch/eng/joining-the-blocks_how-blockchain-could-soon-affect-everyday-lives/43003266.

the only way to comply with the new regulations would be to use refrigeration trucks that make up a significant part of cold chain distribution. These trucks are often four to eight times more expensive than normal logistic services. However, 60 per cent of about 200 million yearly shipments in the EU do not contain products that are temperature sensitive. This means that an estimated US$ 3 billion is wasted annually for unnecessary cooling.[19]

There reportedly are three categories of temperature that medicines need to be stored at: cold (-20°C), cool (2° to °C), and ambient (15° to 25°C). Every medicine, however, has so called 'stability data', which states that the medicine 'can stay for X hours in temperature range Y, [which is] usually 72 hours between 2°C and 40°C'.[20] Modum is focusing on the ambient products. Medicinal shipments that do not require refrigeration are tracked with a Modum sensor to monitor the temperatures of the medicines. This means that no cold chain truck is required. When the medicine reaches the destination, the data is transferred to the Ethereum blockchain.

Blockchain use can also have implications for the real and perceived quality of a firm's products. Blockchain's capabilities for detection and control of counterfeit products and low-quality ingredients in food products are among a number of mechanisms that contribute to a product's quality. Moreover, in a blockchain world consumers are empowered due to the decentralized nature of information flows.

The preceding examples point to an emerging trend in organizations' blockchain adoption to create value. Value also involves choices regarding firm boundaries.[21] Specifically prior researchers have widely recognized the necessity of collaboration and learning outside the borders of a company in order to better utilize innovations and create novel business models.[22] In the context of logistics and supply chain management (SCM) practice, both cooperation and competition between value chains facilitate knowledge acquisition and create

---

[19] R Campbell (2016) 'Modum.io's Tempurature-tracking Blockchain Solution Wins Accolades at Kickstarter Accelerator 2016' *Bitcoinmagazine*, https://bitcoinmagazine.com/articles/modum-io-s-tempurature-tracking-blockchain-solution-wins-accolades-at-kickstarter-accelerator-1479162773/.

[20] Ibid.

[21] JB Barney (1999) 'How Firm Capabilities Affect Boundary Decisions' *Sloan Management Review* Vol 40(1) 19– 32.

[22] H Chesbrough (2006) *Open Business Models: How to Thrive in the New Innovation Landscape* (Harvard Business School Press, Boston, MA, USA); I Nonaka and H Takeuchi (1995) 'Global Organizational Knowledge Creation,' in I Nonaka and H Takeuchi (eds), *Knowledge Creating Company* (Oxford University Press, Oxford, UK) 197–223.

logistics value.[23] Significant benefits may arise when organizations mutually develop and leverage technologies and resources.[24] This is even more true of blockchain. Interorganizational collaboration and cooperation have been the key feature of a number of high profile early blockchain projects.

However, there are a number of key challenges that need to be addressed in interorganizational collaborations. Some scholars have claimed that in highly innovative cooperative contexts the capability to detect opportunistic behaviour is low.[25] This is especially true for companies that engage in coopetition, which involves 'simultaneous cooperation and competition'.[26]

Prior researchers have challenged some of the key assumptions in cooptation – especially those related to opportunism and trust. Regarding the development of trust in a cooperative context, some have noted that the control processes carried out by the partners are weakened and this may result in an incentive, to one or more partners, to behave opportunistically.[27] Pivotal to this view of interorganizational control is the challenge firms face in achieving an optimal balance between cooperation and competition.[28]

It can be argued that blockchain offers the best means to balance cooperation and competition by addressing trust-related concerns in interorganizational collaborations. Blockchain thus provides the most effective control measure in interorganizational relations.

2.3   ILLUSTRATION FROM TWO INDUSTRIES

As illustrative examples of blockchain-led disruptions in business models, we use two industries: the creative contents industry and the food industry.

---

[23]   DW Song and ES Lee (2012) 'Coopetitive Networks, Knowledge Acquisition and Maritime Logistics Value' *International Journal of Logistics Research and Applications* Vol 15(1) 15–35.

[24]   MJ Chen (1996) 'Competitor Analysis and Interfirm Rivalry: Toward a Theoretical Integration' *Academy of Management Review* Vol 21(1) 100–34; C Enberg (2012) 'Enabling Knowledge Integration in Coopetitive R&D Projects – The Management of Conflicting Logics' *International Journal of Project Management* Vol 30(7) 771–80.

[25]   JF Hennart (1988) 'A Transaction Costs Theory of Equity Joint Ventures' *Strategic Management Journal* Vol 9(4) 361–74.

[26]   M Bengtsson and S Kock (2014) 'Coopetition–Quo Vadis? Past Accomplishments and Future Challenges' *Industrial Marketing Management* Vol 43(2) 180–88.

[27]   A Grandori and M Neri (1999) 'The Fairness Properties of Interfirm Networks,' in A Grandori (ed), *Inter-firm Networks* (Routledge, London, UK) 41–66.

[28]   DJ Ketchen, CC Snow and VL Hoover (2004) 'Research on Competitive Dynamics: Recent Accomplishments and Future Challenges' *Journal of Management* Vol 30(6) 779–804.

2.3.1   The Creative Contents Industry

Creative work such as music is undervalued due to transactional frictions.[29] These are associated with high information gathering and contract-enforcement costs. If anyone wants to pay for the right to play a song at a concert or in a movie, it often takes a long time. An upshot of this is that people may use a movie, music or audio recording without paying for it or decide not to use it due to the complexity in making payments. A significant part of the creative work thus remains underutilized.

The current model also enables intermediaries to reap most of the profits. In the music industry, for instance, intermediaries capture most of the value and artists get paid last. According to Musicoin, intermediaries take over 80 per cent of royalty fees.[30] The current model is that streaming services first pay off the record labels, publishers and Public Rights Organizations (PROs) before paying to artists.

The above problems are likely to be overcome because of advances on a number of fronts. Ascribe.io has developed a solution that utilizes a unique cryptographic ID verified with blockchain to authenticate an artwork. Such a system makes it possible to securely transfer ownership rights of creative content to galleries or collectors.[31]

With blockchain, artists will know how much their record label/publisher is paid for their services.[32] Companies such as Mycelia want to address this unfair situation using blockchain. Mycelia was founded by Grammy-winning British singer and songwriter Imogen Heap with an aim to create a 'fair trade' music industry.[33] Mycelia has developed intelligent songs with built in smart contracts. The system enables artists to sell directly to consumers without

---

[29]   Ryo Takahashi (Aug, 2017) 'How Can Creative Industries Benefit from Blockchain?'   http://www.mckinsey.com/industries/media-and-entertainment/our -insights/how-can-creative-industries-benefit-from-blockchain?cid=other-eml-alt -mip-mck-oth-1708&hlkid=ab75fa8be47f4910be97e311b0ba92f0&hctky=2762145& hdpid=e9e4c6cb-5ccd-4eec-b040-5a5a57c078cc.

[30]   R Campbell (2017) 'How the Blockchain Lets Musicians Connect with Fans (and Get Paid)' *Nasdaq*, www.nasdaq.com/article/how-the-blockchain-lets-musicians -connect-with-fans-and-get-paid-cm755712.

[31]   Oscar Lopez (Dec 16, 2016) 'The Tech Behind Bitcoin Could Help Artists and Protect Collectors. So Why Won't They Use It?' *Artsy*, www.artsy.net/article/artsy -editorial-the-tech-bitcoin-could-help-artists-protect-collectors-so-why-won't-they-use -it.

[32]   I Murphy (2017) 'Music Societies Turn to Blockchain' *Enterprise Times*, https:// www.enterprisetimes.co.uk/2017/04/10/music-societies-turn-blockchain/.

[33]   L Kuo (Feb 19, 2016) 'Imogen Heap Wants to use Blockchain Technology to Revolutionize the Music Industry' https://qz.com/620454/imogen-heap-wants-to-use -blockchain-technology-to-revolutionize-the-music-industry/.

the services of a label, financial intermediary, or technology company. The reduced costs could lead to a lower price to consumers of music.

An NFT can provide a further mechanism to create higher value by guaranteeing exclusive ownership of music rights to customers. To take an example, the NFT music platform Royal founded by Justin David Blau (better known by his stage name 3Lau) makes it possible for artists to give their fans direct ownership of their songs. The fans can also receive royalties if the songs they own become popular. In October 2021, 3Lau released a collection of 333 unique art pieces as NFTs. The NFTs also represented 50 per cent of ownership in the streaming rights of 3Lau's song, 'Worst Case'. An NFT of 3Lau's two-minute song 'WAVEFORM' gave its owner 100 per cent of the rights.[34] The NFT was offered as an auction item as part of global auction house Christie's collaboration with NFT marketplace OpenSea. On December 7, 2021, 'WAVEFORM' was sold for 77 ETH (US$ 330,200).[35]

Initiatives have also been developed around issues of rampant piracy in this industry. For instance, Revelator, a cloud-based provider of sales and marketing intelligence for independent music businesses, has developed a blockchain-based system to track music rights and distribute royalties to rights owners. Revelator issues copyright registrations as digital assets, which are secured by multi-signature authentication. It also enforces multi-party terms and jurisdiction compliance rules.[36] The system tracks downloads on music streaming services Spotify, iTunes, and others. Through the platform artists can see their shares on-demand with one click. There is no need to send a request to a manager or an accountant, and wait for a response. This mechanism is likely to boost trust between the involved parties and reduces friction between them.

Likewise, in April 2017, three of the world's largest performance rights organizations (PROs), the American Society of Composers, Authors, and Publishers (ASCAP), France's Société des auteurs, compositeurs et éditeurs de musique (SACEM) and PRS (Paul Reed Smith) for Music announced that they had teamed up to develop a blockchain-based system of managing music copyright information. The system is expected to provide real-time update and

---

[34] R Rivas (Dec 9, 2021) 'Will the Future of the Music Industry Be NFTs and Metaverse Concerts?' https://cryptoslate.com/will-the-future-of-the-music-industry-be -nfts-and-metaverse-concerts/.

[35] S Escalante-De Mattei (Dec 8, 2021) 'Christie's NFT Auction with OpenSea Concludes with Middling $3.6 M. Result' https://www.artnews.com/art-news/market/ christies-opensea-nft-sale-1234612759/.

[36] O Ogundeji (2016) 'Blockchain Music Administrator Revelator Raises $2.5m' *Cryptocoinnews*,   https://www.cryptocoinsnews.com/blockchain-music-administrator -revelator-raises-2-5m/.

tracking capabilities. Data and technology teams from the three organizations were reported to be working with IBM in order to match, aggregate and qualify existing links between music recordings International Standard Recording Codes (ISRCs) and music work International Standard Work Codes (ISWCs). The project is expected to improve royalty matching processes and result in turn in faster licensing, lower errors and reduced costs.[37]

2.3.2 The Food Industry

In order to emphasize the importance of blockchain in the food supply chain, the proponents of blockchain offer an example of the 2015 E. coli outbreak at Chipotle Mexican Grill outlets. The crisis left 55 customers ill. The company suffered a reputation loss due to negative news stories, restaurant shutdowns, and investigations. Sales reduced dramatically and its share price dropped by 42 per cent. The roots of the problem lay partly in the reliance of Chipotle and other food companies on multiple suppliers to deliver parts and ingredients. There was a severe lack of transparency and accountability across complex supply chains. Food companies such as Chipotle are not in a position to monitor their suppliers in real time. It was thus impossible for Chipotle to prevent the contamination or contain it in a targeted way after it was discovered.[38]

Chipotle's value proposition is centred on fresh and locally sourced ingredients. The non-blockchain methods of securing the Chipotle food supply chain are expensive and cumbersome. The process involves manual verification and massive record keeping. Blockchain can reduce the workload and ensure traceability. Besides the obvious value of traceability, huge benefits can be reaped in terms of reduced labour costs and food wastes. The above examples can be generalized to any industry such as aircraft, electronics or drugs. In short, blockchain-led total value chain visibility can offer huge gains to operations for any firm.[39]

Overall blockchain can create customer value in many different ways. Put in the simplest terms, a higher customer value can be created by reducing costs and/or by increasing perceived quality. In Table 2.1, we show how different

---

[37]   *M Magazine* (2017) 'ASCAP, SACEM and PRS for Music Join Forces on Blockchain Project' http://www.m-magazine.co.uk/news/ascap-sacem-prs-music-join -forces-blockchain-.

[38]   MJ Casey and P Wong (2017) 'Global Supply Chains Are About to Get Better, Thanks to Blockchain' *Harvard Business Review*, https://hbr.org/2017/03/global -supply-chains-are-about-to-get-better-thanks-to-blockchain.

[39]   K O'Marah (2017) 'Blockchain: Enormous Potential Demands Your Attention' *Supply Chain Digital*, http://www.supplychaindigital.com/technology/blockchain -enormous-potential-demands-your-attention.

Table 2.1   *Different value delivery mechanisms using blockchain*

	Reducing costs	Increasing perceived quality
Organizational level	• Château Margaux's deployment of Everledger's blockchain-based system • Artists can sell directly to consumers without the services of a label, financial intermediary, or technology company	• Château Margaux's deployment of Everledger's blockchain-based system
Interorganizational level	• Modum's system to ensure the safe delivery of pharmaceutical drugs: reduction in unnecessary usage of valuable resources • Walmart's service to monitor produce in the US and pork in China	• Walmart's service to monitor produce in the US and pork in China

mechanisms might be put to work to deliver higher customer value using blockchain.

2.4   BLOCKCHAIN-ENABLED NOVEL BUSINESS MODELS

Activities and processes can be carried out in novel ways to achieve the overall goal of a firm's business model. This is referred to as 'novelty-centered activity system design'.[40] Key elements of a design include content, structure and governance. In such a design, new activities can be adopted (content), the existing activities can be linked in new ways (structure) or the activities can be governed in new ways (governance).[41]

A novel business model may create a new market or facilitate transactions in a way that is superior to the existing models.[42] Blockchain facilitates the development and implementation of creative and novel business models that can create and capture value from customers.

New activities can be created using blockchain that can improve a business model. As an illustration of this potential, consider a food supply chain. Even supply chain activities involving a small quantity of products such as dumping a few dozen pints of apples or blueberries into a juice press or pouring a mixture of liquid and solids into a strainer in order to remove the solids can be recorded on blockchain in a cost-effective manner. Combining with data related to temperature, humidity, motion, chemical composition or other

---

[40]   Zott and Amit (n 6).
[41]   Ibid.
[42]   Ibid.

relevant indicators that can be collected from IoT (Internet of Things) devices or sensors on equipment, blockchain can cost effectively confirm everything related to the supply chain history of food products.[43]

If a farmer registers foods on blockchain, the distribution company that buys it from the farmer can also register. Everyone in the supply chain up to the grocer can do the same thing. These benefits thus accrue to all the parties involved in the supply chain such as the retail warehouses and individual stores. For instance, stores know the details of arrival of a shipment so they are prepared to receive it.[44] In the food product supply chain, for instance, when it is confirmed that a load of apples will arrive at a juice factory, a code is generated and stored remotely. The code is available for verification at any time. Information about the apples and the factory that receives them is 'chained' together by this code. Theoretically the data can be portrayed as colour-coded maps of inputs, conversion steps and outputs from 'farm to fork'.

The final step in the design of a business model is the governance of the activities using new ways.[45] In Modum's case noted above, a Solidity-based smart contract compares the data against various regulatory requirements.[46]

If all the required conditions are fulfilled, the product is released. If the temperature and other tracked conditions deviate significantly from the regulatory requirements, the sender and the receiver are notified of the deviation. Modum conducted its first pilot project in June 2016.[47] A smart contract provides the most effective governance mechanism.

2.5   MEASURES AT ORGANIZATIONAL AND INTERORGANIZATIONAL LEVELS

The above discussion suggests that blockchain integration entails the creation of new business processes beyond the boundary of the firm. Measures are thus needed at organizational as well as interorganizational levels.

---

[43]   O'Marah (n 39).

[44]   T Groenfeldt (2017) 'IBM and Maersk Apply Blockchain to Container Shipping' *Forbes*, https://www.forbes.com/sites/tomgroenfeldt/2017/03/05/ibm-and-maersk-apply -blockchain-to-container-shipping/.

[45]   Zott and Amit (n 6).

[46]   Campbell (n 19).

[47]   Ibid.

2.5.1   Organizational-Level Measures

Value also involves transaction costs.[48] Cost reduction represents a key mechanism for value delivery. In this regard, in order to illustrate blockchain's potential to reduce costs consider international remittances and other transactions dealing with different currencies across different countries. International money transfers currently take several days and are extremely inefficient. Using blockchain-based applications, it is possible to drastically reduce the cost of a cross-border transaction (see Chapter 6).

In some cases, buyers of creative work may be forced to purchase contents that they do not need. For instance, digital music stores such as iTunes allow consumers to purchase individual song tracks. A smaller unit than this may not be possible in the non-blockchain world. Using blockchain, consumers can buy only small snippets of creative works. Blockchain's 'micrometering' capability can redefine the smallest consumable unit of creative content such as music or a movie.[49] Cryptocurrencies' low transaction costs facilitate micropayments. Putting these two conditions together, it makes it practically feasible to pay a very low price for a few seconds of a song to use in a movie trailer.[50]

Consumers are not required to purchase unneeded parts of creative material. Streamium's disruptive business model allows artists to be remunerated by offering micrometering payment services.[51] Anyone can use the service by creating a live broadcast on Streamium websites with a few clicks. Streamium uses webRTC, which is an Internet communication protocol for peer-to-peer videoconferencing. The broadcast is linked to a Bitcoin address. An artist who broadcasts her concert can share a link with viewers. The viewers are asked to load a Bitcoin balance. With the progress of the broadcast, the viewer's balance is automatically deducted. Viewers know the rate before joining the session.[52] Viewers pay a per-minute rate. There are no intermediaries involved.

One way consumers may benefit from blockchain as discussed above is that this technology may play an important role in reducing deadweight losses. For instance, in many cases consumers are forced to buy more than they want which makes the price of a movie/music outside a consumer's affordability

---

[48]   OE Williamson (1981) 'The Economics of Organization: The Transaction Cost Approach' *Am. J. Sociol* Vol 87(4) 548–77.
[49]   Takahashi (n 29).
[50]   Ibid.
[51]   Ibid.
[52]   Mario Cotillard (May 24, 2015) 'Streamium Allows You to Earn Bitcoin per Minute' https://bravenewcoin.com/news/streamium-allows-you-to-earn-bitcoin-per-minute/.

range. If the supplier lacks the ability to divide a movie/music into smaller consumable units, the difference between the price the consumer is willing to pay and the marginal cost of a copy of the digital service represents deadweight loss.[53] With blockchain, the supplier can bring the price within the affordability range by offering just what the consumer needs and thus overcome the inefficiencies associated with deadweight losses.

Blockchain also provides a means of enhancing the real and perceived quality of a product. In some cases, digital contents are offered through advertising models.[54] It may even be the only available choice. Blockchain makes it possible to offer a high-quality, ad-free experience. For instance, Brave's solution allows Internet users to pay content providers in Bitcoins and get an ad-free experience.[55]

To take another example, a software application designed by start-up Everledger verifies the 'provenance' of rough-cut diamonds. The system can be considered to be a digital expression of the Kimberley Process.[56] Note that the Kimberley Process (KP) is an initiative jointly undertaken by governments, industry and civil society to eliminate the flow of diamonds mined within conflict zones such as Sierra Leone that are used by rebel movements to finance wars against legitimate governments.[57]

Everledger has also developed a blockchain-based system to track wines. In December 2016, wine expert Maureen Downey and Everledger recorded the first certification of a 2001 bottle from French producer Château Margaux. Downey's company Chai Consulting and Everledger developed the Chai Wine Vault system for this purpose (https://www.winefraud.com/chai-wine-vault/). The IBM-based ledger gives each bottle a unique digital identity with over 90 pieces of data related to ownership and storage history. The data include high resolution photographs and information from the label, capsule, cork and glass.[58] As the wine bottle moves along different participants in the supply chain, digital data is updated with ownership and storage records. To verify provenance, retailers, warehouses, auction houses and other sale platforms

[53]   SJ Liebowitz and S Margolis (2005) 'Seventeen Famous Economists Weigh In on Copyright: The Role of Theory, Empirics, and Network Effects' *Harvard Journal of Law & Technology* Vol 18(2) 435–57.

[54]   Marcus O'Dair (July 1, 2016) 'Music on the Blockchain' Blockchain for Creative Industries Research Cluster Middlesex University.

[55]   Takahashi (n 29).

[56]   H Clancy (2017) 'The Blockchain's Emerging Role in Sustainability' *GreenBiz*, https://www.greenbiz.com/article/blockchains-emerging-role-sustainability.

[57]   Kimberly Process (2016) https://www.kimberleyprocess.com/.

[58]   CF Rothschield (2016) 'Wine Vault Offers Security in a Digital Age' *Wine Searcher*, http://www.wine-searcher.com/m/2016/12/wine-vault-offers-security-in-a -digital-age.

can link the bottle to its digital identity. Authentication certificates can be kept private or they can be made public for marketing purposes.

There are substantial frauds related to counterfeit products such as medicines, fine wines and luxury fashions. One estimate suggested that the value of fraudulent fine wine is about US$ 1 billion annually.[59] It was reported that counterfeiters had reverse-engineered the Coravin system so that they can refill a bottle. As of December 2016, Downey's company was in the process of developing a tamper-proof tag with a chip that detects and registers when a bottle's cork is pulled, or when it is pierced by a system such as Coravin.[60] The ID of such a bottle will not 'check in' when logged into the system.[61]

According to Everledger, one-fifth of the sales of international 'fine wine' are of counterfeit bottles.[62] Everledger's tamper-evident radio frequency identification (RFID) tag is attached on the bottle's cork. Everledger's system did not track factors such as bottle temperature. The organization argued that the reputation of the organization storing the wine was sufficient.[63] The diamond industry uses a certificate system. For older wines, factors such as a label's design and paper used by a producer in the stated year of production are used in the authentication.[64]

Policing and other interventions associated with piracy increase companies' costs of doing business. These costs are often passed to consumers, which is likely to result in higher prices of the products.[65] Firms such as Château Margaux can thus pass on lower costs to consumers due to blockchain-led reduction in piracy rates.

2.5.2   Interorganizational-Level Measures

With blockchain firms can generate more value from cooperation and collaboration. To take one example, Walmart has teamed up with its groceries and food products suppliers to implement blockchain. In late 2016, it was reported that Walmart was trial testing a service it developed with IBM to monitor produce in the US and pork in China. The first project involved tracking

---

[59]   Ibid.
[60]   Coravin makes use of a needle and gas to extract wine without opening the bottle.
[61]   Rothschield (n 58).
[62]   MA Mathieson (2017) 'Blockchain Starts to Prove Its Value outside of Finance' *Computer Weekly*, http://www.computerweekly.com/feature/Blockchain-starts-to-prove -its-value-outside-of-finance.
[63]   Ibid., e.
[64]   Ibid.
[65]   S Otim and V Grover (2010) 'E-commerce: A Brand Name's Curse' *Electronic Markets* Vol 20(2), 147–60.

produce from Latin America to the US. The second involved moving pork products from Chinese farms to Chinese stores. As of February 2017, it had completed the two pilots with IBM. Walmart was reported to be confident that a finished version would be ready 'within a few years'.

Blockchain enabled digitally tracking individual pork products in a few minutes compared to many days taken in the past. Details about the farm, factory, batch number, storage temperature and shipping can be viewed on blockchain. These details help assess the authenticity of products, and the expiry date. In the case of food contamination, it is possible to pinpoint the products to recall.[66]

While the test was limited to these two items, it involved multiple stores. If an item is found to be spoiled or the source of a product is shown to be compromised, the system acts proactively. The goal thus is to improve food safety. The information tracked includes the farm where the vegetable or pig originated and their operating practices. RFID tags, sensors and barcodes, which are already widely used across many supply chains, provide the relevant data.[67]

On May 31, 2017, Walmart released the results of the food safety and traceability protocols test that started in October 2016 in China and the US. Walmart reported that blockchain helped to reduce the time taken to track food from days to minutes.[68] Specifically, the tests performed on Chinese pork and US mangos revealed that tracing food origins could be handled in 2.2 seconds, which used to take many weeks with non-blockchain technologies.[69]

Blockchain-based solutions help Walmart provide guaranteed quality and performance. Blockchain also has important cost-saving implications for the retailer. In a crisis involving contaminated food products, Walmart would be able to easily identify the source and engage in strategic removals of affected products instead of recalling the entire product line. Blockchain also enables more effective response if tainted products are discovered. In this way, the

---

[66] F Yiannas (2017) 'A New Era of Food Transparency with Wal-Mart Center in China' *Food Safety News*, http://www.foodsafetynews.com/2017/03/a-new-era-of -food-transparency-with-wal-mart-center-in-china/#.WOB65mcVjIU.

[67] O Kharif (2016) 'Wal-Mart Tackles Food Safety with Trial of Blockchain' *Bloomberg*, https://www.bloomberg.com/news/articles/2016-11-18/wal-mart-tackles -food-safety-with-test-of-blockchain-technology.

[68] S Higgins (2017) 'Walmart: Blockchain Food Tracking Test Results Are Very Encouraging. *CoinDesk*, http://www.coindesk.com/walmart-blockchain-food-tracking -test-results-encouraging/.

[69] J Nation (Jun 1, 2017) 'Walmart Tests Food Safety with Blockchain Traceability' https://www.ethnews.com/walmart-tests-food-safety-with-blockchain-traceability.

company can keep buyers' confidence in other products and avoid the danger of consumers getting ill.[70]

In May 2017, Walmart filed a patent application with the US Patent and Trademark Office (USPTO) entitled 'Unmanned Aerial Delivery to Secure Location'.[71] In addition to blockchain's role in package authentication and tracking, Walmart has outlined its plans to incorporate the technology in authenticating a customer and a courier, measuring the temperatures of containers and products and comparing with acceptable thresholds and other purposes.

2.6   BLOCKCHAIN'S ROLE IN INTERORGANIZATIONAL RELATIONSHIPS

Interorganizational relationships are at the centre of a business model. As noted above, a major goal of a firm's business model is also to contribute to profitability and growth for its partners.[72]

The key value proposition of blockchain is the production of trust. Blockchain can play a major role in shaping how interorganizational trust, conflict, collaboration and cooperation emerge. Valuable insights thus can be obtained by looking at its impact on interorganizational relationships.

A party involved in interorganizational relations can engage in opportunistic behaviour by wilfully disregarding other business partners' goals in pursuit of its own interests. In order to understand the nature and mechanisms of this challenge, we especially look at two types of interorganizational relationships and networks: horizontal (organized across markets), and vertical (organized along the production chain).

Compared to vertical relations, horizontal cooperation tends to experience more opportunistic behaviours that are associated with business partners' self-interests. This is because the latter relations are often characterized by lower reciprocal interdependence.[73]

---

[70]   C De Jesus (Nov 21, 2016) 'Walmart Is Using Blockchain to Find Contaminated Food Sources' https://futurism.com/walmart-is-using-blockchain-to-find-contaminated -food-sources/.

[71]   A Coggine (Jun 7, 2017) 'Walmart to Track Delivery Drones with Blockchain, Soon to Accept Bitcoin?' https://cointelegraph.com/news/walmart-to-track-delivery -drones-with-blockchain-soon-to-accept-bitcoin.

[72]   Zott and Amit R (n 6).

[73]   A Rindfleisch (2000) 'Organizational Trust and Interfirm Cooperation: An Examination of Horizontal Versus Vertical Alliances' *Marketing Letters* Vol 11(1) 81–95.

Researchers have also noted the important role of devoting significant resources and efforts to design, implement, and enforce formal control structures and to monitor their effectiveness.[74] In many cases, these efforts are likely to act against the objectives of lowering transaction costs.[75]

One way to establish and maintain stable, long-term relationships in order to avoid failure and drive cooperation and achieve goals is to use adequate governance mechanisms.[76] Prior researchers have also noted the important role of formalization in a business partner's relationship-specific investments and cooperation efficiency.[77] As a key element of formal control, of special interest here is operational formalization, which 'encompasses the usage of formalized and mutually binding agreements'.[78] Such a control is formalized in a written document that delineates the rules, the responsibilities of each party, and processes and specifies outcomes.[79] It covers the activities and processes of the cooperation on an operational level by defining 'detailed tasks, activities, schedules, and operating procedures for the alliance'.[80] The existence of clearly defined rules and procedures is likely to foster a long-lasting commitment.[81]

The means of operational formalization is often in the form of a contract. However, an important point to bear in mind is that a contract is incomplete, that is, the parties may have an incentive to breach a contract. Indeed breach of contract is not an uncommon practice in economies characterized by a poorly

---

[74]   L Xu and BM Beamon (2006) 'Supply Chain Coordination and Cooperation Mechanisms: An Attribute-Based Approach,' *Journal of* Supply Chain Management Vol 42(1) 4–12.

[75]   C Schmoltzi and CM Wallenburg (2012) 'Operational Governance in Horizontal Cooperations of Logistics Service Providers: Performance Effects and the Moderating Role of Cooperation Complexity' Journal of Supply Chain Management Vol 48(2) 53–74. doi:10.1111/j.1745-493X. 2011.03262.x.

[76]   JH Dyer and H Singh (1998) 'The Relational View: Cooperative Strategy and Sources of Interorganizational Competitive Advantage' *Academy of Management Review* Vol 23(4) 660–79.

[77]   JY Murray and M Kotabe (2005) 'Performance Implications of Strategic Fit between Alliance Attributes and Alliance Forms' *Journal of Business Research* Vol 58(11) 1525–33.

[78]   C Schmoltzi and CM Wallengburg (2012) 'Operational Governance in Horizontal Cooperations of Logistics Service Providers: Performance Effects and the Moderating Role of Cooperation Complexity' *Journal of Supply Chain Management* Vol 48(2) 53–74, 55.

[79]   TK Das and BS Teng (2002) 'Alliance Constellations A Social Exchange Perspective' Academy of Management *Review* Vol 27(3) 445–56.

[80]   Murray and Kotabe (n 77), p. 1527.

[81]   H Patzelt and DA Shepherd (2008) 'The Decision to Persist with Underperforming Alliances: The Role of Trust and Control' Journal *of* Management *Studies* Vol 45(7) 1217–43.

48 *The rise of blockchains*

Table 2.2 *Blockchain-led changes in the nature of relationships with network members*

	Horizontal networks	Vertical networks
Stimulation of new relations	Blockchain provides a unique and innovative way to deliver value by forming new alliances and relationships (e.g., Loyyal's tokenization of loyalty points)	Powerful firms such as Walmart may find it attractive to develop relations with blockchain-ready firms which otherwise are less likely to be a part of the vertical network
Modification of existing relations	Some functions performed by horizontal networks become unnecessary (e.g., an AIA (Agro Industria Associades) member may think that finance related help from other members is unnecessary and may choose a less involved relationship with other AIA members)	Deepen relations with some network members (e.g., Bajaj Electricals and its vendors) Some network members are no longer needed: artists can sell directly to consumers without the services of a label, financial intermediary, or technology company
Replacement of a network member by another	If dominant firms in a horizontal network decide to move some strategic programmes (e.g., loyalty) onto blockchain, firms that are unable or unwilling to adopt blockchain may be excluded from the network Blockchain may make membership in some networks less attractive for some firms (e.g., members for whom access to finance is the main motivation for joining the AIA)	Blockchain would allow firms to reduce reliance on network partners associated with low profitability (e.g., small manufacturers may get working capital loans from banks rather than from factors) Firms that are unable or unwilling to develop blockchain capability may be excluded by powerful players from vertical networks

functioning legal system with weak rule of law, corrupt government officials and judiciaries, or a high cost of enforcement.[82]

The above are exactly the situations in which blockchain has a high degree of usefulness and applicability. This technology helps make sure that business partners do not engage in fraudulent activities and that they play by rules.

Blockchain may change the economics of interorganizational relationships. Some of the key impacts of blockchain on interorganizational relationships are presented in Table 2.2.

[82] Bohnet, Frey and Huck (n 4).

2.6.1   Stimulation of New Relations

The economics of blockchain may make it attractive to form new horizontal and vertical networks. As an example of blockchain-led new horizontal networks, consider loyalty. In traditional schemes, travellers need to wait until the points settle and accrue. Consumers are limited on where and how they can spend points. Blockchain can help tokenize loyalty points, which allows travellers to get instant value by redeeming points on the spot. It would also be of obvious value for consumers to be able to use points more widely through a community of partners. This can be considered to be a marketplace or exchange model. When points are accepted as 'currency' among many providers, consumers get an easier and faster-to-use programme, which can be more relevant to their preferences.

IBM teamed up with the New York-based blockchain startup Loyyal to develop blockchain infrastructure for loyalty and rewards programmes.[83] In October 2016, Loyyal launched the Dubai Points programme. The beta pilot used a smartphone app-based system to provide incentives for tourists visiting places that are of cultural and historic significance. It offers points for different activities such as travelling, visiting museums and staying in specific hotels. Points can then be used to fully or partially cover the cost of attractions being promoted by the provider. The points earned by a tourist are recorded on Loyyal's blockchain. It makes them easy to audit and difficult to counterfeit. Programme administrators have access to a live view of every point, which shows how the points have been earned, and how they are being used.[84] Blockchain can help offer services desired by customers which increases customer value perception. In February 2020, Loyyal signed a commercial production vendor agreement with the Emirates Group. More than 25 million members of Emirates Airline and budget airline flydubai are expected to benefit from the blockchain-based loyalty programme's transparency, efficiency and cost savings.[85]

---

[83]   D Kowalewski, J McLaughlin and AJ Hill (2017) 'Blockchain Will Transform Customer Loyalty Programs' *Harvard Business Review*, https://hbr.org/2017/03/blockchain-will-transform-customer-loyalty-programs.

[84]   L Parker (2016) 'Loyyal Helps Make Dubai the Global Leader in Blockchain Technology' *Bravenewcoin*, https://bravenewcoin.com/news/loyyal-helps-to-make-dubai-the-global-leader-in-blockchain-technology/.

[85]   Loyyal Corporation (Feb 21, 2020) 'Loyyal Signs Three Year Production Agreement with the Emirates Group for Use of Blockchain Loyalty and Rewards Platform' https://www.prnewswire.com/news-releases/loyyal-signs-three-year-production-agreement-with-the-emirates-group-for-use-of-blockchain-loyalty-and-rewards-platform-301008696.html.

Firms' blockchain adoption affects decisions about who to include and who not to include in their networks. Blockchain can also make it attractive to form new vertical networks. One's power arguably 'resides implicitly in the other's dependency'.[86] This view suggests that for a developing world-based firm's Information and Communications Technology (ICT) adoption, as an example, interorganizational pressures from industrialized world-based trading partners are of paramount importance. In the case of a low bargaining power, on the other hand, less powerful firms may resist ICT adoption pressures.

A large body of empirical findings demonstrates the existence and the roles of interorganizational coercive pressures. In the early 2000s, US multinationals such as Walmart and JC Penney started asking their foreign suppliers to transact on the Internet, which led the suppliers from developing Asian countries to adopt the Internet sooner because of such pressure.[87] Likewise, dominant Japanese firms adopted total quality management (TQM) process as a tool for initiating long-term cooperative relations with trading partners.[88] To put things in context, powerful firms such as Walmart may find it attractive to develop relations with blockchain-ready firms which otherwise are less likely to be a part of the vertical network.

2.6.2   Modification of Existing Relations

Blockchain provides an opportunity to deepen relationships with some business partners. India's Yes Bank has teamed up with IBM for a blockchain project to digitize vendor financing for its client, the consumer electrical equipment manufacturing company, Bajaj Electricals. The financial technology (FinTech) start-up Cateina Technologies would work on the business logic and rules, which are captured in a blockchain-based smart contract. Cateina wrote the software code on top of Hyperledger. The bank has used IBM's Hybrid Cloud technology for its vendor financing system. By doing so, the entire process for bill discounting is cut from four days to almost real time. In addition, the system allows transparency for all parties through the shared public ledger. The entire transaction history of a vendor is recorded and is immutable.[89]

---

[86]   RM Emerson (1962) 'Power-dependence Relations' *American Sociological Review* Vol 27(1) 31–41.

[87]   P Woodall (2000) 'Survey: The New Economy: Falling Through the Net' *The Economist*, 23, S34–S39.

[88]   KA Bates (1997) 'The Role of Coercive Forces in Organization Design Adoption' *Academy of Management Review* Vol 22(4), 849–51.

[89]   R Kasteleln (2017) 'China Poised to Dominate Fintech and Blockchain Markets in 2017' *BlockchainNews*, http://www.the-blockchain.com/2017/01/04/indias-yes-bank-enlists-ibm-help-build-blockchain-solutions/.

When Bajaj Electricals processes invoices in an oracle system, the details are transferred to Yes Bank on blockchain. After bill discounting (bank lending against receivables), the funds are automatically disbursed to the vendors of Bajaj Electricals when the conditions in the smart contract are fulfilled. As of February 2017, Bajaj Electricals was doing transactions with one supplier on the blockchain system.[90] In this example, the suppliers would benefit by deepening relations with Bajaj Electricals.

Blockchain may make more choices available to firms. Thanks to such a feature, firms can terminate a relationship with a firm associated with low profitability. For instance, many SMEs rely on factors for trade finance needs. Note that factors are key intermediary players in the global trade finance market. They offer money to the exporter. Based on the promised future payments, exporters borrow from factors. Exporting firms make an outright sale of accounts receivable to factors in order to maintain liquidity. For instance, a Chinese exporter selling to Walmart can take an invoice for those goods to a factor, which can pay the exporter right away. For a US$ 100 invoice, the factor may pay as little as US$ 90. The upshot is that buyers such as Walmart pay a higher price for goods they buy from developed world-based sellers. The global factoring market is estimated at over US$ 2 trillion annually. Venture capital (VC)-funded startup Skuchain and others have created blockchain-based products to address inefficiencies in B2B trade and supply chain finance. The products are expected to eliminate the roles of intermediaries and financiers. Buyers and sellers agree on the terms of a deal. Blockchain can track and manage the transaction from start to finish.

Blockchain can also make some of the relationships less important. Consider Mozambique's Agro Industria Associadas (AIA), which was formed in 2004 as a private sector-led services firm by seven food processing firms. Among the benefits that AIA can give to its members is sending weekly reports with updates on sales, stocks, and receivables to banks. Thanks to the updates, banks reportedly were more comfortable about the perceived risks associated with the sector, which made credit applications a little easier to file. It is argued that the improved access to information would not have been possible for individual processors. There has also been a high degree of inter-firm cooperation existing among the AIA firms. When an AIA member experiences shortage of inputs, other AIA members join in to help and talk with the suppliers on a joint basis.[91]

---

[90]   S Gupta (2017) 'How Bajaj Electricals Uses Blockchain to Pay Suppliers' http://www.livemint.com/Companies/BcqXQgey9fieFps9xVZ   xrK/How-Bajaj-Electricals-uses-blockchain-to-pay-suppliers. html.

[91]   C Webber and P Labaste (2010) *Building Competitiveness in Africa's Agriculture: A Guide to Value Chain Concepts and Applications* World Bank, Washington, DC.

In other parts of the world, blockchain-based platforms have helped SMEs expand their access to finance and other inputs. If an AIA member thinks that such help is unnecessary, it may choose a less involved relationship with other AIA members. Blockchain can give many of the same benefits without the need for a horizontal or vertical collaboration.

2.6.3   Replacement of a Network Member by Another

Due primarily to its trust-producing role, blockchain can reduce transaction costs thereby making some networks unnecessary. SMEs can reap the benefits of low-cost working capital loans from formal financial institutions such as India's Yes Bank. In this way, blockchain would allow firms to reduce reliance on network partners (e.g., factors) that are associated with low profitability.

Attractiveness as a network partner is a function of the importance or desirability the dominant member attaches to blockchain capability. Schware and Kimberley pointed out the cases of companies 'who have gone out of business because of inability, or unwillingness to comply or disbelief in the need to comply' (p. 19).[92] In some cases, when firms use coercive power to force use, the less powerful partners may be left vulnerable.[93] To put things in context, firms that are unable or unwilling to develop blockchain capability may be excluded by powerful players such as Walmart in their vertical networks.

In some cases, blockchain may render interorganizational collaboration unnecessary. Blockchain can perform the same function faster, more accurately and in a more cost-effective way.

A similar point can be made about horizontal networks. In the loyalty programme partnership above, if dominant firms in a horizontal network decide to move onto blockchain, firms that are unable or unwilling to adopt blockchain are excluded from the network. Likewise, blockchain may make some networks less attractive for some firms. Returning to the AIA example above, if access to finance is the main motivation for joining the AIA for some firms, blockchain reduces the relative attractiveness of the AIA for such firms. Horizontal networks such as the AIA would involve too high transaction costs for them. For instance, the member firms had contributed US$ 500 of seed money to start the AIA.[94]

---

[92]   R Schware and P Kimberley (1995) *Information Technology and National Trade Facilitation* (World Bank Office of the Publisher, Washington D.C.
[93]   PW Forster and AC Regan (2001) 'Electronic Integration in the Air Cargo Industry: An Information Processing Model of On-time Performance' *Transportation Journal* Vol 40(4) 46–61.
[94]   Webber and Labaste (n 91).

2.7   CHAPTER SUMMARY AND CONCLUSION

A number of forward-looking companies are revamping their business management strategies and business models using blockchain solutions. They had already designed new, novel, and innovative business models using advanced ICT tools such as cloud computing, big data and IoT. Many of them are developing blockchain applications to enhance trust with consumers, business partners and other key stakeholders.

A wide range of mechanisms and pathways may be involved in the creation of value by using blockchain. Some companies are developing new tools and systems that work on top of blockchain technology in order to deliver higher value by empowering customers. Blockchain can also address the issue of inefficiency, which is more acute when the activities to be performed require a substantial amount of documentation and paperwork, or the current design involves a large number of intermediaries. Some firms have embraced blockchain as a piracy-fighting tool. Such measures are likely to have effects on costs and perceived quality of the product.

An observation is that unlike many other ICT systems such as RFID, blockchain can be deployed without devices, reading hardware or any process to attach tags to cases or pallets. Marginal costs associated with implementing blockchain are thus zero or low, if technologies such as IoT have already been used to detect, measure, and track key SCM processes. Blockchain also combines unit level (instead of batch level) entity identification. Firms can exploit zero or very low marginal costs of digital networks. This combination is likely to bring transformation in supply chains. Thus it makes economic sense to generate a blockchain code even for small transactions. To take one example, Walmart has accelerated the adoption of the IoT. In October 2016, it filed a patent application, that describes the addition of IoT tags to products based on Bluetooth, RFID, infrared, NFC (Near-Field-Communication) and other technologies. The tags will monitor product usage patterns and automatically refill orders. The IoT tags can also track products' expiration dates and product recalls.[95]

One observation that is worth mentioning is that creative services are undervalued and underutilized. Blockchain has the potential to change this situation. Blockchain will make it transparent who the owner of the creative material is. Blockchain makes it possible to offer much smaller units of digital products than was possible in the past. Blockchain can lead to a decrease in transaction costs, which reduces opportunism and adverse selection.

---

[95]   M Alleven (May 5, 2017) 'Walmart Looks to Take On Amazon in the IoT' http://www.fiercewireless.com/wireless/walmart-looks-to-take-amazon-iot.

In the context of the food industry, the example of the 2015 E. coli outbreak at Chipotle Mexican Grill noted above is illustrative of a widespread problem faced by the food supply chain. Blockchain has the potential to effectively address the root causes of problems such as this. Blockchain can help ensure that the food consumers are eating is right and authentic. The case of the Swiss start-up Modum makes it clear that using blockchain, measures can be adopted to reduce the wastage of resources.

The arguments and evidence advanced in this chapter suggest that major strategy may be needed for leading and managing change at the organizational and interorganizational levels in order to incorporate blockchain.

Blockchain can change the nature of relationships with network members. A firm's blockchain adoption may influence the importance of existing horizontal and vertical networks in many different ways. Blockchain-led value change leads customers to explore, maintain or terminate a relationship with its suppliers. It may cause the stimulation of new relations, modification of existing relations and replacement of a given network by another. For instance, tourism organizations such as hotels, airlines car rental agencies, restaurants and attractions can team up to develop effective loyalty programmes (stimulation of new horizontal networks). Blockchain can help foster deeper vertical relations with some partners (modification of existing relations). For instance, blockchain can help improve the systems and methods for providing supply chain financing. Adoption of blockchain also makes some networks less attractive. Firms may replace factors by banks (replacement) to access their working capital needs. Blockchain can help firms connect to a higher quality network, which would lead to better firm performance.

In order to balance cooperation and competition, there is the need to manage tension within the relationship. Thanks to its decentralization, immutability and smart contract features, blockchain is better able to overcome the various sources of tension and conflict between partners involved in interorganizational relations. Blockchain-based solutions link reputations of transacting parties to specific addresses. For instance, the technology allows creative contents' producers and consumers to verify each other. Parties involved in a transaction may modify their behaviour in response to knowing that they are being watched. This could promote a climate of collaboration and cooperation among content creators and consumers.[96]

Blockchain's transformative power is surely not only about changing organizational processes but also bringing drastic changes in the horizontal and vertical networks. Blockchain can help firms develop suitable cooperation that matches their needs and provides added value. Some businesses are together

---

[96]   Takahashi (n 29).

creating innovative business models that are helping to improve value creation and delivery. The existing structures and processes are poorly suited to address trust-related problems. Blockchain decentralization and immutability features make it possible to form new horizontal networks such as a marketplace of loyalty points. Some horizontal networks (e.g., AIA), on the other hand, involve too high transaction costs for small firms and thus become unattractive in the blockchain world. Blockchain-based smart contracts provide an effective way of governing relationships with partners in horizontal and vertical networks. A better balance of cooperation and competition can be achieved in interorganizational collaborations with the help of blockchain. Blockchain thus has potential to overcome challenges such as opportunism and adverse selection.

The benefits of blockchain can be realized not only by large enterprises but also by SMEs. For instance, as noted, the functioning of markets often puts SMEs at disadvantage in terms of access to credit. Blockchain's trust-producing mechanism enables SMEs to establish a new vertical network and access low-cost financing from banks.

Finally, transparency is a key dimension of blockchain-based business models. This means that businesses that have thrived on opaque business models may face challenges to survive and cope with disruptions created by blockchain.

3. Combining with other technologies to amplify blockchain's value creation

3.1 INTRODUCTION

It is argued blockchain has demonstrated some level of success in solving the problem of third-party trust, which is the trust placed in intermediaries such as banks and brokers. But the problems related to the first-party trust and second-party trust[1] still mostly exist. For instance, the original record that has been entered into the blockchain ledger cannot be necessarily trusted because there is no guarantee that blockchain-based systems lead to the creation of error-free or fraud-free records.[2]

There are thus significant first-mile and last-mile problems. In order to understand the first-mile problem, consider the following observation about the mineral and mining industry: 'Mining, at its most simple, is a process of digging up dirt, filtering it for minerals or ore, smelting and then refining to a product.'[3] Blockchain alone cannot ensure that there are no errors, frauds, and irregularities in multiple stages in the supply chain. Especially blockchain cannot effectively address the 'first mile' problem, which is arguably the most

---

[1]   First-party trust is the trust that actors have in themselves. One example of this is the handling of private keys. As a relevant situation of this kind of trust, we can consider mishandling private keys. When a wrong party gets the keys, they can steal the assets. When the private keys are lost or forgotten, the assets are lost. Second-party trust is the trust placed in the entity that a party is transacting with (https://medium.com/hubtoken/hub-frequently-asked-questions-e6f4896310b8). The question here includes 'who the party' is and whether thy behave in a way that is 'agreed upon in the transaction' (https://medium.com/hubtoken/linkedin-cofounder-and-hub-ceo-eric-ly-delivers-keynote-presentation-at-ico-and-the-token-economy-4fef0c2a7aeb).

[2]   J Heminwa and A Sulkowsk (2019) 'Blockchains, Corporate Governance, and the Lawyer's Role' *Wayne Law Review* Vol 65(January), 17–55.

[3]   B Kilbey and F Warwick (2020) 'Blockchain Not Silver Bullet for Mine Operations: Verisk Maplecroft VP' *S&P Global Platts*, https://www.spglobal.com/platts/en/market-insights/latest-news/metals/012920-blockchain-not-silver-bullet-for-mine-operations-verisk-maplecroft-vp.

crucial step in assuring the ore's quality.[4] Some have raised the question of trust at this point because blockchain systems can be corrupted if the actors involved do not engage in trustworthy behaviours. For instance, the government agents who tag bags can collude with smugglers and enter incorrect data.[5]

The last-mile problem refers to the bridge between a physical asset and its digital counterpart on the chain. For instance, blockchain alone cannot ensure that malicious activities such as physical tampering and modification have not taken place when a product moves along a supply chain. A blockchain solution's credibility and effectiveness thus would depend on how the solution can bridge two types of assets.

Many of these challenges can be overcome by combining blockchain with other advanced technologies, mainly so called Fourth Revolution (4R), also known as the Fourth Industrial Revolution (4IR), technologies. Indeed, many of the transformations that blockchain has brought and will continue to bring are not found in isolation. These transformations can be attributed to 'blockchain plus something'.[6] That is, it is possible to bring the changes by combining blockchain with other emerging technologies.[7] For instance, artificial intelligence (AI), which is arguably the most prominent 4R technology, is viewed to have a great potential to address trust issues in blockchain-based solutions.

In this chapter, we provide an analysis of how many of the trust-related challenges in interorganizational relations can be overcome by combining blockchain with other advanced technologies. It gives a special consideration to the potential of significant added value as well as complementary and synergistic effects by combining blockchain with these technologies.

---

[4]   F Brugger (2019) 'Blockchain Is Great, But It Can't Solve Everything. Take Conflict Minerals' *African Arguments*; https://africanarguments.org/2019/04/23/ blockchain-is-great-but-it-cant-solve-everything-take-conflict-minerals/.

[5]   J Cant (2019) 'Block Firm Helps Congo Mine Fight against Blood Diamonds' *Cointelegraph*. https://cointelegraph.com/news/blockchain-firm-helps-congo-mine-to -fight-against-blood-diamonds.

[6]   deloitte.com (July 2020) 'Blockchain and Internal Control: The COSO Perspective New Risks and the Need for New Controls' July https://www2.deloitte .com/us/en/pages/audit/articles/blockchain-and-internal-control-coso-perspective-risk .html.

[7]   Ibid., l.

3.2   ARTIFICIAL INTELLIGENCE AND MACHINE LEARNING

Economists view AI as among the four most important 'general purpose technologies' (GPTs),[8] the other three being steam engine, electric power, and Information Technology (IT). GPTs possess potential to transform household as well as business activities.[9] GPTs such as AI also facilitate complementary innovations and bring transformations and changes in business processes.[10] AI systems can mimic and imitate human cognition to perform tasks that seemed to be possible only with human thinking and logic before. It entails simulating human intelligence by machines. The key processes involved are learning (acquiring information and understanding the rules for using the information), reasoning (applying the rules to reach conclusions), and self-correction.

Machine learning (ML) is a type of AI that helps increase accuracy of software applications in predicting outcomes without explicit programming. The basic idea behind ML is simple: algorithms receive input data and by using statistical analysis they predict output values within acceptable ranges. ML processes are similar to those involved in data mining and predictive modelling, which also look for patterns in data in order to adjust program actions.

The combination of AI and blockchain is likely to bring powerful economic and social effects. Blockchain's ability to cryptographically validate identities and transactions and create immutable records can enhance trust, transparency and accountability. Part of the fascinating character of AI stems from the fact that computers perform better than humans in repetitive tasks. Their judgement and intelligence are not affected by emotions, feelings, and needs. They have better memories and can process huge amounts of information.[11] AI thus enhances efficiency and provides new opportunities for cost savings and revenue generation.

In supply chain management, for instance, AI plays a critical role in optimizing the flows of materials, components and products in the long-haul international routes, the last-mile delivery as well as in the warehouse. AI algorithms use historic supply chain information, and real-time data to estimate

---

[8]   I Gill (2020) 'Whoever Leads in Artificial Intelligence in 2030 Will Rule the World until 2100' *Brookings*, https://www.brookings.edu/blog/future-development/2020/01/17/whoever-leads-in-artificial-intelligence-in-2030-will-rule-the-world-until-2100/.
[9]   B Jovanovic and P Rousseau (2005) 'General Purpose Technologies' *National Bureau of Economic Research*, https://www.nber.org/papers/w11093.
[10]   Gill (n 8).
[11]   L Whitney (2017) 'Are Computers Already Smarter Than Humans?' http://time.com/4960778/computers-smarter-than-humans/.

time of delivery. Based on local conditions such as those related to traffic and weather, they can select optimal routes for vehicles and sequence deliveries. In the warehouse, AI-powered systems can map the capacity and availability of goods and assess the manpower needed.

Using AI, shipments can be consolidated and rearranged more effectively. For instance, AI algorithms can group a large number of items by location, customer, season, freight mode and delivery timelines. They can also consider other prerequisites needed to transport medical and food products that are sensitive to temperature and humidity. By analysing information related to damage claims and other liabilities based on supply chain actions, AI can provide critical insight into key problems. Such information can be used to assess risks and select an appropriate damage mitigation strategy and to re-evaluate the rates charged for cargos with various levels of risk.[12] All these can lead to savings in transportation and warehousing and optimal use of capacity.

Blockchain can also prevent counterfeit, knock-off and fake products from entering a supply chain. The pharmaceutical company Merck has been granted a patent that combines AI with blockchain to enhance supply chains' integrity and eliminate counterfeit products. The process links physical objects to blockchains to create 'crypto-objects'. ML is used to create 'fingerprints' using unique features such as physical patterns, chemical signature and DNA. Once the object becomes a crypto-object with a unique fingerprint, another layer of security can be provided with data such as time or location. The receivers of a crypto-object can compare the discriminating data with corresponding reference data. The latter sets of data are stored in repositories with restricted access.[13]

AI and blockchain thus have strong complementary capabilities that can have dramatic effects on the performance of industries and markets. Each also has a potential to improve the performance and functioning of the other (Figure 3.1).

3.2.1 Effects of Blockchain on AI

Figure 3.1 reveals different mechanisms by which blockchain can influence AI. First, blockchain's ability to cryptographically validate and record each

---

[12] J Hackenberg (2020) 'AI and Blockchain: Solving Supply Chain's Transparency Problem' *Supply Chain Digital*,
  https://www.supplychaindigital.com/technology/ai-and-blockchain-solving-supply-chains-transparency-problem.
[13] N Ruggieri (2019) 'Merck's AI and Blockchain Patent Gives Objects Unique "Fingerprints"' *Ethnews*, https://www.ethnews.com/mercks-ai-and-blockchain-patent-gives-objects-unique-fingerprints.

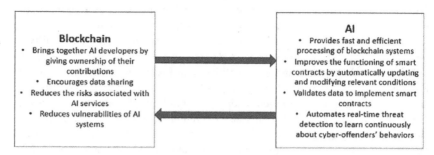

Source: Adapted from: Nir Kshetri (2019). 'Complementary and Synergistic Properties of Blockchain and Artificial Intelligence' *IEEE IT Professional*, 21(6) 60–65.

Figure 3.1   *Synergistic effects of AI and blockchain*

transaction and its clear audit trails can help bring together many smaller AI providers by giving ownership of their contributions via smart contracts. Each may provide different AI services. With a network effect, AI developers are encouraged to contribute, which can lead to the development of a rich AI ecosystem. Each of them will have their own community of equity holders.[14]

Currently small companies lack capabilities and resources for utilizing AI in order to solve extremely difficult problems. Big companies have unfair advantages and privileges. Blockchain's ability to create trustless relationships means that a small company does not need to have full ownership and full control over huge AI teams or huge amounts of data. It is possible to rely on ad hoc communities to solve specific problems that are controlled by smart contracts. If the communities provide more valuable services, more entities can join.[15]

Blockchain's clear audit trails can help the development of the AI marketplace. Blockchain can facilitate buying and selling of data, models, and AI applications in online marketplaces. Blockchain-verified data and model sharing could help lower the barrier to entry of smaller players and stimulate their participation in the AI world.[16]

Second, blockchain's data encryption feature can encourage data owners to share their data with smaller AI developers. A problem in a non-blockchain

---

[14]   Hyperledger (2018) 'Blockchain as the Next Artificial Intelligence Enabler' https://www.hyperledger.org/blog/2018/11/27/blockchain-as-the-next-artificial -intelligence-enabler-2.

[15]   Ibid.

[16]   A Woodie (2018) 'Can Blockchain Help ML and AI?' https://www.datanami .com/2018/06/13/can-blockchain-help-ml-and-ai/.

system is that someone buying data on a marketplace could distribute it. It creates a free-rider problem. With blockchain, consumers feel more confident that their data are not abused.[17] Blockchain makes it possible to identify each block of data and anonymize it.

To take an example, Google's AI lab Google DeepMind is reported to be working on an 'auditing system for healthcare data'. Blockchain makes it possible to share data and ensure that data remain private, secure, accurate, and tamper-free.[18] AI will allow healthcare professionals to obtain analytics on medical predictions that are drawn from patient profiles.[19]

Researchers in New Zealand are reported to be working on a project to develop a New Zealand-focused model of risk stratification. The goal is to identify patients who are most at risk and in need of services. Patients have access to their data via an app. They can input their data and choose how they can share with researchers.[20] In this way, blockchain facilitates access to relevant data for small AI developers.

Data owners often tend to share data with big companies as compared to smaller ones. Blockchain thus offers special benefits to small players that often lack the ability to demonstrate attributes that prove their trustworthiness. Especially they are not in a position to produce characteristic-based trust,[21] which is generated by identifiable attributes linked with trustworthy behaviour. Entities that are known to possess certain well-defined attributes (e.g., large companies) are viewed as trustworthy. Big companies may lose size-dependent trust advantage with the availability of new encryption methods.[22] Thus, a level playing field is achieved for small AI start-ups. Many start-ups are promoting the development of data marketplace for AI:

a. Enigma's data marketplace Catalyst developed by an MIT-based team allows organizations to contribute data. Users can subscribe to and

---

[17] N Kshetri (2018) 'Blockchain and Electronic Healthcare Records' *IEEE Computer* Vol 51(12) 59–63.

[18] C Metz (Nov 3, 2017) 'Google DeepMind's Untrendy Play to Make the Blockchain Actually Useful' https://www.wired.com/2017/03/google-deepminds -untrendy-blockchain-play-make-actually-useful/.

[19] M Yao (Jun 2, 2017) 'Blockchain and AI Are Revolutionizing These 10 Industries'
https://www.freecodecamp.org/news/blockchain-and-ai-are-revolutionizing-these -10-industries-92b07fd12bcd/.

[20] R McBeth (28 Feb, 2019) 'Reducing Health Inequities and Increasing Access to Care Using AI and Blockchain' https://www.healthcareitnews.com/news/reducing -health-inequities-and-increasing-access-care-using-ai-and-blockchain.

[21] LG Zucker (1986) 'Production of Trust: Institutional Sources of Economic Structure, 1840–1920' *Research in Organizational Behavior* Vol 8 53–111.

[22] Hyperledger (n 14).

consume data via smart contracts. Computations can be performed over encrypted data. This means that nodes do not need to see the raw data in order to perform computing.[23]

b. The Blockchain start-up Datum's marketplace allows users to make money from their data. The company had over 90,000 people using its app to monetize their data with pre-screened partners.[24]

c. Computable Labs uses blockchain to build a decentralized data market-place for AI. The goal is to democratize access to data and algorithms needed for AI. It aims to provide a token curated registry (TCR) that serves as a hub for the buying and selling of data.[25] A TCR is an incentivized voting game designed to create trusted lists, which are maintained by the users of data, algorithm and applications. The idea is to use the 'Wisdom of the Crowds' principle. Users vote to decide submissions that are valid and should be included in the list. Tokens are needed to vote (https://education.district0x.io/general-topics/understanding-ethereum/token-curated-registry/).

Third, blockchain can reduce the risks associated with using AI services. This is important because most organizations lack in-house AI capabilities. AI services often lack tools to estimate the quality of providers.

Diffusion of technologies such as AI depends on trialability.[26] That is, organizations are more likely to adopt AI if providers offer risk-free trials. Blockchain increases AI's trialability by making it possible to offer AI deals in which payments are conditional. An AI consumer pays for services only if the provider is right. The provider may actually pay the consumer for wrong predictions.[27]

Most AI models function as 'black boxes'. A few big companies dominate the AI field because they are viewed as reputable and providers of better AI services. When AI models are put on blockchain, predictions are immutable. Reputation of AI providers would depend less on their size and more on their capability to provide high-quality AI services.[28] Blockchain increases the

[23] https://blokt.com/interview/enigmas-privacy-protocol-solves-key-blockchain-issues-preventing-global-adoption.
[24] cbinsights.com (9Aug, 2018) '7 Companies Using Blockchain to Power AI Applications' https://www.cbinsights.com/research/blockchain-ai-startups/.
[25] Ibid.
[26] EM Rogers (1995) *Diffusion of Innovation* (4th edn, Free Press, New York).
[27] Hyperledger (n 14).
[28] Ibid.

trustworthiness of AI. Blockchain can display a clear and impenetrable chain of information for AI to explain its processes.[29]

AI algorithms and data are vulnerable and susceptible to misuse, threat and manipulation. Data manipulation may also go undetected for a long time. In such cases, organizations may face difficulty in recovering the correct data feeding its AI system. Such a scenario could lead to disastrous consequences in systems relying on AI in health care, finance and other sectors.[30] Blockchain can reduce such vulnerability.

Blockchain can ensure that data and algorithms used in AI are secure. Perpetrators need to penetrate several entrance gates to attack a system. Since the database is encrypted, users that have not been granted access cannot view anything.[31]

AI makes it possible to understand and analyse huge amounts of data. While blockchain cannot perform well in terms of analysis, its decentralized feature can help protect data that AI-related systems depend on.[32] Compared to a closed AI system, a blockchain-based system is more transparent. Records that are on a blockchain-based ledger can be reviewed and audited by any authorized party.

3.2.2   Effects of AI on Blockchain

Figure 3.1 portrays how AI can improve the functioning of blockchain-based systems. First, AI can provide fast and efficient processing of blockchain systems. Traditional computers without AI programs require huge amounts of processing power to manage blockchains in order to complete tasks. This is due to the encrypted nature of data and the lack of explicit instruction on how

---

[29]   Dmytro Spilka (Sept 10, 2018) 'Understanding the Power of Blockchain Infused with AI' https://www.techradar.com/news/understanding-the-power-of-blockchain-infused-with-ai.

[30]   cfr.org (Aug 28, 2017) 'The Cybersecurity Vulnerabilities to Artificial Intelligence' https://www.cfr.org/blog/cybersecurity-vulnerabilities-artificial-intelligence.

[31]   Ronald van Loon (27 March, 2018) 'Blockchain Potential to Transform Artificial Intelligence' https://www.digitaldoughnut.com/articles/2018/march/blockchain-potential-to-transform-ai.

[32]   W Thibodeaux (2018) 'A.I. Is Awesome, Blockchain Is a Powerhouse. But Here's What Combining Them Could Do' https://www.inc.com/wanda-thibodeaux/ai-is-awesome-blockchain-is-a-powerhouse-but-heres-what-combining-them-could-do.html.

to process them. With AI, a higher performance can be achieved in blockchain management. More intelligent machines improve the process.[33]

Second, AI improves the functioning of smart contracts by automatically updating and modifying the relevant conditions in such contracts. Smart contracts are created for transactions that may occur in future points of time. However, changes in the business world, political and legal institutions and other factors may make the contracts outdated. AI and blockchain may work together to provide real-time updated contracts. AI is useful if parts of those contracts dictate the fixed terms and some aspects might change with changes in conditions in the business environment.[34]

Third, AI can effectively validate data to implement smart contracts. In a smart contract executed 'above' the blockchain, the software program runs outside and feeds information to the blockchain. In most cases, the Internet of Things (IoT) provides the data. AI's analysis and intelligence conditions represented by the data meet the standards stipulated in the contract. For instance, IBM worked with the UAE's Dubai Customs and Dubai Trade, the telecommunications company Du, a letter of credit (LC) issuing bank, Emirates NBD Bank, the responding bank, Santander, freight company Aramex and an airline to use its blockchain platform Hyperledger in international trades. The plan was to integrate it with IBM Watson's AI after completing the Proof of Concept (PoC). The PoC was designed to track the shipment of fruit from India to Dubai via a cargo ship. In Dubai, the fruit would be processed to produce juice and then exported to Spain by an airplane. To move the transactions to blockchain, Du tracked data via IoT-enabled devices. Aramex would ship the fruit and an airline company would transport the juice.

Finally, AI can be used to automate real-time threat detection to learn continuously about cyber-offenders' behaviours. The importance of this aspect stems from the fact that a number of crypto-exchange platforms have faced cyberattacks. Some solutions have already been proposed for addressing such challenges. A virtual AI security analyst developed at MIT's Computer Science and Artificial Intelligence Laboratory (CSAIL) accurately identified 85 per cent of attacks when it was trained by human experts. By doing so, it exceeded previous benchmarks and reduced false positives by factors of three and five.[35]

[33] Spilka (n 29).
[34] K Matthews (2019) '6 Digitization Trends Coming from AI and Blockchain' https://www.informationweek.com/strategic-cio/digital-business/6-digitization-trends -coming-from-ai-and-blockchain/a/d-id/1334369.
[35] A Conner-Simons (April 18, 2016) 'System Predicts 85 Percent of Cyber-attacks Using Input from Human Experts' http://news.mit.edu/2016/ai-system-predicts-85 -percent-cyber-attacks-using-input-human-experts-0418.

3.3   REMOTE SENSING AND SATELLITE IMAGERY

In some cases, a higher level of trust in data entered in a blockchain ledger than can be achieved by utilizing remote sensing and satellite imagery data. For instance, the TaaS (Traceability-as-a-Service) provider Circulor's mine-to-manufacturer traceability of Tantalum in Rwanda utilizes satellite data to verify the authenticity of mines. A registered mining company that has a concession can apply to use the system. The coordinates of the mine's operations and its historical production are entered in the system. Satellite data is used to verify that the mine is working.[36]

Blockchain and satellite imagery systems can be combined to create a self-sustaining ecosystem to facilitate traceability and monitoring. For instance, blockchain-based smart contracts make it possible for owners of satellites and those that need their services to engage in negotiation autonomously. Transactions can be completed based on criteria that are predetermined. They include the price a customer would pay for an image that they can download when they need. It is also possible for users, satellite owners and the satellites to dynamically create new services and the revenue can be used to pay for launching them, insurance premiums, and other costs.[37]

The utilization of remote sensing and satellite imagery data can help blockchains to interact with data about the natural environment (In Focus 3.1 below). Such data can also be used to develop so called 'green' smart contracts.[38] For instance, the Green World Campaign, which is described as 'an open source charity', and Cornell University were reported to be building smart contracts using satellite data to promote environmental sustainability. People who make land use more sustainable with green agricultural practices such as by increasing tree cover and improving soil are automatically rewarded. To do so, Chainlink oracles supply the proof of land improvement data using satellite imagery to the blockchain. The data is accessed by the smart contract to release a payout.[39]

---

[36]   M Burbidge (2019) 'Proving Provenance' *Brainstorm Magazine*, http://www.brainstormmag.co.za/business/14571-proving-provenance.

[37]   C Stocker (2017) 'The Future May Owe Itself to Blockchain Technology. Here's Why' *Futurism*, https://futurism.com/the-future-may-owe-itself-to-blockchain-technology-heres-why/.

[38]   World Economic Forum (2021) 'Blockchain Can Help Us Tackle Climate Change. Here's How.' [online] Available at: https://www.weforum.org/agenda/2021/06/blockchain-can-help-us-beat-climate-change-heres-how/.

[39]   Max Yakubowski (Sept 5, 2021) 'How Will Blockchain Technology Help Fight Climate Change? Experts Answer' https://cointelegraph.com/explained/how-will-blockchain-technology-help-fight-climate-change-experts-answer.

IN FOCUS 3.1 CHAINLINK'S ORACLE TO PROVIDE WEATHER
              DATA

Google BigQuery, which is a cloud-based big data analytics web service for processing very large read-only data sets, hosts the Global Surface Summary of the Day (GSOD) database from the United States Department of Commerce's scientific and regulatory agency National Oceanic and Atmospheric Administration (NOAA). The NOAA Satellite and Information Service provides access to global environmental data from satellites and other sources, which can be used to monitor and understand the Earth (https://www.noaa.gov/satellites). The GSOD provides daily summaries of weather and climate observations from more than 9,000 stations that are globally distributed. Data provided include each location's temperature, visibility, wind speed, and precipitation. The earliest observations go as far back as 1929. Weather and climate data is sourced from many reputable data providers. Among such providers is the Global Precipitation Measurement (GPM) mission, which was initiated by the National Aeronautics and Space Administration (NASA) and the Japan Aerospace Exploration Agency (JAXA) in 2014. Other GPM members include the Centre National d'Études Spatiales (CNES), the Indian Space Research Organisation (ISRO), NOAA, and the European Organization for the Exploitation of Meteorological Satellites (EUMETSAT).[a] GPM provides global mapping of precipitation at three-hour intervals based on the Integrated Multi-satellite Retrievals algorithm. The algorithm combines information from the constellation of GPM satellites in order to estimate precipitation over the majority of the Earth's surface.[b]

Chainlink has built an adapter that enables smart contracts to query the NOAA GSOD weather data via BigQuery. An external adapter can be viewed as a code (specifically an API (application programming interface) server) that is between a data source and a Chainlink node.[c] Application developers can request data from weather stations within a specific region or for the weather station nearest to a specified point.[d] A Chainlink node's job is to retrieve and provide data and execute payment on a given blockchain. Node operators get paid in LINK tokens for their assignments. The node operators set the price of these assignments. Node operators have to pay LINK to SmartContract.com (Chainlink) – penalty payments – in case of their failure to execute an assignment.[e]

The US company AccuWeather, which provides weather data, forecasts, and warnings to over a billion people worldwide has launched a Chainlink node to provide weather data to smart contracts. The node went live in December 2021.[f]

Notes:
^a nasa.gov (2019) *The Global Precipitation Measurement Mission (GPM) NASA Global Precipitation Measurement Mission.* [online] Available at: https://gpm.nasa.gov/missions/GPM.
^b Ibid.
^c Z Ayesh (2021) *Building My First Chainlink Adapter.* [online] Chainlink Community. Available at: https://medium.com/chainlink-community/building-my-first-chainlink-adapter-996ab51dfe9.
^d A Day (2021) *Hedging against Bad Weather with Cloud Datasets and Blockchain Oracles.* [online] Google Cloud – Community. Available at: https://medium.com/google-cloud/hedging-against-bad-weather-with-cloud-datasets-and-blockchain-oracles-7ba3e0150304.
^e J Huxtable (2018) 'LinkPool: The First Network of Chainlink Nodes Backed by a Smart Contract' [online] *LinkPool.* Available at: https://medium.com/linkpool/linkpool-the-first-network-of-chainlink-nodes-backed-by-a-smart-contract-9dc34593c4d.
^f Brooks Butler (Dec 14, 2021) 'AccuWeather Chainlink Node Goes Live' https://cryptobriefing.com/accuweather-chainlink-node-goes-live/.

3.3.1   Combining Satellite Images, Blockchain and AI

Some companies are also developing solutions involving satellite images, blockchain and AI that reward sustainable farming practices. One such example is Oracle's partnership with the World Bee Project. Oracle and the World Bee Project have also created the hive-monitoring project Global Hive Network. The network aims to generate data by monitoring hives worldwide in order to identify trends in honeybee populations. The network will also monitor the behaviour of honeybees and how they are affected by weather patterns, diseases, pesticides and other factors. Such data can help beekeepers make informed decisions.[40]

The solutions created by Oracle and the World Bee Project help farmers manage bee populations and pollinator habitats. The plan is to take images of the farm with drones or satellites and utilize AI-based image recognition algorithms to evaluate whether the way a farmland is managed supports bee colonies and other pollinators in a sustainable way.[41] Research has indicated that farms that allocate a certain proportion of their land to plant flowering crops such as spices, oil seeds, buckwheat, and sunflowers can increase crop yields by up to 79 per cent due to efficient pollination from bees. An eco-label certificate can be issued to farmers depending on the farm composition. The certification can be stored in a blockchain so that all supply chain partners can see it (e.g., during the farm product's journey to the retailer).It can help ensure that the honey being sold by retailers is authentic, which is important because

---

[40]   Michael Rand (Aug 16, 2021) 'How the Internet is Helping Save the Bees' https://www.zdnet.com/article/how-the-internet-is-helping-save-the-bees/.

[41]   J Charness (2019) 'How Oracle and the World Bee Project Are Using AI to Save Bees' *Oracle AI and Data Science Blog,* https://blogs.oracle.com/datascience/how-oracle-and-the-world-bee-project-are-using-ai-to-save-bees-v2.

more than three-quarters of honey sold has been reported to be over-processed or mixed with cheap ingredients. The solution helps to reduce harmful pesticide use by pinpointing the locations, where such activities have taken place.[42]

3.4   INTERNET OF THINGS

IoT is the network of physical objects or 'things' (e.g., machines, devices and appliances, animals or people) embedded with electronics, software and sensors, which are provided with unique identifiers and possess the ability to transfer data across the Web with minimal human interventions.

According to Gartner, there are three components of an IoT: the edge; the platform; and the user. The edge is the location where data originates or is aggregated. Data may also be reduced to the essential or minimal parts. In some cases, data may be analysed. The data then goes to the platform, which is typically in the cloud. Analytics are often performed in the cloud using algorithms. A real-time data streaming decides if some actions need to be taken right away or if the data needs to be stored for future use. The user engages in a business action.

There are three possible ways in which data that have been analysed can move from the IoT platform to a user: (1) the user deploys an application program interface (API) to call or query the data, which specifies how software components of the user and platform should interact; (2) if the IoT finds a predetermined set of events, it can announce or signal to the business user; (3) it is possible to combine (1) and (2).[43]

According to chip design firm Arm Holdings' 2017 white paper, one trillion IoT devices would be built between 2017 and 2035.[44] The blockchain-IoT combination is likely to transform many industries.[45] For instance, smart IoT devices can carry out autonomous transactions through smart contracts. It may be that by combining blockchain and IoT with AI, and big data solutions, more significant impacts can be produced.

---

[42]   Rich Clayton (Nov 14, 2019) 'Healthy Hives: Cloud Analytics Helps Save the World's Bee Population' https://insidebigdata.com/2019/11/14/healthy-hives-cloud -analytics-helps-save-the-worlds-bee-population/.

[43]   N Laskowski (2016) 'Delving into an Enterprise IoT Initiative? Read This First' *TechTarget*,   http://searchcio.techtarget.com/feature/Delving-into-an-enterprise-IoT -initiative-Read-this-first.

[44]   I Wladawsky-Berger (Jan 10, 2020) 'The Internet of Things Is Changing the World' *Wall Street Journal*. [online] Available at: https://www.wsj.com/articles/the -internet-of-things-is-changing-the-world-01578689806.

[45]   K Christidis and M Devetsikiotis (2016) 'Blockchains and Smart Contracts for the Internet of Things' *IEEE Access*, 4 2292–303.

IN FOCUS 3.2 IOTA FOUNDATION COMBINES DISTRIBUTED LEDGER TECHNOLOGY AND THE INTERNET OF THINGS TO FACILITATE MICROTRANSACTIONS

The IOTA Foundation aims to facilitate microtransactions and data storage to a network of connected devices. The goal is to build the economic layer for the Internet of Things by creating an environment in which machines can trade services and resources with each other.[a] It uses an open source distributed ledger technology called the Tangle rather than blockchain.[b] The IOTA Foundation has stated that its technology solutions are being used in diverse sectors such as automotive and mobility, eHealth, digital identity, smart energy sectors, and supply chain and global trade activities.[c]

A use case of IOTA's Tangle involves building a self-sufficient, energy-positive community in Norway's Trondheim city. In 2019, IOTA developed a Proof of Concept (PoC) in collaboration with the UK car manufacturer Jaguar Land Rover, French energy operator ENGIE Group's R&D centre ENGIE Lab CRIGEN, Norwegian real estate company Entra ASA, which owns buildings in Trondheim, and many tenants including consulting, digital services and software development company Sopra Steria. The PoC followed the energy usage and provenance of Jaguar's all-electric small luxury SUV/crossover Jaguar I-Pace connected to the building through an electric charger. The Jaguar I-Pace is also equipped with a Smart Wallet developed utilizing IOTA's technology. The wallet allows the vehicle to autonomously earn cryptocurrency for reporting data about potholes, weather conditions, traffic and other conditions.[d] Drivers can earn credits by enabling their vehicles to report these data to relevant agencies such as highway departments and road maintenance authorities. Using their mobile phones, drivers can use the credits earned in cryptocurrency to pay for road tolls, smart charging or parking fees.[e]

Notes:
[a] Bitpanda (n.d.) *Five Use Cases of Cryptocurrencies.* [online] Available at: https://www.bitpanda.com/academy/en/lessons/five-use-cases-of-cryptocurrencies/.
[b] Cointelegraph (n.d.) *Iota News by Cointelegraph.* [online] Available at: https://cointelegraph.com/tags/iota.
[c] IOTA Foundation Blog (2021) *Crypto Finance AG and IOTA – The Virtues of Collaboration.* [online] Available at: https://blog.iota.org/crypto-finance-ag-and-iota/.
[d] IOTA Foundation Blog (2019) *IOTA Showcases Sustainable Energy Traceability at Powerhouse Energy Positive Building.* [online] Available at: https://blog.iota.org/iota-renewable-energy-transfer-at-powerhouse-smart-building-dd42bbf799e5/.
[e] Ibid.

By attaching IoT devices to items, real-time tracking can be achieved and visibility and traceability can be increased.[46] Data from IoT devices can also be used to execute smart contracts (In Focus 3.2: IOTA Foundation combines distributed ledger technology and the IoT to facilitate microtransactions). For instance, sensors can tell a smart contract that a product has arrived.[47] In an insurance smart contract, the IoT can provide data related to the insurable events. For example, in case of robbery, using IoT data, it would be possible to check if the warehouse's door was locked. Likewise, if there is a warehouse fire, IoT devices from the fire detection systems could provide the latest data.[48]

Several innovative solutions involving blockchain and IoT have been developed. Platform company NetObjex is installing IoT devices in hotels to keep track of a guest's water and energy consumption. Using oracles, smart contracts interact with the data from IoT devices to automatically calculate and reward guests based on their consumption metrics. A Chainlink oracle network with custom adapters is used to send the consumption data to a smart contract. Reward eligibility is computed and if the guest meets the criteria, the reward is automatically transferred to their account. Rewards are calculated in reference to the average threshold consumption for all travellers. Reward tokens can be cashed out using decentralized crypto exchanges or used to pay for future stays.[49]

To take another example, in June 2021, the capital city of South Korea, Seoul, announced a plan to use IoT data and blockchain to monitor older buildings. The new system will automatically send alerts when risks are detected and thus city staff do not need to visit buildings to conduct safety inspections. The initiative will start with a 46-building pilot in December 2021. From 2022, it will be scaled up to 824 buildings that are over 30 years old or are viewed as potentially hazardous or prone to disasters. IoT sensors attached to walls measure the slope and cracks of a building and other indicators. The data will be stored in blockchain. Seoul Metropolitan Government thinks that block-

---

[46]   SDCE Staff (2020) 'Global Supply Chain Management Software to Reach $9.56 billion by 2024' *Supply & Demand Chain Executive*, https://www.sdcexec.com/software-technology/news/21111458/global-supply-chain-management-software-to-reach-956-billion-by-2024.

[47]   M Hussey (2019) 'What Is a Blockchain Oracle?' *Decrypt*, https://decrypt.co/resources/oracles.

[48]   Chainlink *Cryptonews*, https://cryptonews.com/coins/chainlink/.

[49]   Digital Twin Asset Management with IoT, AI, Blockchain for Automation (2021) *NetObjex Integrates Chainlink Oracles to Power Its IoT-based Automation* [online] Available at: https://www.netobjex.com/netobjex-integrates-chainlink-oracles-to-power-its-iot-based-automation-engine/.

chain will help to ensure the accuracy of information and provide verifiable and objective data in case of accidents and disputes.[50]

3.5   DIGITAL TWIN

A digital twin is 'a virtual representation of an object, a service process, a product or anything else that can be digitized'.[51] For a physical entity, a digital twin is an exact digital replica or representation of the entity (physical twin) and includes the 'properties, condition and behavior of the real-life object through models and data'. The digital twin possesses the capability to simulate actual behaviour of the physical twin in the deployed environment. Digital twins thus give a real-time view of what is happening with physical assets such as equipment.

To take an example, the auction house Sotheby's London has created a digital twin of its London headquarters on New Bond Street. The digital replica is located in Decentraland, which is a decentralised Ethereum-powered virtual reality platform. The virtual gallery consisting of five ground floor spaces will show digital art. A digital avatar of a commisionaire at Sotheby's 'Hans Lomulder' will greet visitors at the door.[52]

In order to create a physical object's digital twin, data from various sources are collected and synthesized. They include data related to physical characteristics, manufacturing and operational data as well as insights from data analytics. Combining with AI algorithms, this information is integrated into a virtual model. With analytics, it is possible to get relevant insights regarding the physical asset.[53]

IoT sensors gather data from the physical object and send it to the digital twin, which can be used to optimize the product's performance.[54] The digital

---

[50]   Cities Today (2021) *Seoul Monitors Building Safety with IoT and Blockchain.* [online] Available at: https://cities-today.com/seoul-monitors-building-safety-with-iot -and-blockchain/.

[51]   C Miskinis (2018) 'What Separates Digital Twin Based Simulations vs a Reality that Is Augmented' *Challenge Advisory,* https://www.challenge.org/insights/digital -twin-vs-augmented-reality/.

[52]   Kabir Jhala (June 7, 2021) 'Crypto-crazed Sotheby's Launches First Virtual Gallery in Digital Metaverse Decentraland' https://www.theartnewspaper.com/2021/ 06/07/crypto-crazed-sothebys-launches-first-virtual-gallery-in-digital-metaverse -decentraland.

[53]   Digital Twins *Happiest Minds,* https://www.happiestminds.com/insights/ digital-twins/#:~:text=How%20do%20Digital%20Twins%20work,an%20asset%20is %20built%20physically.

[54]   B Marr (2019) '7 Amazing Examples of Digital Twin Technology in Practice' *Forbes,* https://www.forbes.com/sites/bernardmarr/2019/04/23/7-amazing-examples

twin also acts as the virtual counterpart during the physical twin's product life cycle.[55] AI and ML are used to analyse the model of operations represented by the digital twin.[56]

Digital twins play a key role in augmented reality (AR), which involves the real-time integration of digital information with the user's environment. The digital twin follows the product's location and movement. Images that are overlaid onto the real world using real-time sensor data and analytics can be used to perform product maintenance and services.[57] The digital twin thus can be a reference point that can be used to check the blockchain information.[58]

3.6   CHAPTER SUMMARY AND CONCLUSION

There are various complementary and synergistic mechanisms by which blockchain and other modern technologies are likely to have powerful impacts on structures, conduct and performance of industries and markets. AI and blockchain probably have the most significant synergistic effects that have the potential to disrupt economies and transform societies. For instance, AI can provide fast and efficient processing of blockchain systems to enable transactions. AI is likely to emerge as the driving force behind smart contracts by automatically updating and modifying the relevant conditions in and validating data to implement such contracts. Blockchain, on the other hand, can enhance access to data, algorithms, and applications to enhance the AI ecosystem. Blockchain can also help provide a level playing field in the AI world in many different ways. Combined together, AI and blockchain can drastically strengthen the cybersecurity landscape. Overall, their synergistic actions can enhance trust, transparency, efficiency, and accountability.

As discussed above, technologies such as remote sensing and satellite imagery, and the IoT perform various functions including acting as a source of information for executing smart contracts. Digital twins, on the other hand, simulate actual behaviour of the physical twin in the deployed environment.

Other technologies such as quick response (QR) codes, computer vision and machine vision are not discussed in this chapter but will be considered in other

-of-digital-twin-technology-in-practice/#765de5f76443.
[55]   S Haag and R Anderl (2018) 'Digital Twin – Proof of Concept' *Manufacturing Letters* Vol 15 64–66.
[56]   Marr (n 54).
[57]   'The Digital Twin – What Is It and How Does It Work?' *Essentra Components*, https://www.essentracomponents.com/en-gb/news/product-resources/the-digital-twin -what-is-it-and-how-does-it-work.
[58]   J Kelly (2019) 'Blockchain Is No Silver Bullet against the Black Market' *Financial Times*, https://www.ft.com/content/7414d28a-7d52-11e9-8b5c-33d0560f039c.

chapters. Overall, combinations of blockchain and other advanced technologies enable a high level of control on the actions of participants involved at all stages in the supply chain. By doing this it is possible to ensure that malicious users cannot abuse the system.

PART II

Key application areas of blockchain

4. Supply chain management

4.1 INTRODUCTION

Supply chain management (SCM) is emerging as an ideal use case for block-chain. For instance, in the annual Blockchain 50 list published in February 2020 by *Forbes*, which consisted of the world's biggest brands with over US$ 1 billion in annual revenue that were using blockchain, most companies in the list had used blockchain for supply chain and related logistical operations. An analysis of the Netherlands-based market intelligence platform for blockchain and DLT (distributed ledger technology) firm Blockdata found that six of the Blockchain 50 companies specifically developed SCM use cases. Blockdata also found that companies in the Blockchain 50 were more likely to use blockchain for traceability and provenance, which are closely related to supply chain, compared to payments and settlement.[1] Blockdata's analysis indicted that 15 had used blockchain solutions in traceability and provenance, whereas 13 had used such solutions for payments and settlements.[2]

PwC has identified provenance as the number one use case of blockchain and estimated that by helping organizations to verify the sources of their goods and track their movement and enhancing supply chain transparency, the technology has the potential to increase the global GDP (Gross Domestic Product) by US$ 962 billion by 2030.[3]

Supply chains entail flows of various categories of crucial resources such as physical goods, information and finance (e.g., payments). The last two categories of non-physical flows play supporting roles in SCM.[4] Blockchain deployment can improve the flows of both non-physical layers: non-financial

---

[1]   A Fenton (2020) 'Blockchain Traceability Overtakes Payments among Major Corporations' *Cointelegraph*, https://cointelegraph.com/news/blockchain-traceability-overtakes-payments-among-major-corporations.

[2]   Blockdata (2020) 'Forbes Blockchain 50 – Products Data Deep Dive' *Blockdata*, https://blog.blockdata.tech/2020/04/forbes-blockchain-50-products-data-deep-dive/.

[3]   Pwc (2020) 'Time for Trust: The Trillion-dollar Reasons to Rethink Blockchain' *PWC*, https://image.uk.info.pwc.com/lib/fe31117075640475701c74/m/2/434c46d2-a889-4fed-a030-c52964c71a64.pdf.

[4]   CR Carter, DA Rogers and TY Choi (2015) 'Toward the Theory of the Supply Chain' *Journal Supply Chain Management* Vol 51(2) 89–97.

information and financial information. Blockchain-based SCM may incorporate additional useful non-financial information related to different attributes of an object, such as shape and colour as well as environmental conditions such as temperature and humidity. Supply chain-related data also may be collected continuously rather than at discrete intervals. Second, information in traditional supply chains flows only in backward and forward directions. Some blockchain-based supply chain systems have nodes such as certification agencies and regulators, which were not a part of the information flows in traditional SCM. Third, blockchain-based supply chain systems make reasonable efforts to ensure the veracity of the information entered in the system. For instance, supply chain participants cannot use fake custom clearance certificates since such certificates are directly uploaded by relevant government agencies. In some cases, it is also possible to evaluate the veracity of the information recorded in blockchain databases. If a farmer claims that he has planted organic palm trees in a certain plot of land and the information is entered into the blockchain records, interested participants such as certification agencies can visit the site and compare data recorded in the blockchain against the real-world situation. The record can also be confirmed with other sources of information such as satellite imagery. There is thus a strong disincentive for a supply chain participant to provide false information in a blockchain system.

4.2   SUPPLY CHAIN AS AN IDEAL USE CASE FOR BLOCKCHAIN

Blockchain can connect various participants in a supply chain without giving any specific participant a higher level of competitive advantage. CEO and founder of traceability-as-a-service provider Circulor,[5] Doug Johnson-Poensgen noted that supply chain is among applications that can really benefit from blockchain and DLTs. Supply chains have many features that cannot be solved with a huge database alone. Complex global supply chains have no central authority. They need commercial confidentiality of data and an immutable record of transactions. Johnson-Poensgen went on to say that raw materials have the potential business problem that would most likely scale with blockchain.[6]

Thus, the whole supply chain benefits from the deployment of this technology. Blockchains make it possible to tokenize an asset when the asset moves

---

[5]   spendmatters.com (2020) 'How a Circular Economy Can Build a Sustainable Supply Chain for Batteries' *AzulPartners*, https://spendmatters.com/uk/how-a-circular-economy-can-build-a-sustainable-supply-chain-for-batteries/.

[6]   M Bennett (2019) 'Blockchain App for Miners in Rwanda Ensures the Minerals in Your iPhone are Conflict-free' *Diginomica*, https://diginomica.com/blockchain-app-for-miners-in-rwanda-ensures-the-minerals-in-your-iphone-are-conflict-free.

through a supply chain. The process involves issuing a blockchain-based digital token, which represents a tangible or an intangible asset. When the asset moves from one location to another, the token is removed from the original location and put into the new one (In Focus 4.1: Bext360 tokenizes coffee supply chains). This process stimulates the flow of information across a network. The information that flows is likely to be more accurate. In the non-blockchain world, banks tokenize money, but it is not a standard procedure in supply chains, in which many companies interact.[7].

IN FOCUS 4.1 BEXT360 TOKENIZES COFFEE SUPPLY CHAINS

Denver, Colorado-based start-up Bext360 has tokenized coffee supply chains using blockchain. Its kiosks in Uganda evaluate coffee beans using its Bextmachines, which are Coinstar-like devices. Smart image recognition, technology machine vision and artificial intelligence grade coffee beans by taking a three-dimensional scan of each bean's outer fruit.[a] Bigger and riper cherries are valued and paid more.

Bextmachines analyze farmers' coffee cherries and coffee parchment deposited at collection stations and sort them to assess quality. Bext360's systems store data relate to time, date and location of transactions and amount of payment. It also includes indicators related to sustainable sourcing and satellite images to show if producers are polluting water.[b]

The Bextmachines link the output to cryptotokens, which represent the coffee's value. New tokens are automatically created when the product passes through the supply chain. The values of tokens increase at each successive stage of the supply chain.[c]

Notes:
[a] Z Cadwalader (2018) 'Trace Your Coffee Using Blockchain' *Sprudge*, https://sprudge.com/132380-132380 .html.
[b] C. Zhong (2019) 'Innovator BanQu Builds Blockchain and Bridges for Traceability, Small Farmers' Livelihoods' *Greenbiz*, https://www.greenbiz.com/article/innovator-banqu-builds-blockchain-and-bridges -traceability-small-farmers-livelihoods.
[c] Moyee Coffee (2018) 'World's First Blockchain Coffee Project' *Moyee Coffee*, https://moyeecoffee.ie/ blogs/moyee/world-s-first-blockchain-coffee-project.

[7] P Brody (2021) *Why Blockchain Benefits the Supply Chain.* [online] Available at: https://www.coindesk.com/policy/2021/11/15/why-blockchain-benefits-the-supply -chain/.

A McKinsey.com article asserted that blockchain's value creation potential lies mainly in three areas.[8] These areas fit squarely into supply chains. First, in applications such as supply chains, blockchain can address problems relating to inefficiency, opacity, and fraud. Second, in some sectors, blockchain can help modernize value by helping the digitization process, simplifying value creation process and facilitating collaboration. Some specific areas include smart contracts in the global shipping industry, trade finance, and payments applications. Third, blockchain is being used in supply chains by some firms to enhance reputational value by demonstrating their ability to innovate. Indeed, many of the most promising blockchain applications are in supply chains.

4.3   CURRENT STATUS OF BLOCKCHAIN DEPLOYMENT IN SUPPLY CHAIN MANAGEMENT

Figure 4.1 presents Blockchain 50 companies that had developed use cases for SCM and related areas as reported by Blockdata. Since SCM is viewed as a more general use case, we discuss the other four use cases presented in Figure 4.1 in this section.

4.3.1   Traceability

As noted earlier, companies in the Blockchain 50 list were more likely to use blockchain for traceability and provenance compared to payments and settlement.[9] Traceability entails following a product's path along the direction of the upstream supply chain to its origin, while tracking involves following the downstream supply chain, that is, from raw materials to the end product.[10] The lack of traceability in traditional supply chains is mainly due to data silos. That is, supply chain data is accessible by one participant but is isolated from other supply chain participants. In order to be able to trace ingredients across

---

[8]   M Higginson, M Nadeau and K Rajgopal (2019) 'Blockchain's Occam Problem' *McKinsey & Company*, https://www.mckinsey.com/industries/financial-services/our-insights/blockchains-occam-problem?cid=other-eml-alt-mip-mck&hlkid=f1 ff7216a70e4041951d60293978a0ea&hctky=2762145&hdpid=95e9bdfa-0709-4b4d -8252-f401bcaac86d.

[9]   A Fenton (2020) 'Blockchain Traceability Overtakes Payments among Major Corporations' *Cointelegraph*, https://cointelegraph.com/news/blockchain-traceability -overtakes-payments-among-major-corporations.

[10]   F Dabbene, P Gay and C Tortia (2014) 'Traceability Issues in Food Supply Chain Management: A Review' *Biosyst. Eng* Vol 120 65–80.

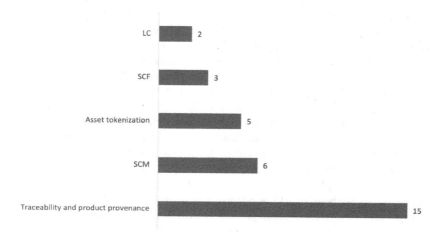

Note: LC (Letter of Credit); SCM (Supply Chain Management); SCF (Supply Chain Finance).
Source: Blockdata (2020) Forbes Blockchain 50 – Products Data Deep Dive. *Blockdata,*
https://blog.blockdata.tech/2020/04/forbes-blockchain-50-products-data-deep-dive/.

Figure 4.1   *Number of products related to supply chain-related use cases offered by Blockchain 50*

multiple tiers of a supply chain, data must be shared in a tamper-proof way and must be accessible to relevant parties.[11]

While other technologies make it possible to trace and track products, blockchain will lead to confidence and trust in a wide range of products such as fresh produce, raw materials and diamonds. When goods change hands, relevant records can be added. Some companies with blockchain-based traceability solutions included in the list were IBM, Nestle, Foxconn, Honeywell, Walmart, Amazon, BMW and Mastercard. Blockdata's analysis found that ten of the products were already in production and five were in the pilot phase. Use cases were found in such diverse industries as agriculture, mining, aerospace, food and automotive.

The above issues are important due primarily to the fact that consumers highly value transparency, which can be facilitated by traceability. A study conducted by the SaaS (Software-as-a-Service) company Label Insight in

---

[11] M Westerkamp, F Victor and A Küpper (2020) 'Tracing Manufacturing Processes Using Blockchain-based Token Compositions' *Digital Communications and Networks* Vol 6(2) 167–76, https://www.sciencedirect.com/science/article/pii/S235286481830244X.

2016 found that 94 per cent of consumers were likely to be loyal to a brand that offers complete transparency. The company's 2016 Transparency ROI (Return on Investment) Study also found that 73 per cent of the respondents were willing to pay more for products that have completely transparent supply chains.[12] Similar findings have been reported in recent studies. A survey conducted by IBM found that 73 per cent of consumers surveyed placed importance on traceability of products and 71 per cent of them would pay a premium for it.[13] Blockchain's key features such as decentralization and immutability make it an ideal tool to improve supply chain traceability[14] by addressing various shortcomings of traditional supply chains.[15] Despite traditional supply chain information systems' capability to uniquely identify products, they perform poorly in traceability.

The importance placed on traceability in SCM is also apparent in scholarly literature. An analysis of 613 academic articles related to blockchain use in logistics and supply chain management (LSCM) indicated that 'traceability' was the fourth most used title word (after blockchain/ blockchain technology, supply chain/supply chain management, and applications) and fifth most used keyword (after blockchain/blockchain technology, supply chain/supply chain management, smart contract and IoT (Internet of Things)).[16] Indeed, early academic papers focusing on the use of blockchain in LSCM, mainly dealt with traceability and product provenance.[17]

---

[12] M Mannak (2019) 'Good for the Planet, Suppliers, and Balance Sheet' *Financial Management Magazine*, https://www.fm-magazine.com/issues/2019/aug/supply-chain-transparency-strategy.html.

[13] ibm.com (2020) 'Meet the 2020 Consumers Driving Change' *IBM*, https://www.ibm.com/thought-leadership/institute-business-value/report/consumer-2020.

[14] HM Kim and M Laskowski (2018) 'Toward an Ontology-driven Blockchain Design for Supply-chain Provenance' *Intell. Syst. Account. Finance Manag* Vol 25(1) 18–27.

[15] K Toyoda, PT Mathiopoulos, I Sasase and T Ohtsuki (2017) 'A Novel Blockchain-based Product Ownership Management System (POMS) for Anti-counterfeits in the Post Supply Chain' *IEEE Access* Vol 5 17465–77. doi.10.1109/ACCESS.2017.2720760.

[16] B Müßigmann, H von der Gracht and E Hartmann (2020) 'Blockchain Technology in Logistics and Supply Chain Management – A Bibliometric Literature Review from 2016 to January 2020' *IEEE Transactions on Engineering Management*, https://ieeexplore.ieee.org/abstract/document/9138446.

[17] F Tian (2017) 'A Supply Chain Traceability System for Food Safety Based on HACCP, Blockchain and Internet of Things' *Proc. Int. Conf. Service Syst. Service Manage.* 1–6; HM Kim and M Laskowski (2018) 'Toward an Ontology-driven Blockchain Design for Supply-chain Provenance, Intelligent Systems in Accounting' *Finance Manage*, Vol 25(1) 18–27; B Mukri (June, 2018) 'Blockchain Technology in Supply Chain Management: A Review' *Int. Res. J. Eng. Technol.* Vol 5(6) 2497–500.

Various types of transformation parameters can be used in blockchain-based traceability.[18] In single item traceability, a consumer can see the history of the item as it moves along the supply chain. Blockchain can be combined with RFID (radio frequency identification) or QR codes.[19] Single item traceability is appropriate for expensive prescription products such as life-saving drugs.[20]

In a batch traceability system, batch-managed products are tracked and traced from raw materials to finished goods. SAP (Systems, Applications & Products in Data Processing) Global Batch Traceability (GBT) allows companies to create a 'product batch genealogy'. To do so, batches of products are tracked and linked with business activities (e.g., purchase orders, production orders and deliveries) throughout a supply chain.[21]

Mass Balancing methodology takes into account the materials or masses that enter and leave a system. This approach is widely used in fields such as chemical engineering. For instance, the systems and solutions provider for aseptic packaging, SIG, requires its supplier to purchase certain amounts of certified plant-based feedstock for a given amount of polymer output.[22] Certified mass balance systems are used to verify the amount of bio-based feedstock that goes into the manufacturing of polymers.[23]

[18]   B Kilbey and F Warwick (2020) 'Blockchain Not Silver Bullet for Mine Operations: Verisk Maplecroft VP' *S&P Global Platts*, https://www.spglobal.com/platts/en/market-insights/latest-news/metals/012920-blockchain-not-silver-bullet-for-mine-operations-verisk-maplecroft-vp.

[19]   G Benatar and R Gurwitz (2018) 'Small Item Picking (SIP) Solutions Suitable to the South African Market. Is Automation or Mechanization an Option?' *SAPICS*, https://conference.sapics.org/wp-content/uploads/2018/06/Benatar-Gurwitz.pdf.

[20]   Reckitt Benckiser International Ltd (2008) 'Response to Public Consultation in Preparation of a Legal Proposal to Combat Counterfeit Medicines for Human Use – Key Ideas for Better Protection of Patients against the Risk of Counterfeit Medicines as Proposed by the European Commission, Enterprise and Industry Directorate-General, Consumer Goods, Pharmaceuticals' https://ec.europa.eu/health/sites/health/files/counterf_par_trade/doc_publ_consult_200803/18_reckitt_benckiser_en.pdf.

[21]   'SAP Global Batch Traceability' *Movilitas*. [online] Accessed June 23, 2022, https://www.movilitas.com/solutions/track-trace/sap-global-batch-traceability/.

[22]   SIGnals (2017) 'Understanding the Mass Balancing System behind Signature Pack' *SIGnals*, https://www.sig.biz/signals/en/articles/understanding-mass-balancing.

[23]   technology.risiinfo.com (2019) 'SIG's Signature Pack Wins Award in "Environmental" Category at French Packaging Award 2019' *RISI*, https://technology.risiinfo.com/packaging-technology/europe/sigs-signature-pack-wins-award-environmental-category-french-packaging-award-2019.

4.3.2   Asset Tokenization

Asset tokenization involves the issuance of blockchain tokens that represent tradable assets. To take an example, Paris-based NFT platform for the luxury and fashion industries Arianne uses blockchain to track and trace luxury goods. Luxury brands can use the Arianee platform to tokenize their assets and create a digital passport for their products. Founded in 2017 as a nonprofit consortium, Arianne aims to 'implement a global standard for the digital certification of luxury goods'.[24] Members of the Arianee Consortium include Audemars Piguet, ba&sh, Breitling, Constantin, Dubuis, Manufacture Royale, Olistic, Richemont, Roger MB&F, Satoshi Studio, Vacheron Panerai and Verlan.[25] Arianee uses NFTs that are based on the Ethereum's ERC-721 standard.[26] The passport guarantees a product's authenticity and allows the brands to maintain a 'perpetual' relationship with the product owner. All the events and transactions during a product's life cycle are recorded.[27]

The luxury watch brand Breitling has teamed up with Arianee to issue digital passports as certificates of authenticity for its luxury watches. Each watch has a unique digital passport that certifies its origin.[28] A buyer of a Breitling watch gets a guarantee card that they can scan. They can do so by downloading the Arianee wallet app. The watch then can be added to the buyer's digital wallet. A customer can see the watch's serial number and the activation date of the digital warranty.[29]

In March 2020, Breitling launched a pilot of the solution for its watch, Top Time. The pilot was viewed as a success and in October 2020 Breitling became the first luxury watchmaker to offer blockchain-based tokenization to track and trace all its watches.[30]

Breitling customers can use the digital passport to verify authenticity of their watch and prove their ownership. By proving the authenticity, the digital certificates can also be helpful in reselling a watch if the owner wishes to do so. They can also transfer ownership of their Breitling watch to another owner.

---

[24] Ledger Insights (2020) *Breitling Expands Blockchain Digital Passports to All Watches.* [online] Ledger Insights – Enterprise Blockchain. Available at: https://www.ledgerinsights.com/breitling-expands-blockchain-digital-passports-to-all-watches/.
[25] Arinee (2021) *Digital Passports for Luxury Fashion Items.* [online] Available at: https://www.innovationintextiles.com/digital-passports-for-luxury-fashion-items/.
[26] R Dillet (2020) *Luxury Watch Maker Breitling Issues Digital Certificates on the Ethereum Blockchain.* [online] Available at: https://techcrunch.com/2020/10/15/luxury-watch-maker-breitling-issues-digital-certificates-on-the-ethereum-blockchain/.
[27] Arinee (n 25).
[28] Ibid.
[29] Dillet (n 26).
[30] Ledger Insights (n 24).

Breitling has also linked the passport to its warranty programme, which allows customers to track repairs to their watches. As of October 2020, Breitling was planning to add other functionality to the passport, which would allow users to extend the warranty period and add theft or loss insurance.[31]

4.3.3 Supply Chain Finance

Supply chain finance (SCF) solutions represent technologies and financial services to connect various supply chain partners. The goal is to improve the effectiveness of financial supply chains by decreasing or even preventing the cost-shifting practices, which involve shifting inventory-related and other costs to supply chain partners. While such tactics are effective in reducing the company's internal costs in the short term, they have adverse effects in the total supply chain costs in the long run.[32] In order to improve the functioning of financial supply chains, downstream supply chain partners need to improve the visibility and availability, as well as costs of cash for upstream participants.[33] A related term is trade finance, which encompasses financing to suppliers in order to help them manufacture goods and as well as to buyers to help buy those goods.

With blockchain, supply chain participants can have access to detailed and authentic data on other participants about previous transactions, which can be used by a financial institution to assess risks. Using data from satellite, global positioning system (GPS) or radio-frequency identification technology, blockchain solutions can make it possible for interested parties to see the status of goods. In the Australian government's 'National Blockchain Roadmap', announced in 2020, which identified supply chain tracking as a key use case, there have been some innovative uses of data to facilitate SCF. Alibaba Group's mobile and online payment platform Alipay Australia is responsible

---

[31]   breitling.com (Oct 13, 2020) 'Breitling Becomes the First Luxury Watchmaker to Offer a Digital Passport Based on Blockchain for All of Its New Watches' *Breitling*,   https://www.breitling.com/us-es/news/details/breitling-becomes-the-first -luxury-watchmaker-to-offer-a-digital-passport-based-on-blockchain-for-all-of -its-new-watches-33479#:~:text=10%2F13%2F20-,BREITLING%20BECOMES %20THE%20FIRST%20LUXURY%20WATCHMAKER%20TO%20OFFER %20A%20DIGITAL,ALL%20OF%20ITS%20NEW%20WATCHES&text= From%20October%2013%2C%202020%2C%20all,their%20authenticity%20and %20seamless%20accessibility.

[32]   scdigest.com (2013) 'Supply Chain News: What Are the Barriers to Lean Success?' *Scdigest*, http://www.scdigest.com/ontarget/13-01-30-2.php?cid=6680.

[33]   J Lamoureux and T Evans (2011) 'Supply Chain Finance: A New Means to Support the Competitiveness and Resilience of Global Value Chains' *SSRN*, https:// papers.ssrn.com/sol3/papers.cfm?abstract_id=2179944.

for handling payment for products exported to China. Alipay Australia uses logistics-related data generated by IoT devices and other sources. The data are stored in Chinese blockchain company VeChain's VeChainThor network. The information is used to provide loans to suppliers to meet their working capital needed.[34] Mastercard was designated for handling payments for products destined for other countries.

Retailers and other downstream supply chain players are also considering 'milestone' payments to various parties when the shipments move along the supply chain. This means that manufacturers do not need to wait for a long time for their accounts to settle. That is, instant payments are made to a digital wallet. It could be argued that benefits of such payment models are especially important in situations such as those created by COVID-19, which has negatively affected companies' cash flows. For example, under the 'milestone' payments model, 30 per cent of the total payment can be made to an Australian manufacturer when the shipment clears customs in Australia and the information is recorded in blockchain. An additional 30 per cent is paid when the shipment clears customs in China and the rest is transferred when the product is delivered.[35]

4.3.4 Letter of Credit

A 2020 JP Morgan report on enterprise blockchain and digital currencies identified letter of credit (LC) as the most promising application.[36] The US computer technology corporation Oracle has claimed that in general, by automating key components of trade finance such as LC issuance, processing times can be cut by 60 per cent, and time required to enter and scrutinize data can be shortened by 70 per cent.[37] With blockchain, it is also possible for all parties to see instantly all data related to transactions.

[34] J Simmons (2020) 'CREAM Co-founder: That's Why VeChain Is the No. 1 Enterprise Blockchain' *Crypto News Flash*, https://www.crypto-news-flash.com/cream-co-founder-thats-why-vechain-is-the-no-1-enterprise-blockchain/.

[35] A Fenton (2019) 'VECHAIN: Why Does Good News Kill the Price of This Altcoin?' *Micky*, https://micky.com.au/vechain-why-does-good-news-kill-the-price-of-this-altcoin/.

[36] Ledger Insights (2020) 'JP Morgan Blockchain Report Picks Trade Finance as Winner, says Libra's Release "Failed"' *Ledger Insights*, https://www.ledgerinsights.com/jp-morgan-blockchain-trade-finance-libra-release-failed/.

[37] Oracle (2020) 'Transform the Future of Trade Finance' *Oracle Corporation*, https://www.oracle.com/a/ocom/docs/industries/financial-services/trade-finance-process-management-br.pdf.

In 2019, Euromoney reported that there were about 30 consortia that focused on using DLT in trade finance.[38] Blockchain consortium Contour was established in 2018 by eight banks, including ING, BNP Paribas and HSBC. The goal is to eliminate LC-related paperwork.[39] Contour has claimed that it reduces process for presenting documentation against an LC to under 24 hours. Traditionally the process can take up to two weeks to process documentations for an LC.[40]

4.4 BLOCKCHAIN'S EFFECT ON KEY SUPPLY CHAIN MANAGEMENT OBJECTIVES

SCM plays a key role in a firm's ability to deliver customer value.[41] One of the key goals of an effective SCM involves getting the product in the right condition, in a timely manner and at the lowest possible cost.[42] Measurement of SCM performance is often described in terms of objectives such as quality, speed, risk reduction,[43] [44] dependability, cost and flexibility.[45]

---

[38] euromoney.com (2019) 'Trade Finance and Blockchain: Now Is the Time for a Network of Networks' *Euromoney*, https://www.euromoney.com/article/b1h041crxm5dks/trade-finance-and-blockchain-now-is-the-time-for-a-network-of-networks.
[39] finextra.com (2020) 'DBS Joins Contour Trade Finance Network' *Finextra*, https://www.finextra.com/newsarticle/35796/dbs-joins-contour-trade-finance-network.
[40] euromoney.com (2019) 'Trade Finance and Blockchain: Now Is the Time for a Network of Networks' *Euromoney*, https://www.euromoney.com/article/b1h041crxm5dks/trade-finance-and-blockchain-now-is-the-time-for-a-network-of-networks; finextra.com (n 39); (20 May, 2021) 'Contour increases global footprint with Addition of SMBC to Digital Trade Network' https://contour.network/press-release/contour-increases-global-footprint-with-addition-of-smbc-to-digital-trade-network/.
[41] JT Mentzer, DJ Flint and GTM Hult (2001) 'Logistics Service Quality as a Segment-customized Process' *Journal of Marketing* Vol 65(4) 82–104.
[42] D Flint (2004) 'Strategic Marketing in Global Supply Chains: Four Challenges' *Industrial Marketing Management* Vol 33(1) 45–50.
[43] I Baird, I Skromme and H Thomas (1991) 'What Is Risk Anyway? Using and Measuring Risk in Strategic Management,' in: RA Bettis and H Thomas (eds), *Risk, Strategy and Management* 24, (Jai Press Inc., Connecticut).
[44] RA Bettis and V Mahajan (1985) 'Risk/Return Performance of Diversified Firms' *Management Science* Vol 31(7) 785–99.
[45] GP White (1996) 'A Survey and Taxonomy of Strategy-related Performance Measures for Manufacturing' *International Journal of Operations & Production Management* Vol 16(3) 42–61; A Meyer and P Hohmann (2000) 'Other Thoughts; Other Results? – Remei's BioRe Organic Cotton on Its Way to the Mass Market' *Greener Management International* Vol 31 59–70; M Goldbach, S Seuring and S Back (2003) 'Coordinating Sustainable Cotton Chains for the Mass Market – The Case of the German Mail Order Business' *OTT Greener Management International*

In addition to the above objectives, prior researchers have addressed the role of SCM for sustainable products.[46] This trend is partly driven by consumers' increasing concern about the source of products they use such as food and beverages, pharmaceuticals and cosmetics.[47] Social and environmental issues such as those related to noise pollution, congestion, and carbon dioxide emissions have become increasingly important and prominent.[48] Researchers have also argued that sustainability-related issues in supply chains, which often deal with natural environment and social causes are less quantifiable.[49] In this regard, it is hoped that blockchain, in combination with other technologies, can help obtain more quantifiable and objective data to tackle these issues.

Global supply chains are complex and face multiple uncertainties.[50] A major objective of SCM is also to reduce risks. Among the various risks that organizations face are relational risks such as a business partner's engagement in opportunistic behaviour (e.g., cheating, distorting information).[51] [52]

The sources of risks in supply chains can be classified into two main categories, namely, atomistic or holistic.[53] In order to deal with atomistic sources of risk, a selected and limited part of the supply chain needs to be looked at in order to assess risk. This approach is suitable for components and materials that are of low value, less complex, and easily available. On the other hand, holistic sources of risk require an overall analysis of the supply chain. This

Vol 43 65–78; G Kovács (2004) 'Framing a Demand Network for Sustainability' *Progress in Industrial Ecology: An International Journal* Vol 1(4) 397–410; P Rao and D Holt (2005) 'Do Green Supply Chains Lead to Competitiveness and Economic Performance?' *International Journal of Operations & Production Management* Vol 25(9) 898–916.

[46]   FE Bowen, PD Cousins, RC Lamming and AC Faruk (2001) 'The Role of Supply Management Capabilities in Green Supply' *Production and Operations Management* Vol 10(2) 174–89.

[47]   M Scott (2017) 'Innovation Percolates When Coffee Meets the Blockchain' *Nasdaq*, http://www.nasdaq.com/article/innovation-percolates-when-coffee-meets-the-blockchain-cm774790.

[48]   HJ Quak and MBM de Koster (2007) 'Exploring Retailers' Sensitivity to Local Sustainability Policies' *Journal of Operations Management* Vol 25(6) 1103–22.

[49]   JD Linton, R Klassen and V Jayaraman (2007) 'Sustainable Supply Chains: An Introduction' *Journal of Operations Management* Vol 25(6) 1075–82.

[50]   I Manuj and JT Mentzer (2008) 'Global Supply Chain Risk Management' *Journal of Business Logistics* Vol 29(1) 133–55.

[51]   Baird (n 43).

[52]   Bettis and Mahajan (1985) (n 44).

[53]   G Svensson (2000) 'A Conceptual Framework for the Analysis of Vulnerability in Supply Chains' *International Journal of Physical Distribution & Logistics Management* Vol 30(9) 731–49.

approach is preferable for high-value, complex, and rare components and materials.[54]

To achieve the various objectives noted above, it is important to evaluate suppliers. Due to increased competition, globalization and outsourcing, the number of players in a typical supply chain has increased significantly. In response, firms have introduced supplier evaluation programmes using environmental and social criteria.[55] [56] Some use supplier self-evaluation, in which supply chain partners declare how they have tackled environmental and social issues.[57] To take an example, the global apparel retailer C&A requires its suppliers to respect its ethical standards which include fair and honest dealings with employees, subcontractors and other stakeholders.[58] There are, however, implementation challenges due to the technical impracticality of assessing various stakeholders' sustainability practices.

Blockchain can help address many of the challenges facing modern supply chains. Table 4.1 below provides illustrative examples of how blockchain can contribute to key SCM objectives such as cost, quality, speed, dependability, risk reduction, sustainability and flexibility.

4.4.1   Reducing Costs and Risks

A study conducted by Cointelegraph Consulting and Swiss blockchain firm Insolar found that blockchain can reduce supply chain-related costs by 0.4–0.8 per cent.[59] Among the most obvious cost components, manual paper-based processes and humans carrying documents such as air courier expenses are eliminated.

To take an example, a study conducted by the Danish shipping company Maersk, which is the world's largest container carrier, found that significant

---

[54] Svensson, Ibid.

[55] J Koplin, S Seuring and M Mesterharm (2007) 'Incorporating Sustainability into Supply Management in the Automotive Industry: The Case of the Volkswagen AG' *Journal of Cleaner Production* Vol 15(11–12) 1053–62.

[56] P Beske, J Koplin and S Seuring (2008) 'The Use of Environmental and Social Standards by German First-tier Suppliers of the Volkswagen AG' *Corporate Social Responsibility & Environmental Management* Vol 15(2) 63–75.

[57] P Trowbridge (2001) 'A Case Study of Green Supply-chain Management at Advanced Micro Devices' *Greener Management International* Vol 35 (Autumn 2001), 121–35.

[58] JJ Graafland (2002) 'Sourcing Ethics in the Textile Sector: The Case of C&A' *Business Ethics A European Review* Vol 11(3) 282–94.

[59] sdcexec.com (2019) 'Blockchain Technology Saved European Supply Chains $450 Billion' *Supply & Demand Chain Executive*, https://www.sdcexec.com/software-technology/news/21104426/blockchain-technology-saved-european-supply-chains-450-billion.

costs savings can be achieved by fully digitizing the documents in international supply chains. In 2014, Maersk tracked a shipment of avocados and roses from East Africa to Europe in order to understand the costs and inefficiencies associated with physical processes and paperwork in cross-border trades.[60] In some cases, shipping containers can be held up in port for many days due to a piece of missing paperwork. A single container to handle a simple shipment of goods from East Africa to Europe required stamps and approvals from as many as 30 people and needed over 200 different interactions and communications.[61] A blockchain proof of concept (POC) done in September 2016 by IBM and Maersk, which tracked a container of flowers from the Kenyan coast city of Mombasa to Rotterdam in the Netherlands, found that the time and costs can be dramatically reduced with the technology.[62]

Blockchain deployment results in even higher cost savings in some niche areas. For instance, according to IDC, by 2023, a quarter of original equipment manufacturers (OEMs) will utilize blockchain to source spare parts. This will improve accuracy of usable parts by 60 per cent and reduce costs by 45 per cent.[63] Blockchain systems also lower costs by reducing errors. (See In Focus 4.2).

Blockchain can also help address various supply chain risks. Blockchain provides immutable information that can be made readily accessible to relevant supply chain partners, which helps to know who is performing what actions. Additionally, the time and location of the actions can be determined. For instance, the identities of individuals participating in transactions can be validated. Especially in permissioned blockchain, only parties mutually accepted in the network can engage in transactions in specific touchpoints.

Blockchain facilitates valid and effective measurement of outcomes and performance of key SCM processes. Once the inputs tracking data are on a blockchain ledger, they are immutable. Other suppliers in the chain can also track shipments, deliveries, and progress. In this way, blockchain produces trust among suppliers and reduces risks.

---

[60]   P Baipai (2017) 'How IBM and Maersk Will Use the Blockchain to Change the Shipping Industry.' Retrieved from http://www.nasdaq.com/article/how-ibm-and-maersk-will-use-the-blockchain-to-change-the-shipping-industry-cm756797.

[61]   T Groenfeldt (2017) 'IBM and Maersk Apply Blockchain to Container Shipping' *Forbes*, https://www.forbes.com/sites/tomgroenfeldt/2017/03/05/ibm-and-maersk-apply-blockchain-to-container-shipping/.

[62]   Ibid.

[63]   S Ellis (2019) 'Top 10 Predictions for Worldwide Supply Chains in 2020' *MH&L*, https://www.mhlnews.com/technology-automation/article/22055896/top-10-predictions-for-worldwide-supply-chains-in-2020.

Blockchain can also help address various cybersecurity risks in supply chains. More details are discussed in Chapter 5. For instance, blockchain can ensure that a software file downloaded from a source has not been breached, which is an extremely valuable application for some companies. In 2017, the world's largest defence contracting firm Lockheed Martin Aeronautics announced plans to leverage blockchain in its operations. In order to integrate blockchain into its external software supply chain, Lockheed Martin teamed up with the cybersecurity provider Guardtime Federal.[64] Guardtime Federal has helped Lockheed Martin integrate Keyless Signature Infrastructure (KSI) blockchain across the external software supply chain.[65] Blockchain's role is to ensure data integrity by verifying that data in the network is not compromised. For instance, when a third-party routine maintenance is performed, KSI helps detect unauthorized software.[66]

IN FOCUS 4.2 WALMART CANADA'S DLT

Walmart Canada's distribution centres have more than 4,500 employees that include more than 350 drivers. Thousands of items are transported daily from sites in Calgary, Mississauga and Cornwall to over 400 retail stores across Canada. More than 853 million cases of merchandise are moved annually. Winnipeg, Manitoba-based Bison Transport was the carrier partner in the pilot of the project.[a]

The system integrates and synchronizes all data on a shared ledger in real time. The solution can be accessed via a web portal or a mobile application.[b]

Walmart Canada owns a fleet of 180 tractors and 2,000 trailers. It also relies on a third-party fleet owned by about 60 carriers to move close to 500,000 loads annually. Each third-party trailer generates about 200 data points per shipment related to a number of variables from demurrage fees (which are assessed on laden containers that are inside a port beyond the number of free days agreed upon) to accessorial charges (fees added to a shipper's invoice for services the carrier performed beyond the standard

---

[64] S Higgins (2017) 'Defense Giant Lockheed Martin Integrates Blockchain' *CoinDesk*, http://www.coindesk.com/defense-giant-lockheed-martin-integratesb lockchain/.

[65] lockheedmartin.com (2020) 'Lockheed Martin and Guardtime Federal Join Forces to Thwart Software Cyber Threats' *Lockheed Martin Aeronautics*, https:// news.lockheedmartin.com/2020-02-20-Lockheed-Martin-and-Guardtime-Federal-Join -Forces-to-Thwart-Software-Cyber-Threats.

[66] C Biesecker (2020) 'Lockheed Martin Contracts with Guardtime Federal to Secure Software Supply Chain' *IIOT Connection*, https://www.iiotconnection.com/ lockheed-martin-contracts-guardtime-federal-secure-software-supply-chain/.

pickup and delivery operations). It is not unusual to have conflicting pieces of information. During peak periods Walmart Canada needed to dispute about 70 per cent of the related invoices.[c]

In 2019, Walmart Canada teamed up with Toronto-based DLT Labs to create a solution known as DL Freight. It is described as the largest industrial-grade blockchain in the world. The solution involves a common electronic ledger to host every document or piece of data associated with a shipment. The blocks of timestamped information cannot be changed, which creates a 'single source of truth'. The system is used to track deliveries, verify transactions, automate payments and perform reconciliations with carriers.[d]

The system went live in February 2020. By August 2020, it had processed over 150,000 invoices. Fewer than 2 per cent resulted in disputes.[e]

In a few months after the deployment, disputes with third-party carriers reduced by 97 per cent.[f] The solution was among the six finalists in the Council for Supply Chain Management Professionals' Supply Chain Innovation Award in September 2020.[g]

Notes:
[a] C Brett (Nov 21, 2019) 'Walmart Canada and DLT Labs Launch Production Blockchain' https://www.enterprisetimes.co.uk/2019/11/21/walmart-canada-and-dlt-labs-launch-production-blockchain/.
[b] I Putzger (Feb 13, 2020) 'Blockchain a Growing Trend in Supply Chain Visibility, but Is It Just "Hype"?' https://theloadstar.com/blockchain-a-growing-trend-in-supply-chain-visibility-but-is-it-just-hype/.
[c] J Smith (Sept 11, 2020) 'Walmart Canada Leverages Blockchain to Solve a Billing Nightmare' https://www.trucknews.com/features/walmart-canada-leverages-blockchain-to-solve-a-billing-nightmare/.
[d] Brett (n [a]).
[e] R Wolfson (Sept 9, 2020) 'Walmart Canada's Blockchain Freight Supply Chain Proving Its Value' https://cointelegraph.com/news/walmart-canada-s-blockchain-freight-supply-chain-proving-its-value.
[f] Smith (n [c]).
[g] Walmart Canada (Sept 1, 2020) 'Walmart Canada and DLT Labs Recognized for Supply Chain Innovation' https://www.newswire.ca/news-releases/walmart-canada-and-dlt-labs-recognized-for-supply-chain-innovation-848551895.html.

4.4.2 Demonstrating Quality and Sustainability

Blockchain solutions also allow faster response and quicker feedback to supply chain partners, which can have a major impact on quality of products and the promotion of sustainable practices (See In Focus 4.3). For instance, the British–Dutch multinational consumer goods company Unilever utilizes blockchain technology Provenance's platform to connect with farmers. Among many benefits, Unilever has been able to address product quality issues in its tea leaf supply chain.

Table 4. 1   *The roles of blockchain in achieving various strategic supply chain objectives*

Supply chain performance dimension	Explanation/context	Example
Reducing costs and risks	• Elimination of paper records • Easier identification of the source of a problem and engagement in strategic removals of affected products instead of *recalling the entire* product line • Possible to ensure that only known parties can engage in transactions • Possible to ensure that software file has not been breached	• Maersk: significant costs savings by fully digitizing the documents in international supply chains • Foolproof method for confirmed identity can reduce cybersecurity-related risks (Lockheed Martin)

Demonstrating quality and sustainability	• Real-time feedback can improve product quality and *promote sustainable practices*	• Quality-related issues were down by 20 per cent in Unilever's tea supply chain in Malawi and helped promote sustainable practices
		• Carrefour has incorporated blockchain in supply chains to help achieve its sustainability goals:
		    1) to have 100 per cent of natural raw materials in its exclusive brand products by 2030;
		    2) to sourcing 50 per cent of cotton textile organically by 2025

Increasing speed of operations in supply chain systems	• Digitizing communications and other important processes: there is no need for paper documents to be stamped and approved • Pinpointing the exact location where specific supply-chain related actions took place or a product originated from	• 2020: Walmart provided detailed information related to the original source of potential contamination to the FDA within an hour
Improving dependability and flexibility	• Exerting pressure on supply chain partners to be more responsible and accountable • COVID-19 forced firms to adopt blockchain solutions to increase flexibility	• Gemalto's delivery of temperature-sensitive medicines from drug manufacturer to hospitals located in hot climates • SMBC joined komgo and Contour to exchange documents required for LC

Financial incentives are provided to the tea farmers for feeding social or ecological data into the blockchain system.[67] Provenance, blockchain-enabled FinTech (financial technology) start-up Halotrade and real estate development company Meridia have developed what is referred to as the 'Trado Model'. It facilitates data sharing among producers, consumers and supply chain players.[68] The Trado model was first piloted in the Lujeri Tea Estate in Malawi, which made it possible for Unilever to directly access farming data from smallholder farmers. Data related to various indicators such as tea leaf production, social impact and sustainability credentials are recorded in the Provenance blockchain platform. The data helped Unilever to release payments earlier.[69]

IN FOCUS 4.3 CARREFOUR USES BLOCKCHAIN TO PROMOTE SUSTAINABILITY AND ASSURE CUSTOMERS OF PRODUCT QUALITY

The French retailer Carrefour aims to have 100 per cent of natural raw materials in its exclusive brand products by 2030. The retailer also has set a goal of sourcing 50 per cent of cotton textile organically by 2025.[a] To help achieve these sustainability goals, Carrefour has incorporated blockchain in supply chains.

In 2018, Carrefour announced a plan to track its own branded products in France, Spain and Brazil and expand to other countries by 2022.[b] The company launched Europe's first food blockchain in March 2018. The free-range Carrefour Quality Line (CQL) Auvergne chicken was the first product to be tracked by blockchain. The company sells one million units of this product every year.[c]

In November 2018, it launched a Hyperledger-based food tracking solution to track free-range chickens in Spain branded as 'Calidad y Origen'.[d] By December 2018, other product lines tracked by blockchain included Auvergne farmyard fattened chicken and CQL oranges.[e] In March 2019, Carrefour expanded blockchain solutions to track its milk

---

[67]   sappi.com (2019) 'Sappi Teams Up with Major Global Brands to Explore the Potential of Innovative Blockchain Technology in Enhancing the Sustainability of Global Supply Chains' *Sappi*, https://www.sappi.com/sappi-teams-up-with-major -global-brands-to-explore-the-potential-of-innovative-blockchain-technology.

[68]   N Kshetri (2021) *Blockchain and Supply Chain Management* (Elsevier, Amsterdam, Netherlands, Oxford, UK, and New York, USA).

[69]   S George (2019) 'Blockchain-enabled Supply Chain Sustainability Scheme Hailed "Successful" by Business Giants' *Edie Newsroom*, https://www.edie.net/ news/8/Blockchain-enabled-supply-chain-sustainability-scheme-hailed--successful- -by-business-giants/.

supply chain. The retailer announced that consumers can see GPS coordinates of farms where milk was collected, as well as information about when the milk was collected and packaged. Details are also provided about various stakeholders involved in the supply chain.[f] It offered complete product traceability to its new blockchain-powered product, CQL micro-filtered full-fat milk.

Carrefour tags some products with QR codes, which allow consumers to learn details about the origination of foods they buy.[g] Carrefour reported that blockchain's deployment to track meat, milk and fruit from farms to stores led to an increase in sales of these products.[h] For instance, in terms of sales growth blockchain-tracked chickens outperformed chickens that were not tracked.[i]

Blockchain's positive effects on sales can be attributed with the fact that this technology assures customers of the quality of products they buy. Consumers can thus avoid food items that contain genetically modified organisms, antibiotics or pesticides.[j] Such verification is not possible without blockchain.

Notes:

[a] https://www.ledgerinsights.com/carrefour-expands-blockchain-traceability-to-textile-products/.

[b] C Biscotti (2018) 'IBM's Food Blockchain Is Going Live with a Supermarket Giant on Board' *Hawthorncaller*, https://hawthorncaller.com/ibms-food-blockchain-is-going-live-with-a-supermarket-giant-on-board.

[c] D Tuaño (Mar 15, 2018) 'Carrefour's Iconic Chicken Launches Europe's First Food Blockchain' https://www.petrolplaza.com/news/8313.

[d] H Partz (2019) 'Retail Giant Carrefour Applies Blockchain for Tracking Milk Product Supply Chain' *CoinTelegraph*, https://cointelegraph.com/news/retail-giant-carrefour-applies-blockchain-for-tracking-milk-product-supply-chain.

[e] https://www.carrefour.com/en/newsroom/carrefour-now-using-blockchain-technology-auvergne-farmyard-fattened-chicken-and-carrefour.

[f] Partz (n [d]).

[g] 'Carrefour (Apr 26, 2019) 'Carrefour Applies Blockchain Technology to Its Eighth Product – Rocamadour, the First Carrefour Quality Line Cheese to Use It' https://www.carrefour.com/en/newsroom/carrefour-applies-blockchain-technology-its-eighth-product-rocamadour-first-carrefour.

[h] E Thomasson (2019) 'Carrefour Says Blockchain Tracking Boosting Sales of Some Products' *Reuters*, https://www.reuters.com/article/us-carrefour-blockchain/carrefour-says-blockchain-tracking-boosting-sales-of-some-products-idUSKCN1T42A5.

[i] Forbes (Dec 23, 2019) 'The Food on Your Holiday Table May Have Been Verified by Blockchain' https://www.forbes.com/sites/ibm/2019/12/23/the-food-on-your-holiday-table-may-have-been-verified-by-blockchain/?sh=7dad6e807b39.

[j] Thomasson (n [h]).

Blockchain in supply chains can promote sustainability by helping take actions that are sustainable, that is, economically viable, environmentally sustainable and socially responsible.[70] For instance, in Bext360's solution, using a mobile app, relevant parties can negotiate a fair price.[71] Farmers get paid immediately via the app. The app also determines the identity of the person selling the products. Using Bext360's API (application programming interface), intermediaries such as wholesalers and retailers embed the technology into their websites, marketing and point of sales. This level of transparency may not be possible without blockchain. Blockchain thus makes it possible to make indicators related to sustainability more quantifiable and more meaningful for consumers.

Bext360 is expanding into other sectors. It announced a partnership with Amsterdam-based start-up accelerator Fashion for Good, which focuses on social and environmental impact in the fashion industry. The goal is to track the entire value chain of cotton. Clothing companies are facing pressures to ensure fair trading practices. Market pressure has also forced these companies to use organic cottons.[72]

Blockchain solutions can also force dominant actors in a supply chain to take actions that are socially responsible. Even companies with poor labour practices and a poor track record in protecting human rights are joining blockchain-based traceability systems due to pressures from regulators, activists and other actors. Dominant actors in a supply chain are less likely to engage in unjust acts due to fear of being denounced and penalized. In smart contracts, due to the rigidness of codes, these actors are unable to change the contract's terms unilaterally.

A main challenge most supply chains face concerns an asymmetric dependence.[73] In such relationships, the dominant partners often benefit from the vagueness in contracts and measurements. Blockchain-based systems promote transparency and the codes' rigidity means that decisions are based on objective verifiable indicators, which benefit marginalized actors and less powerful members in supply chains. That is, increased accuracy of measurements and rigid contracts lower the risks of being manipulated by others.

---

[70] N Kshetri (2021) 'Blockchain and Sustainable Supply Chain Management in Developing Countries' *International Journal of Information Management* Vol 60(October), 102376.
[71] Bitcoin Magazine (2017) 'Innovation Percolates When Coffee Meets the Blockchain' *Nasdaq*, http://www.nasdaq.com/article/innovation-percolates-when-coffee-meets-the-blockchain-cm774790.
[72] A Knapp (2018) 'AgTech Blockchain Startup Bext360 Raises $3.35 Million to Provide Traceability to Commodities' *Forbes*, https://www.forbes.com/sites/alexknapp/2018/06/01/agtech-blockchain-startup-bext360-raises-3-35-million-to-provide-traceability-to-commodities/#7ee591276d25.
[73] J Pfeffer and GR Salancik (1978) *The External Control of Organizations: A Resource Dependence Perspective* (Harper & Row, New York).

4.4.3 Increasing Speed of Operations in Supply Chain Systems

The speed with which various operations are performed can be increased with blockchain. Digitization of physical process and reduction in interactions and communications are important mechanisms to increase the speed. Blockchain solutions can also help pinpoint the exact location where specific supply chain-related actions took place or a product originated from. In this way, blockchain facilitates traceability, which can help respond to and even prevent crises such as food contamination.

In 2016, in a well-publicized story, Walmart's then vice president of food safety, picked up a package of sliced mangos from one of the company's stores, and asked his team to find where it originated from. It took the team six days, 18 hours, and 26 minutes to find an answer.[74] Since then, the company has started blockchain trials to address problems such as this. In 2020, Walmart helped the Food and Drug Administration (FDA) in six investigations related to food safety. Thanks to blockchain, the retailer was able to provide detailed information related to the original source of potential contamination within an hour.[75]

4.4.4 Improving Dependability and Flexibility

With blockchain, supply chain partners can expect a high level of dependability since immutable data related to measurement for various indicators such as quality and physical state such as temperature, moisture content and location (e.g., with GPS) are available for verification. To take an example, cybersecurity company Gemalto, which was acquired in 2019 by Thales, teamed up with an insurance company to deliver temperature-sensitive medicines from drug manufacturers to hospitals that are located in hot climates. Digital thermometers record the temperature of drugs regularly. Data related to temperature and other relevant indicators are added on the blockchain ledger, which can be seen by all relevant parties. Such a process exerts pressure on supply chain partners to be more responsible and accountable as the drugs move along a supply chain. Drugs are more likely to be delivered in a state that meets regulatory requirements. Due to blockchain's 'super audit trail', data in a blockchain ledger are more accurate and authentic compared to self-reported data provided by supply chain partners.

---

[74] R Hackett (2017) 'Why Big Business Is Racing to Build Blockchains' *Fortune*, http://fortune.com/2017/08/22/bitcoin-ethereum-blockchain-cryptocurrency/.
[75] M del Castillo (Mar 5, 2021) 'Blockchain 50 2021' [online] *Forbes*. Available at: https://www.forbes.com/sites/michaeldelcastillo/2021/02/02/blockchain-50/?sh=45a0832231cb.

Blockchain solutions can also help achieve a higher degree of flexibility in supply chains. Flexibility can be defined as a supply chain's ability to adapt to the changing environment in order to provide products and services in a timely and cost-effective manner.[76] In a discussion of a changing environment the COVID-19 pandemic deserves mention.

COVID-19 forced firms to search for solutions that can provide a higher degree of flexibility. One upshot is that the adoption of blockchain solutions has increased due to COVID-19. To take an example, Berlin, Germany-based blockchain solutions provider Minespider reported that there was an increased interest in the company's traceability services during the COVID-19 pandemic.[77]

Exchanging paper documents is an extremely slow process. This issue became especially apparent during the COVID-19 pandemic. Documents such as LC, bills of lading, invoices and others are normally carried in the cargo holds of passenger aircrafts, which did not operate during the pandemic. Documents related to cross-border trade transactions needed to find alternative means such as ships to reach their destinations. However, they could not be delivered since banks were closed. Consequently many banks started accepting scanned signatures and documents. However, electronic documents that are not based on blockchain are fraud prone. Blockchain has a clear usefulness in relation to security.[78]

As an example, in July 2020, Japan's Sumitomo Mitsui Financial Group (SMBC) announced that it would join blockchain consortia komgo and Contour, which focus on LC. A major motivation to join the networks was COVID-19-led complexity in exchanging documents required for LC.[79] As noted above, Contour uses R3's Corda technology and komgo has been built on Ethereum. Komgo mainly deals with energy and soft commodities, Contour has a general focus on trade and trade financing.

SMBC joined the Contour network in September 2020, when the network was in a beta phase. Contour went live in October 2020 to be the 'world's first open-to-all, decentralized trade finance network' according to the network. As

---

[76]   P Swafford, S Ghosh and N Murthy (Nov 2000) 'A Model of Global Supply Chain Agility and Its Impact on Competitive Performance' *Proceedings of the 31st National DSI Meeting*, Orlando, Florida, 1037–39.
[77]   C Leonida (2020) 'Blockchain: A New Level of Trust for Miners' *Engineering and Mining Journal* Vol 221(5) 48–51.
[78]   P Tan (2020) 'Coronavirus Hastens Trade Finance's Blockchain Moment' *BBN Times*, https://www.bbntimes.com/technology/coronavirus-hastens-trade-finance -s-blockchain-moment.
[79]   Ledger Insights (2020) 'SMBC Joins Two Blockchain Trade Finance Consortia Komgo, Contour' *Ledger Insights*, https://ledgerinsights.com/smbc-blockchain-trade -finance-consortia-komgo-contour/.

of mid-2021, 13 institutions were utilizing Contour's technology.[80] As noted above, Contour reduces the process for presenting documentation against an LC to under 24 hours.

4.5   CHAPTER SUMMARY AND CONCLUSION

Blockchain facilitates valid and effective measurement of outcomes and performance of key supply chain processes. In general, the more important the issue of traceability is to key stakeholders such as the government, consumers, and retailers, the greater should be the value of blockchain. For this reason, the food industry is most likely to be impacted by blockchain. The example of the 2015 E. coli outbreak at Chipotle Mexican Grill discussed above is illustrative of a widespread problem faced by food supply chains. This example indicates that there is a deep thirst for dependable suppliers in the food industry. In this regard, a key element of the blockchain-based model is that all the transactions are auditable, which is particularly important in gaining the trust of all interested parties. With blockchain, consumers know if the food they are eating is right and authentic. Various measures can be used to increase transparency in fish and seafood supply chains.

Blockchain can also help achieve robust cybersecurity measures and reduce cyber-risks. Trust and security can thus be improved with blockchain. At the same time, more resources need to be devoted to addressing concerns such as participation of diverse supply chain members and enrichment of the existing blockchain ecosystem in order to realize the full potential of blockchain.

---

[80]   emeriobanque.com (2021) 'Contour to Consider Marco Polo with Shift into Open Account Trade Finance' https://www.emeriobanque.com/news/contour-to-consider-marco-polo-with-shift-into-open-account-trade-finance.

5.   Security, privacy and compliance

5.1   INTRODUCTION

Blockchain is viewed as a technology that can provide a strong cybersecurity solution and a high level of privacy protection. Its proponents argue that this technology is secure by design.[1] In a blockchain model, there is no need to store information with third parties. The records are on many interlocked computers that hold identical information. If one computer's blockchain updates are breached, the system rejects it.[2] In addition, multi-signature (Multisig) protection or the requirement of more than one key to authorize a transaction process can further improve security and privacy.

Even if a hacker penetrates a network and tries to steal funds from an account, multiple redundant and identical copies of the same ledger are stored across many computers that are interlocked. If one is breached, there are many others as backups that can provide the funds in the hacked account.

The security features of many of the important systems across many industries rely on what is known as the 'security through obscurity' approach in security engineering. The idea in this approach is to keep a system's security mechanisms and implementation secret. However, a major drawback of this method is that the entire system may collapse when someone discovers the security mechanism.

Blockchain-based systems help avoid the attacks such as noted above. There is no single point of failure or vulnerability in blockchain. Moreover, some blockchain storage companies such as Yottachain use sharding, which involves breaking up data into two or more smaller chunks. They make redundant copies of each shard. The shards are then encrypted and distributed to multiple storage nodes. The storage blockchain will have records of where each node ends up and changes to data. Only metadata is stored in the blockchain and not data itself. The benefit of this type of storage is that there is no

---

[1]   N Kshetri (2017) 'Blockchain's Roles in Strengthening Cybersecurity and Protecting Privacy' *Telecommunications Policy* Vol 41(10) 1027–38.
[2]   R Kestenbaum (2017) 'Why Bitcoin Is Important for Your Business' *Forbes*, Retreived from https://www.forbes.com/sites/richardkestenbaum/2017/03/14/why-bitcoin-is-important-for-your-business/3/#2da6d4c72b3b.

central data storage repository for nefarious actors to target. Any hacker able to access a particular storage node would be able to access only encrypted shards of data, rather than the data.[3]

It is also important to point out that while Bitcoin, the most well-known Blockchain application, has had a bad public perception regarding security, the hacking attacks occurred only to other systems that attempted to hold and store Bitcoin private keys. They are not related to Bitcoin transactions sent from one party to another.

Moving to the issue of privacy protection, many of the causes that lead to privacy violation in a non-blockchain world do not apply to blockchain. For instance, most privacy violations in the so-called paper age are associated with primary data collection. Most of such violations in the cyber age, on the other hand, have resulted from secondary usage of information, which has been mostly legally collected.[4] Organizations store huge volumes of personal data so that potential innovative uses can be discovered. Mayer-Schönberger and Cukier[5] emphasize that 'most innovative secondary uses haven't been imagined when the data is first collected'. It is also worth noting that most consumers are against secondary uses of their personal information. Moreover, these concerns are linked with the collection and storing of data as well as data sharing and accessibility by third parties and various user types. Additionally, firms may need to outsource to cloud services providers (CSPs) which may give rise to privacy and security issues.[6] In blockchain-based solutions, personal data can be seen only with the subject's permission and such data cannot be stored by a third party. Moreover, the proof of identity is stored in a cryptographic format. This means that blockchain-based systems can be designed to provide a high level of privacy protection. Indeed, secure storage and transmission of digitally signed documents are viewed as the most likely killer application of blockchain. Due to blockchain's 'super audit trail', such applications have been built and tested in diverse areas such as supply chain

---

[3] P Rubens (2021) 'Blockchain Technology Can Have a Starring Role in Cybersecurity.' [online] Available at: https://www.enterprisenetworkingplanet.com/news/blockchain-technology-can-have-a-starring-role-in-cybersecurity/.

[4] A Etzioni (2015) 'A Cyber Age Privacy Doctrine: More Coherent, Less Subjective, and Operational' *Brooklyn Law Review* Vol 80(4) Article 2.

[5] V Mayer-Schönberger and K Cukier (2013) *Big Data: A Revolution that Will Transform How We Live, Work and Think* (Houghton Mifflin Harcourt, Boston) p. 153.

[6] N Kshetri (2014) 'Big Data's Impact on Privacy, Security and Consumer Welfare' *Telecommunications Policy* Vol 38(11) 1134–45.

and trade financing,[7] logistics and shipping, and insurance in order to validate the identity of individuals as well as digital and physical assets.[8]

In order to illustrate this point, consider the Canadian identity and authentication provider SecureKey, which has received investments from Canada's big banks including CIBC, BMO, Desjardins, TD, and Scotiabank.[9] SecureKey's network Verified.Me, which is available on both mobile and desktop, helps users verify their identity to access bank services. It was released in May 2019. The Verified.Me service is built on the IBM Blockchain Platform, which uses the Linux Foundation's Hyperledger. Users can prove that they are who they say they are faster and with a high level of privacy protection.[10] The company uses a blockchain-based 'triple blind' privacy protocol to connect individuals to partnering online services using an existing credential. The 'triple blind' mechanism means that consumers can use their bank credentials to log in and access their cellular phone services. The bank cannot see the data's destination and the recipient cannot see the bank used or bank account information. SecureKey, as a middleman, is also 'blind' and cannot see information about the user of the services.[11]

Blockchain can also improve reliability of financial and other reporting, and compliance with various laws and regulations.[12] By maintaining immutable records of the process and history of transactions, this technology can make regulatory reporting and compliance simpler, more automated and more

---

[7]   N Kshetri (2021) *Blockchain and Supply Chain Management* (Elsevier, Amsterdam, Netherlands, Oxford, UK and New York, USA).

[8]   M Mainelli (2017) 'Blockchain Will Help Us Prove Our Identities in a Digital World' *Harvard Business Review*, Retrieved from https://hbr.org/2017/03/blockchain-will-help-us-prove-our-identities-in-a-digital-world.

[9]   J Galang (2017) 'With IBM Partnership, SecureKey Enters Next Phase of Developing Secure Digital Identity Network' *Betakit*, Retrieved from http://betakit.com/with-ibm-partnership-securekey-enters-next-phase-of-developing-secure-digital-identity-network/.

[10]   Christina Comben (May 9, 2019) 'Why Canadian Banks Are Choosing the SecureKey Blockchain System' https://coinrivet.com/canadian-banks-choosing-securekey-blockchain-system/.

[11]   S Ho (2017) 'Canada's SecureKey Receives U.S. Grant to Build Digital Identity Network' *The Globe and Mail*, Retrieved from http://www.theglobeandmail.com/technology/canadas-securekey-wins-us-grant-to-help-build-digital-identity-network/article34022647/.

[12]   deloitte.com (July, 2020) 'Blockchain and Internal Control: The COSO Perspective New Risks and the Need for New Controls' https://www2.deloitte.com/us/en/pages/audit/articles/blockchain-and-internal-control-coso-perspective-risk.html.

efficient.[13] (See In Focus 5.1 The American Association of Insurance Services uses Hyperledger Fabric for regulatory reporting).

IN FOCUS 5.1 THE AMERICAN ASSOCIATION OF INSURANCE SERVICES USES HYPERLEDGER FABRIC FOR REGULATORY REPORTING

The American Association of Insurance Services (AAIS) created the open source project Open Insurance Data Link (OpenIDL) to reduce the cost of regulatory reporting for insurance carriers. It is built with Hyperledger Fabric. Before starting the OpenIDL, IBM invited insurance carriers and regulators to participate in workshops to understand how blockchain can enhance regulatory reporting for the insurance industry. A concern among insurers was related to the transfer of large data files. Moreover, the statistical reporting process was developed more than 80 years ago, which does not meet insurers' needs. The regulators also needed to go directly to the carriers when there is a need for more specific, timely data (e.g., after a hurricane or wildfire).[a] OpenIDL provides a standardized data repository for analytics. A connection point for third parties delivers new applications to members.[b] Major insurance companies such as Selective Insurance Group and the Hanover Insurance Group have backed the project. Technology and service providers, such as KatRisk, Chainyard and MOBI help share business processes and data within the insurance industry.[c]

In Hyperledger Fabric, if members want to share their data with certain parties, a private channel can be created.[d] Such a channel is used to keep every company's data secure. Access control mechanism provided by Fabric ensures that only admitted organizations can access data and resources on a private channel.[e] This means that no other insurer can access data of an insurer. State regulators can request data from their state's insurers. Insurers can review and answer these requests.[f]

Currently carriers supply data and regulators consume it. IBM noted that the permissioned blockchain network makes it possible to include new members that can add value to insurers and the regulators. It is thus possible to add new participants with new sources of data such as weather companies, Internet of Things companies and even data modelling companies that provide additional insights into the data that regulators need.[g]

---

[13] *The Fintech Times* (2021) 'Hardbacon: 5 Fintech Trends that Will Reshape the Financial Services Landscape.' [online]. Available at https://thefintechtimes.com/hardbacon-5-fintech-trends-that-will-reshape-the-financial-services-landscape/.

Notes:

[a] IBM Supply Chain and Blockchain Blog (2019) 'How AAIS Uses Blockchain to Ease Regulatory.' [online] Reporting IBM Supply Chain and Blockchain Blog. Available at: https://www.ibm.com/blogs/blockchain/ 2019/07/how-aais-uses-blockchain-to-ease-regulatory-reporting/.

[b] S Bhartiya (2021) 'What Is OpenIDL, the Open Insurance Data Link platform?' [online] Linux.com. Available at: https://www.linux.com/news/what-is-openidl-the-open-insurance-data-link-platform/.

[c] J Guzman (2021) 'Crypto: Linux Unveils a Blockchain-based Platform – All About It!' [online] interactivecrypto.com. Available at: https://www.interactivecrypto.com/linux-unveils-a-blockchain-based -platform-all-about-it.

[d] Indium Software (2019) 'Multi Organization in Hyperledger Fabric.' [online] Available at: https://www .indiumsoftware.com/blog/multi-organization-in-hyperledger-fabric/.

[e] H Kang, T Dai, N Jean-Louis, S Tao and X Gu (n.d.) *FabZK: Supporting Privacy-Preserving, Auditable Smart Contracts in Hyperledger Fabric.* [online] Available at: http://dance.csc.ncsu.edu/papers/DSN19.pdf.

[f] Hyperledger (n.d.) *OpenIDL Case Study.* [online] Available at: https://www.hyperledger.org/learn/ publications/openidl-case-study.

[g] IBM Supply Chain and Blockchain Blog (2019) 'How AAIS Uses Blockchain to Ease Regulatory Reporting.' [online] IBM Supply Chain and Blockchain Blog. Available at: https://www.ibm.com/blogs/ blockchain/2019/07/how-aais-uses-blockchain-to-ease-regulatory-reporting/.

This chapter evaluates blockchain from security, privacy and compliance considerations. Since most of the data is currently stored in cloud data centres, we also compare how blockchain performs vis-à-vis the cloud in various aspects of security and privacy. It gives special consideration to some of the key underlying mechanisms related to blockchain's impact on Internet of Things (IoT) security.

5.2   COMPARING BLOCKCHAIN AND CLOUD COMPUTING

The adoption of the cloud is rapidly increasing among businesses and individuals. According to the security firm Barracuda Networks' study, 45 per cent of IT (Information Technology) infrastructure used by companies was in the public cloud in 2020, which is expected to increase to 76 per cent by 2025.[14] Thus, it makes sense to compare blockchain and cloud computing from the standpoint of security and privacy.

Table 5.1 below compares blockchain and cloud computing in terms of the ways security and privacy issues are dealt with. Both the cloud and blockchain are designed to provide cost-efficient security solutions. Cloud's options of private, community and public deployment models can be mapped to permissionless and permissioned chains.

---

[14]   L Ingham (March 11, 2020) 'Public Cloud Will Be Home to 76% of IT Infrastructure by 2025, but Security Concerns Remain' *Verdict*, Retrieved from https:// www.verdict.co.uk/public-cloud-security/.

Organizations have realized that a one-size-fits-all approach may not work for cloud adoption. For instance, organizations may have to make decisions concerning combinations of public and private clouds. A public cloud is effective for an organization handling high-transaction/low-security or low data value (e.g., sales force automation). A private cloud model, on the other hand, may be appropriate for enterprises and applications that face significant risk from information exposure such as financial institutions and health care providers or federal agency. For instance, for medical-practice companies dealing with sensitive patient data, which are required to comply with the US Health Insurance Portability and Accountability Act (HIPAA) rules, private cloud may be appropriate.

As explained in Chapter 1, in order to meet security, privacy, and other requirements, permissionless and permissioned chains exist in the blockchain world. The idea in permissioned blockchains is that by controlling access to only trusted users on the platform, developers can avoid problems faced by permissionless chains. For instance, Ethereum is being used in a number of private, permissioned chains in individual projects or in larger consortia such as R3 CEV or the Hyperledger Project. Moreover, blockchain's ability to target specific members in the value delivery chain, including regulators and auditors deserves mention.

Both the cloud and blockchain arguably have security protection 'baked into' them. The data is fully encrypted in both cases. Some cloud services providers follow a so-called 'zero trust' model for security. Note that a 'zero trust' network is based on the premise that trustworthiness needs to be considered for every single device. This means that if a device is hacked, the threat does not spread throughout the whole network. A user often has access only to certain things. In order to get access to the entire network, the attackers need to attack multiple devices at once.[15] Some refer to this improved model as 'security micro-segmentation'.[16] For example, Google follows such an approach.[17]

Some security challenges associated with the cloud can be addressed with blockchain. Blockchain ensures that each party is held accountable for its individual roles in the overall transaction. Especially blockchain's

---

[15] L Armasu (May 13, 2015) 'Google Adopts Zero Trust Network Model for Its Own Cloud.' Retrieved from http://www.tomsitpro.com/articles/google-zerotrust-network-own-cloud,1-2608.html.

[16] N Tausanovitch (2016) 'Zero-trust Security for Cloud Data Centers – How Much Does It Cost?' *Netronome*, Retrieved from https://www.netronome.com/blog/zero-trust-security-for-cloud-data-centers-how-much-does-it-cost/.

[17] D Pauli (2016) 'Google Reveals Own Security Regime Policy Trusts No Network, Anywhere, Ever' *The Register*, Retrieved from https://www.theregister.co.uk/2016/04/06/googles_beyondcorp_security_policy/.

```

*Table 5.1*    **A comparison of the cloud and blockchain from security and privacy considerations**

|  | Cloud | Blockchain |
|---|---|---|
| Mechanisms related to efficiency, and cost-effectiveness | Pay as you go model. Cloud's efficiency: infrastructure-as-a-service | Blockchain removes the need for third parties in transactions by creating a distributed record which is possessed and verified by other users |
| Deployment models | Private, community and public clouds are available | Permissionless and permissioned chains to meet security and privacy requirements |
| Mechanisms to strengthen cybersecurity | Data is fully encrypted. Create a 'cyber risk-free zone': constant monitoring for suspicious activities and real time response[a]. Some companies also employ 'Zero Trust' network: fine-grained control | Data is fully encrypted. Cryptographic hashfunctions are used. Public–private key cryptography to ensure that the data is received only by the intended recipient |
| Some challenges | Many cloud providers rely on the firewall model, which involves monitoring incoming and outgoing network traffic. Based on a defined set of rules, decisions are made whether to allow or block a specific traffic. Criminals exploit new ways to break such systems | Newness: well-developed security mechanisms have not been developed for some systems |

*Note:*   [a] J Bertrand (2017) 'Blockchain and Cloud Kissing Cousins' *Finextra*, Retrieved from https://www.finextra.com/blogposting/13780/blockchain-and-cloud-kissing-cousins.

*Source:*   Adapted from N Kshetri (2017) 'Blockchain's Roles in Strengthening Cybersecurity and Protecting Privacy' *Telecommunications Policy* Vol 41(10) 1027–38.

decentralized and consensus-driven structures enhance security when the network size increases.

## 5.3    AN ILLUSTRATION FROM THE HEALTHCARE INDUSTRY AND MARKET

Cyberattacks against healthcare providers are a serious concern. According to a study conducted by cybersecurity technology company Crowdstrike and healthcare-dedicated medical device security, asset management and operational analytics company Medigate, 82 per cent of healthcare providers
```

experienced cyberattacks from March 2020 to September 2021.[18] Healthcare data also create significant privacy risks. According to a study conducted by cybersecurity company Kaspersky, which focused on telehealth, 81 per cent of healthcare providers were concerned about how patient data are used and shared from telehealth sessions. Among key telehealth issues, doctors and nurses were concerned about data security, and potential HIPAA violations.[19] The current infrastructure cannot guarantee privacy and security of patient data. The failure to prevent access to healthcare information by unauthorized persons can harm patients.

The current model of handling electronic healthcare records (EHRs) has yet another problem: healthcare organizations often act as custodians or stewards of patient data. This leads to inefficiency and delay in patient care. For instance, a patient's treatment may be delayed simply because medical information sent from one service provider does not reach another in a timely manner.

Blockchain may have a potential to address these limitations in current EHR practices. Blockchain initiatives have already been undertaken by governments and the private sector. There are also public–private partnership (PPP) projects. As an example, the Food and Drug Administration (FDA) and IBM Watson Health teamed up to investigate the potential benefits of blockchain in health care. Initial effort will focus on oncology-related data and a blockchain framework.

Blockchain enables the collection of data from a variety of sources and keeps it in an audit trail of transactions. Blocks hold transactions and other data. Accountability and transparency of transactions is achieved in this data exchange process. FDA and IBM believe that blockchain can support the exchange of data from multiple sources on agreed terms and for purposes that a patient approves and agrees to. They include EHRs, clinical trials, genomic data, and information gathered from new sources, such as mobile devices, wearables, and IoT devices.[20] Especially permissioned blockchains can be more effective in sharing and managing EHR. Using permissioned blockchains it is possible to share real-time data among participants of health-

---

[18] Crowdstrike and Medigate (2021) 'Healthcare IoT Security Operations Maturity, a Rationalized Approach to a New Normal' https://explore.medigate.io/healthcare-iot-security-operations-maturity?submissionGuid=54ca3a0d-14f8-4d78-b4f2-729ae4d02ea1.

[19] 'Telehealth Take-up: The Risks and Opportunities' http://media.kasperskycontenthub.com/wp-content/uploads/sites/43/2021/11/22125239/Kaspersky_Healthcare-report-2021_eng.pdf.

[20] F Bazzoli (Jan 31, 2017) 'FDA, IBM Watson Health to Study Application of Blockchain Technology' *Health Data Management*, https://www.healthdatamanagement.com/news/fda-ibm-watson-health-to-study-application-of-blockchain-technology.

care systems and conduct secure transactions. After a transaction is complete through consensus, a permanent record is produced and added to the existing blockchain as a new block.[21]

5.3.1 Challenges of the Current EHR Approach

Current EHR models have problems providing efficient health care, and guaranteeing security and privacy of patient data. We list a few of them below.

5.3.1.1 Data storage

Current models rely on passwords that involve shared secrets that are exchanged and stored on potentially insecure clouds. This approach has led to well-publicized cyber-disasters. In 2021 alone the healthcare sector experienced 78 compromises and the data of more than 7 million persons were breached.[22] Such compromises are less likely to occur in a blockchain model because data is not centrally stored.

5.3.1.2 Data sharing

In a non-blockchain world, healthcare organizations typically follow three models to facilitate interoperability of medical data: push, pull, and view.[23] In a push model, medical information is sent from one provider to another (e.g., from an emergency room physician to a primary care doctor). In a pull model, a provider asks another provider about information (e.g., a cardiothoracic surgeon asking a primary care doctor). Finally, in the view model, a provider looks at another provider's record. For instance, a cardiologist may examine a patient's X-ray that has been taken at an urgent care centre.

Access to healthcare data needs to be accompanied by obligations to the data. It is important for healthcare companies handling identifiable information to structure such obligations by associating metadata, or information about information, using data sets.[24] In the current infrastructure, this is easier said than done. A major drawback of the models describing patient data is that they

---

[21]   M Pratap (Aug 6, 2018) 'Remodelling the Existing Technical Healthcare Infrastructure'   https://hackernoon.com/blockchain-in-healthcare-opportunities -challenges-and-applications-d6b286da6e1f.

[22]   Maria Henriquez (Dec 9, 2021) 'The Top Data Breaches of 2021' https://www .securitymagazine.com/articles/96667-the-top-data-breaches-of-2021.

[23]   JD Halamka, A Lippman and A Ekblaw (March 3, 2017) 'The Potential for Blockchain to Transform Electronic Health Records' https://hbr.org/2017/03/the -potential-for-blockchain-to-transform-electronic-health-records.

[24]   PM Schwartz and DJ Solove (2011) 'The PII Problem: Privacy and a New Concept of Personally Identifiable Information' *New York University Law Review* Vol 86(6) 1814–94.

are not audited in a standardized way. A lack of audit trails means that there is no guarantee of data integrity from the point of data generation to the point of data usage. It is difficult to pinpoint violators of data breaches. Some hospitals still rely on paper medical records and even paper towels.

Frauds are rampant in the medical industry. Some employees of healthcare organizations were reportedly stealing patients' personal data and misusing them.[25] There have been cases of fraudulent claims to insurance providers using false patient medical information and fake identities of doctors. In one scam, a group was able to defraud US$ 50 million in fraudulent healthcare claims using electronic health records of patients without authorization at a Long Island, New York-based hospital (https://tinyurl.com/y9lrhaqt).

Current healthcare systems also fail patients when it comes to informed consent.[26] In the pull model, consent often occurs on an informal and ad hoc basis. Due to time constraints, doctors often are not in a position to help patients understand the processes related to consent. Patients may not know what questions and whom to ask. It may not be possible to get direct and straightforward answers. While patients have the right to put restrictions as to whom their information may be exchanged with, some healthcare organizations lack the capacity to record and implement such restrictions.

5.3.1.3 Efficiency

On the efficiency front, current practices leave a great deal to be desired. For instance, in the push model, if a patient is transferred to a different hospital, the new hospital may not be able to access the data that was 'pushed' from the first hospital. Patients often feel the frustration of providing the same information again and again to different healthcare providers or even to different people at the same healthcare provider.[27]

Current approaches fail to manage medical records that are generated by multiple healthcare institutions. Since data are scattered across various medical institutions, patients may also lose data.[28]

---

[25] HIPAA Journal (Dec 10, 2015) 'Five New Cases of Healthcare Employee Data Theft Reported' https://tinyurl.com/y7b8rfta.

[26] N Bazemore (Mar 28, 2016) 'Not All Doctors Get Informed Consent – Here's Why It's Hurting Patients'
https://www.forbes.com/sites/amino/2016/03/28/not-all-doctors-get-informed -consent-heres-why-its-hurting-patients/?sh=152cd089496c.

[27] M Miliard (Sept 18, 2017) 'Why Blockchain Could Transform the Very Nature of EHRs' https://www.healthcareitnews.com/news/why-blockchain-could-transform -very-nature-ehrs.

[28] Ibid.

Regulations and policies governing the above approaches vary greatly across jurisdictions based on inter alia, local practice, and national privacy policy enforcement. For instance, even in the US, laws differ across states in areas such as requirement to sign a consent form to disclose patient records, the types of medical records that patients have the right to access, and producing patients' records to a third party.[29]

5.3.2   Blockchain Benefits

To understand blockchain's potential in addressing security and privacy issues, not only related to EHRs, we consider blockchain from the perspective of identity and access management which involves controlling information on computer networks about a subject such as patient identity. The key issues in identity and access management concern: (a) information authenticating the subject's identity, (b) information describing the information (metadata), and (c) actions that various participants are authorized to perform and know.

The first three rows in Table 5.2 below show current issues related to identity and access management in health care which might be aided using blockchain. As already noted, there are drawbacks to existing identity management techniques that rely on password-based systems. In a blockchain model, a patient's entire medical records may be stored in a blockchain ledger's key ring. These records can be encrypted with the patient's private key. While a blockchain-based system is not 100 per cent foolproof (e.g., a person's private key can be stolen), it is considered to be more secure than most other systems that exist today.

Blockchain offers audit trails. This means that there is documentation of the events related to the creation, modification, and deletion of electronic records. This offers transparency. For instance, researchers from MIT Media Lab and Beth Israel Deaconess Medical Center proposed MedRec, which is a blockchain-based decentralized record management system to handle EHRs. MedRec is reported to manage 'authentication, confidentiality, accountability, and data sharing'.[30] Patients can access their medical information across different providers and treatment sites. An immutable log of all transactions

---

[29]   JD Holloway (2003) 'What Takes Precedence: HIPAA or State Law?: In Most Cases, State Laws Will Not Be Preempted by HIPAA' *Monitor* Vol 34(1) http://www .apa.org/monitor/jan03/hipaa.aspx.
[30]   A Ekblaw, A Azaria, JD Halamka and A Lippman (2016) 'A Case Study for Blockchain in Healthcare: "MedRec" Prototype for Electronic Health Records and Medical Research Data' White Paper. MIT Media Lab, Beth Israel Deaconess Medical Center.

Security, privacy and compliance 109

Table 5.2 *Blockchain's potential to improve security and efficiency in health care*

	Explanation and examples	Challenges with the current system	Blockchain's potential to address the challenge
Information authenticating the subject's identity	Information to verify that someone is who they claim to be (e.g., a username and password or a thumbprint)	Current identity management techniques in hospitals rely on password-based systems, which involve shared secrets that are exchanged and stored on insecure systems	In blockchain-based authentication, each transaction is signed by the correct private key of the patient
Information describing the information	Information about different pieces of data flow (e.g., between healthcare vendors and patients) and records of data transaction. Information about users' preferences (e.g., how their data can be used) Consent management records between patients and healthcare services provider[a]	No audit trails (e.g., who accessed patients' data). Some hospitals rely on paper medical records	Due to an audit trail complete documentation of events related to the creation, modification, and deletion of records
Actions that various participants are authorized to perform	An access policy specifies access rights and privileges of each participant (e.g., insurance companies cannot have access to patients' medical records)	Parties are authorized to take actions based on patients' data. Patients have no control over their own data	Prevents unauthorized access to data Patients have ownership and control over their information
Efficiency	Inefficient administrative, logistical, and service delivery processes increase costs, and time, and reduce benefits[b]	Inefficient procedures to transfer data across services providers Policy and regulatory differences across jurisdictions	A consumer has access to their up-to-date healthcare information and can forward to a healthcare service provider as and when it is needed

Notes:
[a] (Nov 2, 2017) 'JLINC Labs Announces JLINC Protocol to Align with Flourishing Information Sharing Agreements' https://www.prnewswire.com/news-releases/jlinc-labs-announces-jlinc-protocol-to-align-with-flourishing-information-sharing-agreements-300548235.html.

^b H de Koning, JPS Verger, J van den Heuvel, S Bisgaard and R Does (2006) 'Lean Six Sigma in Healthcare' *Journal for Healthcare Quality* Vol 28(2) 4–11.
Source: Adapted from N Kshetri (2018) 'Blockchain and Electronic Healthcare Records' *IEEE Computer* Vol 51(12) 59–63.

involving a patient's information is created and provided to the patient.[31] MedRec does not store patients' health records. The system stores the record's signature in a blockchain. The signature provides an assurance that the record's unaltered copy is the one that is obtainable.

Using blockchain, patients hold ownership and ultimate control over their information. For instance, the patient can decide where their records can travel. In this way, the locus of control is shifted from the institution providing the health care to the patient. For patients that do not want to manage their data, service organizations may evolve allowing the patients to delegate that task to them.[32]

Assuring that healthcare providers authorize the right person and only the right person represents a current challenge in applying blockchain-based models in EHRs in most countries. By adopting a unique digital ID for identification and authentication of patients, nations can achieve a higher degree of effectiveness of such models. By doing so, they can also improve the quality of health care, eliminate fraud in insurance and enhance administrative efficiency.[33] Table 5.2 above shows how blockchain enhances efficiency. In blockchain-based EHR, there is no organization between the patient and their medical records and there is no need to create custom functionality for each EHR vendor.[34] For instance, a patient's treatment will not be delayed simply because medical information sent from a service provider to a hospital was not received The patient can securely share the information with different providers throughout their lifetime.[35] If there is any change in the patient's condition, data related to these changes are communicated to the ledger by authorized parties.[36] Thus, timely access to accurate and up-to-date information should improve efficiency in patient care.

---

[31]   Ibid.
[32]   Halamka, Lippman and Ekblaw (n 23).
[33]   World Bank (2018) 'The Role of Digital Identification for Healthcare: The Emerging Use Cases', Washington, DC: World Bank License: Creative Commons Attribution CC BY 3.0 IGO, http://pubdocs.worldbank.org/en/595741519657604541/DigitalIdentification-HealthcareReportFinal.pdf
[34]   Halamka, Lippman and Ekblaw (n 23).
[35]   Ibid.
[36]   N Kshetri (2018) 'Blockchain and Electronic Healthcare Records' *IEEE Computer* Vol 51(12), 59–63.

5.4   BLOCKCHAIN AND IOT SECURITY

IoT security has received substantial consideration recently. As an example, consider the 2016 cyberattacks on the US-based domain name system (DNS) provider Dyn. The attacks reportedly originated from 'tens of millions of IP addresses' and was among the largest ever attacks.[37] Some of the traffic came from IoT devices such as webcams, baby monitors, home routers and digital video recorders (DVRs), which had been infected with control software called Mirai, which is an easy-to-use program that even unskilled hackers can exploit. It controls online devices and uses them to launch distributed denial of service (DDoS) attacks. The process involves using phishing emails to infect a computer or home network. Then it spreads to other devices such as DVRs, printers, routers and Internet-connected cameras used by stores and businesses for surveillance.[38]

The above flaws comprise severe privacy and security risks. For instance, based on information gathered from a ubiquitous device such as presence or absence of noise or light in the house, criminals can know whether there is someone at home or not. By exploiting vulnerabilities in the Ubi or Wink Relay devices, it is possible for attackers to turn on their microphones and listen to conversations. Vulnerabilities in the Chamberlain MyQ system allow thieves to know when the garage door is opened or closed.[39]

Severe consequences can occur if an IoT device is hacked. Consider the diffusion of smart water meters and associated cybersecurity risks. As of early 2017, 20 per cent of residents in the US state of California had smart water meters, which collect data and send alerts on water leakages and usage to consumers' phones.[40] The Washington Suburban Sanitary Commission (WSSC) was also reported to be taking measures to integrate IoT into its water supply system. Water-usage data can tell hackers and criminals when residents are not

---

[37]   NBCNewYork (2016) '3rd Cyberattack "Has Been Resolved" after Hours of Major Outages: Company.' Retrieved from http://www.nbcnewyork.com/news/local/Major-Websites-Taken-Down-by-Internet-Attack-397905801.html.

[38]   E Blumenthal and E Weise (2016) 'Hacked Home Devices Caused Massive Internet Outage' *USA Today*, Retrieved from http://www.usatoday.com/story/tech/2016/10/21/cyber-attack-takes-down-east-coast-netflix-spotify-twitter/92507806/.

[39]   L Constantin (2015) 'Researchers Show that IoT Devices Are Not Designed with Security in Mind' *IDG News Service*, http://www.networkworld.com/article/2906953/researchers-show-that-iot-devices-are-not-designed-with-security-in-mind.html.

[40]   R Hackett (2017) 'How Blockchains Could Save Us from Another Flint-like Contamination Crisis' *Venturebeat*, Retrieved from http://venturebeat.com/2017/02/25/how-blockchains-could-save-us-from-another-flint-like-contamination-crisis/.

home. It is possible that the perpetrators can then burglarize homes when their residents are away.[41]

It may be that blockchain is especially appropriate and promising for tackling privacy and security problems associated with the IoT. Some point out that blockchain can possibly provide military-grade security for IoT devices.[42] Below we consider the key processes and mechanisms as well as some initiatives that potentially contribute to stronger IoT security.

5.4.1   Measures to Integrate Blockchain in IoT Security

Blockchain's incorporation in IoT is being supported through a wide variety of measures. Filament, a blockchain-based solutions provider for the IoT, has launched wireless sensors, called Taps. A Filament Tap allows IoT devices to communicate with computers, phones or tablets within a radius of ten miles.[43]

Filament runs over the so-called 'Telehash' communications protocol, which means a central hub such as the cloud is not needed. Instead, the Filament nodes are deployed in a mesh configuration.[44] That is, the Taps create low-power autonomous mesh networks. This means that each node relays data for the network and all mesh nodes cooperate in the distribution of data in the network. Some potential applications include managing physical mining operations or water flows over agricultural fields. Device identification and intercommunication are done by blockchain that holds the unique identity of each participating node.[45]

One key application of Filament Taps is likely to be in the next generation of industrial network technology. Filament's blockchain-based applications in industrial networks pair cutting-edge sensors connected in a decentralized system that use autonomous smart contracts. Devices are likely to communicate securely, exchange value with each other and execute intended actions in an automatic manner. For instance, Filament's 'Tap' sensors can be attached

---

[41]   Ibid.

[42]   J Coward (2016) 'Meet the Visionary Who Brought Blockchain to the Industrial IoT' *IOT World News*, Retrieved from http://www.iotworldnews.com/author.asp?section_id=495&doc_id=728962.

[43]   P Rizzo (2015) 'Filament Nets $5 Million for Blockchain-based Internet of Things Hardware' *CoinDesk*, Retrieved from http://www.coindesk.com/filament-nets-5-million-for-blockchain-based-internet-of-things-hardware/.

[44]   D Jones (April 4, 2017) 'Verizon & Friends Light Up Filament with $15M.' Retrieved from http://www.lightreading.com/iot/industrial-iot/verizon-and-friends-light-up-filament-with-$15m/d/d-id/731812.

[45]   B Dickson (2016b) 'How Blockchain Can Change the Future of IoT' *VentureBeat*, Retrieved from http://venturebeat.com/2016/11/20/how-blockchain-can-change-the-future-of-iot/.

to a large drilling rig in a remote location. Based on predefined conditions, the drilling rig may sense that it requires an important piece of machinery. It could then automatically send request messages to an autonomous drone, asking to deliver the replacement part. The contracts do not run in a blockchain.[46] Blockchain's role is just to verify inputs and outputs.[47] Such applications are especially useful and valuable with the rapid rise in the number of IoT devices that exchange value among themselves.[48]

Measures are also being taken at interorganizational and industry levels. A group of technology and financial companies announced in January 2017 that they had formed a group to set a new standard for securing IoT applications using blockchain. Companies joining the group include Cisco, application maker Bosch, Bank of New York Mellon Corp., Foxconn Technology, cybersecurity company Gemalto and blockchain start-ups Consensus Systems, BitSE and Chronicled.[49] The group's aim was to establish a blockchain protocol as a shared platform to build IoT devices, applications and networks.[50] In April 2017, the group announced that it had created an API (application programming interface) that supports technologies offered by major Ethereum-based blockchain systems such as JP Morgan's Quorum and the Linux-led Hyperledger project. Using the protocol, users can register multiple weaker identities such as serial numbers, QR (Quick Response) codes, and UPC (Universal Product Code) code and bind them to stronger cryptographic identities. Using blockchain, the newly created cryptographic identities are immutably linked across physical and digital worlds. As of April 2017, the software development kits (SDKs) were in beta phase and were available via the Chronicled and Hyperledger libraries on GitHub.[51]

---

[46] R Lewis (May 18, 2017) 'Internet of Things and Blockchain Technology: How Does It Work?' *Cointelegraph*, Retrieved from https://cointelegraph.com/news/internet -of-things-and-blockchain-technology-how-does-it-work.

[47] M Scott (March 14, 2017) 'Fusing Blockchain and IoT: An Interview With Filament's CEO.' Retrieved from https://bitcoinmagazine.com/articles/fusing -blockchain-and-iot-interview-filaments-ceo/.

[48] S Pajot-Phipps (2017) 'Op Ed: Energizing the Blockchain – A Canadian Perspective.' Retrieved from https://bitcoinmagazine.com/articles/op-ed-energizing -blockchain-canadian-perspective/.

[49] J Brown (2017) 'Companies Forge Cooperative to Explore Blockchain-based IoT Security' *CioDive*, Retrieved from http://www.ciodive.com/news/companies-forge -cooperative-to-explore-blockchain-based-iot-security/435007/.

[50] E Young (2017) 'Tech Giants and Blockchain Startups Unite to Make IoT Apps More Secure.' Retrieved from https://cointelegraph.com/news/tech-giants-and -blockchain-startups-unite-to-make-iot-apps-more-secure.

[51] P Rizzo (2017) 'Cisco, Bosch Reveal New Details on IoT-Blockchain Projects.' Retrieved from http://www.coindesk.com/cisco-bosch-reveal-new-details-iot -blockchain-projects/.

5.4.2   Blockchain-based Identity and Access Management Systems

Blockchain-based identity and access management systems can help strengthen IoT security. Such systems have already been used to securely store information about goods' provenance, identity, credentials, and digital rights. Blockchain's immutability can be achieved by making sure that the original information entered is accurate.[52] In this regard, a key challenge that arises in some applications is that it is difficult to ensure that the properties of physical assets, individuals (credentials), resource use (energy and bandwidth through IoT devices), and other relevant events are stored securely and reliably. This aspect can be relatively easily handled for most IoT devices. For instance, a private blockchain can be used to store cryptographic hashes of individual device firmware (software specifically designed for the device). Such a system is likely to create a permanent record of device configuration and state. This record can be possibly used to verify that a given device is genuine and that its software and settings have not been tampered or breached. Only then the device is allowed to connect to other devices or services.

In the Dyn attack, IP (Internet Protocol) spoofing attacks were launched, especially in the later versions of the Mirai botnet. Blockchain-based identity and access management systems can provide stronger defence against attacks involving IP spoofing or IP address forgery. Since blockchain cannot be altered, it is not possible for devices to connect to a network by disguising themselves by injecting fake signatures into the record. The above example involving Filaments' Taps serves to illustrate this point.

5.4.3   Centralized Cloud Model versus Decentralized Blockchain Model: The Case of IoT

The large and rapidly growing IoT market poses a special challenge from the cybersecurity standpoint. Tens of billions of IoT devices such as home routers, webcams, DVRs, and other appliances with Internet capabilities built into them generate a vast amount of data. One estimate suggested that such devices will generate 79.4 zettabytes (79.4×10^{21} bytes) of data in 2025.[53] The substantial number of IoT devices makes it difficult to fight against cyberattacks.

[52]   C Catallini (2017) 'How Blockchain Applications Will Move beyond Finance.' Retrieved from https://hbr.org/2017/03/how-blockchain-applications-will-move-beyond-finance.

[53]   Help Net Security (June 21, 2019) '41.6 Billion IoT Devices Will Be Generating 79.4 Zettabytes of Data in 2025.' Retrieved from https://www.helpnetsecurity.com/2019/06/21/connected-iot-devices-forecast/.

Especially the reliance on a centralized cloud model is likely to become more problematic when the number of network nodes grows bigger. Centralized models can be expensive and difficult to manage, especially when applied to data-intensive applications involving IoT. Therefore, a decentralized, blockchain-based approach could be more appropriate.

We return to the above examples and comparison of cloud and blockchain models in the context of the IoT. It is important to discuss some key challenges associated with the current centralized cloud model of IoT security. IoT devices are identified, authenticated and connected through cloud servers, where processing and storage are often carried out. Even if IoT devices are just a few feet apart from each other, connections between them often go through the Internet.

First, IoT networks have rocketed to a new level and high costs are a big concern in the centralized cloud model when the existing IoT solutions grow in scale. The amounts of data and communications that needed to be handled when IoT devices grow to the tens of billions increase costs exponentially. Large server farms and networking equipment are needed. Infrastructure and maintenance costs associated with centralized clouds grow rapidly. The future is thus even more challenging with the current cloud-based centralized model.

Second, even if device manufacturers and cybersecurity firms address the economic and manufacturing challenges, the IoT architecture is susceptible to failure. For instance, IoT devices can face DDoS attacks, data thefts, and hijackings. Most IoT devices send data into the cloud and messages can be sent from the cloud to the devices. This aspect is especially important with regard to IoT security. If an IoT device connected to a server is hacked, all devices connected to the server may be affected.

Third, the centralized cloud model of IoT is susceptible to manipulation. Collecting real-time data does not necessarily ensure that the data is put to good use. Consider the water supply system example discussed above. If state officials or water service companies have reason to believe that the evidence of a problem may result in high costs or lawsuits, they can engage in activities to censor, edit, or delete data and associated analyses. They can also manipulate the findings in a particular direction. For instance, consider the water crisis in the city of Flint, Michigan, which began in 2014. The city of about 100,000 people had switched its water supply from a Detroit-area system to the Flint River. The river water was not properly treated, which led to lead contamination in the drinking water. Despite the contamination, Flint authorities had insisted for a long time that the city's water was safe to drink.[54] Citing official documents and findings of researchers who conducted

---

[54] Hackett (n 40).

extensive tests, a *CNN* article asserted that Michigan officials might have altered sample data to lower the city's water lead-level.[55] It was reported that the Michigan Department of Environmental Quality and the city of Flint collected only 71 samples from homes to test lead level while they were required to collect 100 samples. Moreover, the final report from the Department only accounted for 69 of the 71 samples. A researcher noted that the two samples that were discarded from the analysis had high levels of lead. Including them in the analysis would have increased the level above 15 parts per billion (PPB). According to the Environmental Protection Agency (EPA), water supply companies are required to alert the public and take actions if lead concentrations exceed the 'action level' of 15 PPB in drinking water (https://www.epa .gov/dwreginfo/lead-and-copper-rule). An environmental toxicologist noted: 'Flint was a failure of government at every level, from local Flint officials to the highest level of EPA. There were many governmental safeguards put into place, and they all failed'.[56] In 2021, a judge approved a US$ 600 million settlement to resolve thousands of claims, which was the largest settlement of its kind in the state's history.[57]

Blockchain's proponents have forcefully argued that this new technology can save us from 'another Flint-like contamination crisis'.[58] Projects such as the WSSC's integration of the IoT in supply system can be probably upgraded with sensors such as near-infrared reflectance spectroscopy (NIRS) to include data on chemical levels. If such a system was installed in Michigan, Flint's water service company could have found the lead contamination when it exceeded a healthy level. Blockchain-based systems can thus possibly provide the 'second layer of crisis prevention' in such cases.[59]

Blockchain can eliminate many of the above drawbacks. IoT solutions can use blockchain to enable secure messaging between devices in a network. In a blockchain model, message exchanges between devices can be treated in a similar way as financial transactions in a Bitcoin network. To exchange

---

[55]   D Debucquoy-Dodley (2016) 'Did Michigan Officials Hide the Truth about Lead in Flint?' Retrieved from http://www.cnn.com/2016/01/14/us/flint-water -investigation/.

[56]   Susan Goldhaber (Jan 4, 2022) 'The Flint Water Dept. Failed Its Chemistry Test' https://www.acsh.org/news/2022/01/04/flint-water-dept-failed-its-chemistry-test -16034.

[57]   Shirin Ali (Nov, 11, 2021) 'A Historic $600 Million Settlement in Flint's Water Scandal Will Help the Children. About 80 Percent of the Settlement Will Go to Children and Adolescents that Were Impacted During the Flint Water Crisis' https://thehill.com/ changing-america/respect/accessibility/581173-a-historic-600-million-settlement-in -flints-water.

[58]   Hackett (n 40).

[59]   Ibid.

messages, devices will leverage smart contracts which model the agreement between two parties.[60] Blockchain cryptographically signs transactions and verifies those cryptographic signatures to ensure that only the originator of the message could have sent it. This can eliminate the Man-In-The-Middle and replay attacks.[61]

5.4.4   Blockchain's Roles in Ensuring Security of Supply Chain

As discussed in Chapter 4, a key trend that has emerged in the blockchain arena has been the development of sophisticated applications to manage supply chains. This trend is likely to have a major implication for the security of IoT devices.

Blockchain can improve security of both forward and backward linkages in supply chains. In this way, it can be an effective tool to track the sources of insecurity in supply chains (Figure 5.1). If an IoT security breach is discovered, this technology is likely to make it possible to contain the breach in a targeted way. Blockchain can thus facilitate handling and dealing with crisis situations such as product recalls due to security vulnerability.

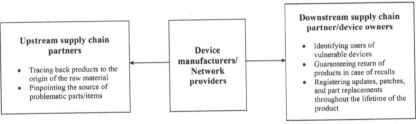

Source: Adapted from N Kshetri (2017) 'Blockchain's Roles in Strengthening Cybersecurity and Protecting Privacy' *Telecommunications Policy* Vol 41(10) 1027–38.

Figure 5.1   *Blockchain's role in improving cybersecurity in supply chain networks*

Blockchain can make it possible to trace back every product to the origin of the raw materials. Transactions can also be linked to identify users of

---

[60]   A Banafa (2017) 'IoT and Blockchain Convergence: Benefits and Challenges' *IEEE. Internet of Things*, Retrieved from http://iot.ieee.org/newsletter/january-2017/iot-and-blockchain-convergence-benefits-and-challenges.html.

[61]   J Coward (2016) 'Meet the Visionary Who Brought Blockchain to the Industrial IoT' *IOT World News*, Retrieved from http://www.iotworldnews.com/author.asp?section_id=495&doc_id=728962.

vulnerable IoT devices. Thus, IoT-linked security crises such as the October 2016 cyberattacks on Dyn can be handled in a better way if the supply chains associated with the infected devices are connected to blockchain networks. For instance, China-based Hangzhou Xiongmai Technologies, which makes Internet-connected cameras and accompanying accessories, recalled its products sold in the US that were vulnerable to the Mirai malware. However, in the current non-blockchain environment it is difficult to track down the owners of the devices and contact them if items with security vulnerability are not returned. This could be resolved with blockchain. Blockchain is suitable for complex workflows such as that can be observed in the technology production and supply chain. An application is that blockchain can be used to register time, location, price, parties involved, and other relevant information when an item changes ownership. The technology can also be used to track raw materials as they move through the supply chain, are transformed into circuit boards and electronic components, are integrated into products, and then sold to customers. Blockchain can also be used to register updates, patches, and part replacements applied to any product or device throughout its lifetime. This would make it easier to track progress in addressing vulnerabilities and security problems and send warnings and notifications to product owners.[62] In this way, blockchain can also provide an effective post-breach resilience plan and implementation.

5.5   BLOCKCHAIN AND COMPLIANCE ISSUES

In order to ensure a widespread diffusion of blockchain solutions, it is important for them to address various compliance issues. As noted above, blockchain can improve financial and other reporting, and compliance with various laws and regulations. However, sufficient progress has not been made on this front. The intergovernmental body for preventing money laundering and terror financing, Financial Action Task Force (FATF) noted that not a single crypto service provider in any jurisdiction was fully compliant with the cryptocurrency 'travel rule', which states that the sender and recipient of crypto funds must be properly identified.[63] In 2015, for instance, a federal investigation found that the US cryptocurrency company Ripple Labs had not properly

---

[62]   B Dickson (2016a) 'Blockchain Could Help Fix IoT Security after DDoS Attack.' Retrieved from http://venturebeat.com/2016/10/29/blockchain-could-help-fix-iot-security-after-ddos-attack/.

[63]   Nasdaq.com (2021) 'DeFi Has Accounted for over 75% of Crypto Hacks in 2021.' [online] Available at: https://www.nasdaq.com/articles/defi-has-accounted-for-over-75-of-crypto-hacks-in-2021-2021-08-10.

followed anti-money laundering (AML) laws and rules about getting accurate customer identification information.

The European Commission (EC) launched a European Financial Transparency Gateway (EFTG) pilot project to assess the feasibility of using blockchain as the basis for a dedicated platform for sharing data. The goal is to offer a single view for regulated financial information of companies listed on the European Union (EU) regulated markets. The information is currently stored within different Member States' infrastructures.[64] The pilot was launched following a successful Proof of Concept (PoC) using blockchain. The European Securities and Markets Authority (ESMA) told the EC that the pilot may not be feasible under General Data Protection Regulations (GDPR). A concern is related to the immutability of data stored on blockchain. Immutability means that the information stored in the European Single Access Point (ESAP) may not be deleted once entered in the blockchain. The GDPR requires information submitted in the company registers to be deleted (e.g., after ten years, in case of errors, etc).[65]

Regulatory compliance has been a key component of many countries' recent central bank digital currency (CBDC) initiatives. It is the responsibility of most central banks to meet the AML and combating the financing of terrorism (CFT) standards of the FATF. A common approach to meet these standards has been to apply proportionality rules. For example, the users of China's Digital Currency Electronic Payment (DCEP)/Digital Yuan (eCNY) that hold less than ¥10,000 and engage in transactions that are smaller than ¥2,000 (daily transaction up to ¥5,000) are identified only by their mobile phone SIM cards. For larger transactions, consumers are required to provide full names, addresses and phone numbers, and link the CBDC wallet with their bank accounts. Likewise, the European Central Bank experimented with a CBDC that involved elements of programmable money. Under this model, individuals are allotted 'anonymity vouchers' to use for small transactions. Larger transactions, on the other hand, would be visible to financial intermediaries and the authorities that are responsible for AML and CFT.

5.6   BLOCKCHAIN'S LIMITATIONS

Blockchain, however, is not without drawbacks and limitations. Due to blockchain's newness, well-developed security mechanisms do not exist for some

---

[64]   eftg.eu (n.d.) *EFTG*. [online] Available at: https://eftg.eu/.
[65]   Finextra Research (2021) 'ESMA Queries Use of Blockchain for EC's Ambitious Financial Data Platform.' [online] Available at: https://www.finextra.com/newsarticle/37587/esma-queries-use-of-blockchain-for-ecs-ambitious-financial-data-platform.

systems. There have been some hacking attacks against digital currencies and crypto products such as DeFi (decentralized finance). According to Elliptic, during the first ten and a half months of 2021, losses caused by DeFi exploits amounted to US$ 12 billion. Fraud and theft accounted for US$ 10.5 billion.[66]

One estimate suggested that on the average, there are between 15 and 50 defects per 1,000 lines of software code. For Ethereum this number is estimated to be at least twice as many. *The Economist* quoted a blogger, who said that Ethereum contracts are 'candy for hackers'.[67] In June 2016, a high-profile hacking case that breached the DAO[68] (decentralized autonomous organization) was revealed. Note that the DAO was launched by a group of Ethereum developers on April 30, 2016. The project had a 28-day funding window. By the end of the funding period, the DAO had raised more than US$ 150 million from over 11,000 funders.[69] It was arguably the biggest crowdfunding project undertaken until that time. On June 17, 2016, someone exploited vulnerability in the DAO's code and stole 3.6 million Ether from the fund. Depending on whether the total value of the stolen fund is calculated before or after the hack, it ranged from US$ 64 million to US$ 101 million.[70]

Since blockchains have not been used and adopted widely enough, they have not yet been seriously tested. An additional problem has been the way blockchain systems are being designed. Organizations in most networks run the same code.[71] This means that if a hacker finds a vulnerability in a blockchain, all systems using the blockchain may face attacks.

The cybersecurity risks associated with attacks on cryptocurrency wallets of users and cryptocurrency exchanges are also increasing. For instance,

---

[66]   R Browne (2021) 'Criminals Have Made Off with over $10 Billion in "DeFi" Scams and Thefts This Year.' [online] *CNBC*. Available at: https://www.cnbc.com/2021/11/19/over-10-billion-lost-to-defi-scams-and-thefts-in-2021.html.

[67]   *The Economist* (2016) 'Not-so-clever Contracts: For the Time Being At Least, Human Judgment Is Still a Better Bet than Cold-hearted Code.' Retrieved from http://www.economist.com/news/business/21702758-time-being-least-human-judgment-still-better-bet-cold-hearted.

[68]   DAOs are run through smart contracts and do not need centralized management and the direct control of self-interested institutions.

[69]   S Siegel (2016) 'Understanding the DAO Hack for Journalists.' Retrieved from https://medium.com/@pullnews/understanding-the-dao-hack-for-journalists-2312dd43e993#.9dt17ge8c.

[70]   J Ore (2016) 'How a $64M Hack Changed the Fate of Ethereum, Bitcoin's Closest Competitor: Cryptocurrency Alternative to Bitcoin Was Co-founded by 19-year-old Canadian-Russian in 2015' *CBC News*, Retrieved from (http://www.cbc.ca/news/technology/thereum-hack-blockchain-fork-bitcoin-1.3719009).

[71]   W Knight (April 18, 2017) 'Blockchain's Weak Spots Pose a Hidden Danger to Users.' Retrieved from https://www.technologyreview.com/s/604219/blockchains-weak-spots-pose-a-hidden-danger-to-users/.

a number of security and privacy concerns were reported in EL Salvador's 'Chivo' Bitcoin Wallet (See In Focus 5.2 below). Likewise, Blockchain analysis company Chainalysis estimated that North Korean hackers stole about US$ 400 million worth of cryptocurrency in 2021 using several techniques including hacking organizations' 'hot' wallets.[72]

IN FOCUS 5.2 EL SALVADOR'S 'CHIVO' BITCOIN WALLET FACES A NUMBER OF SECURITY AND PRIVACY CONCERNS

The Central American country of El Salvador has adopted Bitcoin as legal tender. In June 2021, the country's Congress passed the Bitcoin Law by a supermajority vote.[a] In September 2021, El Salvador launched its proprietary 'Chivo' (a slang term for 'cool' in El Salvador) Bitcoin Wallet.[b] There were a number of security and privacy concerns with the wallet.[c]

Each wallet has been loaded with US$ 30 worth of Bitcoin, which was provided by the government in order to encourage El Salvadoreans to use the cryptocurrency. Between October 9 and October 14, 2021, El Salvador's human rights organization Cristosal received 755 notifications of Salvadorans, who complained of identity theft with their Chivo Wallets.[d]

In order to register for the wallet, a user requires a Unique Identity Document (DUI), phone number, date of birth and needs to upload a photo. Chivo's official website states that users are required to scan the front and back of the DUI and perform facial recognition to check the user's identity.

Several Salvadorans reported a serious flaw in the verification process. Chivo's verification process did not check photos and anyone could register with a DUI and a matching date of birth.[e]

To take an example, Salvadoran YouTuber Adam Flores tried to open a Chivo Wallet for his grandmother as a test case to see whether the verification process is effective. He only had a photocopy of his grandmother's DUI. The application accepted the photocopy as valid. For the real-time facial recognition verification to prove that it is his grandmother who was applying, he took a photo of Sarah Connor, a character in the *Terminator* movies, from a poster on his wall. The application for Chivo Wallet for the YouTuber's grandmother was approved and the US$ 30 incentive was released.[f]

---

[72] bbc.com (Jan 14, 2022) 'North Korea Hackers Stole $400m of Cryptocurrency in 2021, Report Says' https://www.bbc.com/news/business-59990477.

Notes:

[a] Arjun Kharpal (June 9, 2021) 'El Salvador Becomes First Country to Adopt Bitcoin as Legal Tender after Passing Law', https://www.cnbc.com/2021/06/09/el-salvador-proposes-law-to-make-bitcoin-legal-tender .html.

[b] Andjela Radmilac (Sept 9, 2021) 'El Salvador's "Chivo" Bitcoin (BTC) Wallet Allegedly has Privacy Issues: A Privacy Bug Found in the Country's Bitcoin Wallet Has Been Promptly Resolved by Its Development Team After Being Highlighted by a Twitter User, but Other Issues Seem to Persist' https://cryptoslate.com/el-salvadors-chivo-bitcoin-wallet-allegedly-has-privacy-issues/.

[c] Ibid.

[d] Andrés Engler (Oct 29, 2021) 'Identity Thieves Exploit El Salvador's Chivo Bitcoin Wallet's Setup Process' https://www.coindesk.com/business/2021/10/29/identity-thieves-exploit-el-salvadors-chivo-bitcoin -wallets-setup-process/.

[e] David Gerard (Sept 17, 2021) 'El Salvador's Bitcoin Law Is a Farce' https://foreignpolicy.com/2021/09/17/el-salvador-bitcoin-law-farce/.

[f] Engler (n [d]).

Finally, Web 3.0 and the metaverse, where technologies such as blockchain and decentralized apps are displacing centralized social networks, have their own cybersecurity risks. Such risks range from the sale of fake NFTs (non-fungible tokens) to domain name squatting (See In Focus 5.3 below). While some have correctly argued that the assets in the metaverse are virtual so they do not exist in 'reality', an important point that should be considered is that these assets are linked to an individual's real-world wealth and identity.[73] As of December 2021, transactions worth US$ 96 million for virtual land and other items were conducted on the blockchain-based virtual world Decentraland, which allows users to 'create, experience and monetize' content and applications. The largest sale involved a land plot which was sold for US$ 2.4 million. Likewise, 1.2 million traders in the blockchain-based game Axie Infinity made 9.8 million transactions with an average price of US$ 352.[74] Thus the metaverse is attractive for cybercriminals and raises several important concerns about security and privacy.

IN FOCUS 5.3 A SCAMMER USES BANKSY'S NAME TO CREATE AND SELL A FAKE NFT

Pseudonymous British street artist, political activist and film director Banksy attracted media attention in August 2021 when an NFT listed on the

---

[73]   C Metinko (Dec 6, 2021) 'Securing the Metaverse – What's Needed for the Next Chapter of the Internet' https://news.crunchbase.com/news/metaverse-cybersecurity -startups-investment/?utm_source=cb_daily&utm_medium=email&utm_campaign= 20211203&utm_content=intro&utm_term=content.

[74]   seekingalpha.com (Dec 17, 2021) 'Crypto Categories: Enter the Metaverse' https://seekingalpha.com/article/4475696-crypto-categories-enter-the-metaverse.

OpenSea marketplace appeared to link to Banksy's website. A vendor, who went by the name of gaakmann had listed the NFT. An NFT collector named Pranksy offered 100 ETH (more than US$ 330,000) to buy the NFT, which was accepted by the vendor. The NFT's title was *Great Redistribution of the Climate Change Disaster*. It consisted of an 8-bit image styled like a CryptoPunk, the popular NFT collection on the Ethereum blockchain launched in 2017 by the Canadian software company Larva Labs studio. The digital image in the fake Banksy NFT was of a man smoking a cigarette in front of industrial smokestacks. Since Banksy had been vocal about climate crisis in the past, the fake NFT was convincing enough to fool some NFT collectors.[a]

Banksy's spokesperson said that the artist Banksy had not created any NFT artworks. A few hours later, the perpetrators sent Pranksy 97.69 ETH back (100 ETH minus OpenSea's transaction fee). Pranksy believed that he received the refund after identifying the hacker and following them on Twitter.[b]

Scammers are also likely to use .eth domains, which are crypto versions of Internet domain names. These domains are built on the Ethereum network and thus are not dependent on web hosting partners names. .eth domain name squatting is reported to be growing in prevalence. Cybercriminals may register misspellings or similar-looking domain names as that of established businesses to create fake Ethereum domain names and smart contracts. Transactions are only as secure as the entity enforcing them, and on the Internet, it can be hard to tell who exactly you are dealing with.[c]

Notes:
[a] Anny Shaw (Aug 31, 2021) 'Were Banksy and Pranksy Both Pranked in $330,000 NFT Sale?' https://www.theartnewspaper.com/2021/08/31/were-banksy-and-pranksy-both-pranked-in-dollar330000-nft-sale.
[b] Samuel Haig (Sept 1, 2021) 'NFT Whale "Pranksy" Pranked by Fake Banksy for 97.7 ETH' https://cointelegraph.com/news/nft-whale-pranksy-pranked-by-fake-banksy-for-97-7-eth.
[c] Nahla Davies (Dec 10, 2021) 'Cybersecurity and the Metaverse: Pioneering Safely into a New Digital World' https://www.globalsign.com/en/blog/cybersecurity-and-metaverse-pioneering-safely-new-digital-world.

5.7 CHAPTER SUMMARY AND CONCLUSION

Blockchain can help strengthen cybersecurity and privacy in a wide range of settings such as health care, finance and the IoT devices. With this technology, all access to data can be monitored and logged and unmonitored access to identifiable information is not allowed. Among the most promising is that individuals are able to control their own personal data.

In many healthcare organizations, mechanisms do not exist for assuring that patient data are not accessed by unauthorized users. The current EHR infrastructure may not meet patients' privacy demands. Blockchain can solve the broader problem of systems relying on password-based security and authentication. The blockchain ledger includes an audit trail and data that are time-stamped, which allows the patient to know (within reason) who made what changes and when. Third parties such as healthcare providers can see the patient's data with their permission, but they are not required or expected to store the data. In this way, a blockchain-based model is superior to existing data governance models.

In recent years, significant initiatives have been undertaken in a range of settings to use blockchain to strengthen security and privacy of healthcare data. The main focus of many of those initiatives has been on audit trails. Blockchain may also lead to more efficient healthcare by addressing existing inefficiencies that cause lost time, poorer care, and higher costs.

Blockchain-based transactions are also easily auditable. Due primarily to this and other features, blockchain can possibly play a key role in tracking the sources of insecurity in supply chains as well as in handling and dealing with crisis situations such as product recalls in case of a security vulnerability. Blockchain-based identity and access management systems can address key IoT security challenges such as those associated with IP spoofing.

Overall, blockchain can make it harder for cybercriminals, data manipulators and others to mishandle personal data. Thus a promising future can be foreseen for the use of blockchain in addressing various aspects of security and privacy.

6. Payment and settlement systems

6.1 INTRODUCTION

Since Bitcoin's peer-to-peer payment was the first popular blockchain application, blockchain is often regarded as a technology for financial services to facilitate payment and settlement systems. Blockchain's key features can make FinTech (financial technology) products based on this technology and cryptocurrencies attractive. It is argued that blockchain can enhance efficiency of some types of payment systems. The decentralized nature of the network means that all operations are accessible to all relevant members of the network. Processes such as ordering, settlement and payments can be implemented on a (near) real-time basis.

Recently, cryptocurrencies' use in payment and settlement has gained popularity. A study of over 8,000 consumers in the US released by payments-focused publication Pymnts in August 2021 found that more than 60 per cent of crypto owners were 'very' or 'extremely' interested in using crypto as a payment method in order to make online purchases more private or secure.[1]

Major companies have started accepting payments for their products and services in cryptocurrencies. In 2020 and 2021, major companies such as Microsoft, Tesla, Expedia and WeWork started payment acceptance in cryptocurrencies.[2] In countries characterized by high inflation rates, vendors actually prefer to be paid in cryptocurrencies. Despite the volatility in the prices of cryptocurrencies, in economies experiencing hyperinflation, cryptocurrencies are more stable than fiat currencies. To take one example, in 2018, Venezuela's annual inflation rate in 2018 was 65,374 per cent.[3] In Venezuela, street vendors

---

[1]   Helen Partz (Aug 3, 2021) 'New Study Reveals High Demand for Payments in Cryptocurrency' https://cointelegraph.com/news/new-study-reveals-high-demand-for-payments-in-cryptocurrency.
[2]   Daniel Webber (Apr 21, 2021) 'Cryptocurrency in Cross-border Payments: After Coinbase's Success, Can Crypto Flourish beyond Assets?' https://www.forbes.com/sites/danielwebber/2021/04/21/cryptocurrency-in-cross-border-payments-after-coinbases-success-can-crypto-flourish-beyond-assets/?sh=7a02b53d416f.
[3]   Aaron O'Neill (Nov 23, 2021) 'Venezuela: Inflation Rate from 1985 to 2022 (Compared to the Previous Year)' https://www.statista.com/statistics/371895/inflation-rate-in-venezuela/.

accept payments in digital coins in some bigger cities like Caracas, Maracaibo or Valencia.[4] Likewise, the Argentinian e-commerce company Avalancha offers a 10 per cent discount for payments in Bitcoin. That makes sense because the Argentinian peso lost half its value in the first eight months of 2018. If a customer pays with a credit card, Avalancha may not get its money for a month – and that money may not be worth what it once was.[5]

Another notable trend is that employees in some companies receive their payroll in cryptocurrencies. In 2021, Twitter, the City of Miami and the City of Jackson, Tennessee in the US, the American professional basketball team Sacramento Kings,[6] Australian Baseball League team the Perth Heat and others announced their plans to pay compensation to employees in Bitcoin. Among several reasons, some employees prefer to be paid in cryptocurrencies.[7]

Other payment and settlement activities being transformed by blockchain include international remittance and supply chain and trade financing. In 2019, *Euromoney* reported that there were about 30 consortia that focused on using DLT (distributed ledger technology) in trade financing.[8] On the remittance front, as of April 2021, the Mexican crypto company Bitso had one million users in Latin America.[9] Mexicans working in the US sent more than US$ 1 billion in remittances to their home country using Bitso's services, which was 2.5 per cent of remittances sent from the US to Mexico.[10] Likewise, crypto company Ripple's blockchain-based money transfer network RippleNet

---

[4]   Nicolas Martin (Apr 16, 2021) 'Venezuelans Try to Beat Hyperinflation with Cryptocurrency Revolution' https://www.dw.com/en/venezuelans-try-to-beat -hyperinflation-with-cryptocurrency-revolution/a-57219083.

[5]   N Kshetri (June 25, 2019) 'Facebook's Libra May Be Quite Attractive in Developing Countries' *Conversation* https://theconversation.com/facebooks-libra-may -be-quite-attractive-in-developing-countries-119206.

[6]   Fisher Phillips (May 3, 2021) 'Cryptocurrency Clamor: Paying Employees in Bitcoin Has Reached the Mainstream' https://www.jdsupra.com/legalnews/ cryptocurrency-clamor-paying-employees-1276795/.

[7]   bmmagazine.co.uk (June 3, 2019) 'Companies Are Paying Employees in Bitcoin and They're Loving It' https://bmmagazine.co.uk/in-business/companies-are-paying -employees-in-bitcoin-and-theyre-loving-it/.

[8]   euromoney.com (2019) 'Trade Finance and Blockchain: Now Is the Time for a Network of Networks' *Euromoney*, https://www.euromoney.com/article/ b1h041crxm5dks/trade-finance-and-blockchain-now-is-the-time-for-a-network-of -networks.

[9]   Andalusia Knoll Soloff, (Apr 26, 2021) 'The New Wave of Crypto Users: Migrant Workers' https://restofworld.org/2021/crypto-remittances/?utm_source= morning_brew.

[10]   H Field (Aug 5, 2021) 'Crypto Has Cross-border Promise' https://www .morningbrew.com/emerging-tech/stories/2021/08/05/cryptocurrency-gaining-steam -crossborder-payments.

reported fivefold growth in transactions between 2019 and 2020. Other key players in the money transfer industry such as Western Union and MoneyGram have started teaming up with crypto companies.[11]

Another emerging use of blockchain has been in central bank digital currencies (CBDCs), which are likely to have a powerful impact on economies and societies (see In Focus 6.1). In late 2020, the international financial institution owned by central banks, Bank for International Settlements (BIS), surveyed more than 60 central banks about their engagement in digital versions of fiat currency work and found that 86 per cent were exploring CBDCs.[12] Many of the CBDCs are likely to be blockchain-based. For instance, in October 2020, Central Bank of the Bahamas (CBB) launched blockchain-based digital Bahamian Dollar (B$), known as 'the sand dollar'.[13] It was the world's first CBDC.[14] Parties transacting in the sand dollar benefit from the legal-tender status since it uses a liability of the CBB, which is viewed as the safest form of payment in the country. the digital B$. Likewise, Nigeria launched Africa's first digital currency, the eNaira in October 2021.

This chapter provides a perspective on how substantial efficiency gains can be achieved by using blockchain for digital assets' settlement process by decreasing transaction costs and reducing various risks. It presents a variety of examples of payment and settlement systems being transformed by blockchain.

IN FOCUS 6.1 NIGERIA'S CBDC ENAIRA

The eNaira app for using the Nigerian CBDC went live on October 25, 2021.[a] Two apps – eNaira Speed Wallet and eNaira Merchant Wallet – can be downloaded from the Google and Apple app stores.[b] By November 2015, 488,000 consumer wallets had been downloaded and transactions valued at 62 million naira (US$ 150,000) were conducted.[c] About 78,000 merchants from 160 countries also had signed up for the merchant wallet.[d]

eNaira's theme is: 'Same Naira, more possibilities'. The goal is not to replace cash but provide a safe and efficient alternative means of payment

[11]   Ibid.
[12]   C Boar and A Wehrli (2021) 'Ready, Steady, Go? Results of the Third BIS Survey on Central Bank Digital Currency' *Bank for International Settlements*, https://www.bis.org/publ/bppdf/bispap114.pdf.
[13]   DR Stevens (2020) 'The Bahamas Launches Its Central Bank Digital Currency.' [online] *Decrypt*. Available at: https://decrypt.co/45740/bahamas-launches-its-central-bank-digital-currency.
[14]   V Bharathan (2020) 'Central Bank Digital Currency: The First Nationwide CBDC in the World Has Been Launched by the Bahamas' *Forbes*, https://tinyurl.com/yvz9sdpu.

system.[e] The CBN said that eNaira is more reliable than cryptocurrencies and urged all Nigerians to embrace the digital currency. Bitt Inc. has announced plans to launch a new mobile application for the unbanked population to access eNaira.[f]

Barbados-based FinTech company Bitt, which also worked on the Eastern Caribbean central bank's digital currency developed eNaira. The eNaira, which is pegged at parity with Naira, uses blockchain. It is stored in digital wallets and can be used for payment transactions. It can be transferred digitally and at virtually no cost to anyone in the world that has an eNaira wallet. The eNaira features stringent access right controls by the central bank. Unlike some crypto assets such as Bitcoin the eNaira is not a financial asset in itself. It is a digital form of a national currency and draws its value from the physical naira.

The CBN (Central Bank of Nigeria) thinks that the eNaira can bring multiple benefits. The first benefit is an *increase in financial inclusion*. It is expected to expand to anyone with a mobile phone. A large proportion of Nigerians do not have bank accounts (38 million, 36 per cent of the adult population). They will be able to use eNaira with a mobile phone. Second, it is expected to *facilitate remittances*. The Nigerian diaspora can obtain eNaira from international money transfer operators and transfer them to recipients in Nigeria by wallet-to-wallet transfers. Third, it *reduced informality*. Unlike token-based crypto asset transactions, the eNaira is account-based, and transactions are fully traceable. It may bring greater transparency to informal payments and strengthen the tax base.[g]

The country's President Muhammadu Buhari stated that the eNaira has a potential to generate an additional US$ 29 billion in economic activity within a decade by broadening the tax base and increasing business efficiency.[h] There is the possibility of direct government welfare payments with eNaira. The eNaira Speed Wallet went offline two days later after over 100,000 downloads. It was removed from app stores to upgrade. Users had complained that several features of the app were not working.[i]

Several measures have been taken to mitigate the risks, there are daily transactions and balance limits to transfer funds from bank deposits to eNaira wallets. This measure is expected to reduce the risks of diminishing the roles of banks and other financial institutions. In order to prevent money laundering and other illicit activities, a tiered-identity verification system has been implemented. More stringent controls are applied to less verified users. Highest tier holders cannot hold more than 5 million naira (US$ 12,200). Low-tier categories of holders have tighter transactions. As of November 2021, only people with a bank verification number can open a wallet. Over time, the coverage is expected to expand to people with registered SIM cards and those with mobile phones but no ID numbers.[j]

Notes:

a VOA (2021) 'Nigeria Launches Africa's First Digital Currency.' [online] Available at: https://www .voanews.com/a/nigeria-launches-africa-s-first-digital-currency/6286460.html.

b J Crawley (2021) 'Nigeria's eNaira CBDC Goes Live.' [online] Available at: https://www.coindesk.com/ policy/2021/10/25/nigerias-enaira-cbdc-goes-live.

c bloomberg.com (2021) 'Bloomberg – Are You a Robot?' [online] Available at: https://www.bloomberg .com/news/articles/2021-11-15/e-naira-lures-about-half-a-million-people-weeks-after-its-launch.

d E Gkritsi (2021) 'Nigeria's eNaira Wallet Nears 500,000 Downloads in First 3 Weeks: Report.' [online] Available at: https://www.coindesk.com/policy/2021/11/16/nigerias-enaira-wallet-nears-500000-downloads -in-first-3-weeks-report/.

e African Business (2021) 'Nigeria Launches eNaira – Africa's First Digital Currency.' [online] Available at: https://african.business/2021/10/finance-services/nigeria-gears-up-for-enaira/.

f Nairametrics (2021) 'eNaira Completed N46.3 Million Worth of Transactions in Less than 2 Weeks – CBN.' [online] Available at: https://nairametrics.com/2021/11/09/cbn-enaira-completed-n46-3million-worth -of-transactions-in-less-than-2weeks/.

g Department J.R.I.A. (n.d.) 'Five Observations on Nigeria's Central Bank Digital Currency.' [online] IMF. Available at: https://www.imf.org/en/News/Articles/2021/11/15/na111621-five-observations-on-nigerias -central-bank-digital-currency.

h CoinGeek (2021) 'After Initial Glitches, eNaira Gains Traction in Nigeria.' [online] Available at: https:// coingeek.com/after-initial-glitches-enaira-gains-traction-in-nigeria/.

i Cointelegraph (n.d.) 'eNaira Slowly Gains Traction Post-launch amid Glitches.' [online] Available at: https://cointelegraph.com/news/enaira-slowly-gains-traction-post-launch-amidst-glitches.

j Calvin (2021) 'We Are Ready to Work with Nigeria to Share the e-Naira Experience, Says International Monetary Fund (IMF).' [online] BitcoinKE. Available at: https://bitcoinke.io/2021/11/imf-on-the-enaira/.

6.2 BLOCKCHAIN'S BENEFITS OVER TRADITIONAL PAYMENT AND SETTLEMENT SYSTEMS

Blockchain systems offer a number of benefits over traditional payment and settlement systems. First, in many cases, blockchain-based systems are a low cost means of payment and settlement. It was reported that most migrants who use international transfer companies such as Western Union, MoneyGram and Vigo charge US$ 10 on average to send US$ 200. Commissions of companies such as Mexican crypto exchange Bitso are as low as US$ 1 per US$ 1,000 sent.[15]

IN FOCUS 6.2 THE WORLD FOOD PROGRAMME'S BUILDING BLOCKS

The World Food Programme's (WFP) Innovation Accelerator started the 'Building Blocks' pilot in early 2017. In the first stage, food and cash assistance was provided to needy families in Pakistan's Sindh province. Starting

---

15 Soloff (n9).

in May 2017, the WFP started distributing food vouchers in Jordan's refugee camps by delivering cryptographically unique coupons to participating supermarkets. Supermarket cashiers are equipped with iris scanners to identify the beneficiaries and settle payments. UN databases verify biometric data about refugees. Building Blocks' ledger records the transactions on a private version of the Ethereum blockchain: the Parity Ethereum. No banks are involved and beneficiaries thus receive goods directly from the merchants.

The Parity Ethereum used in the system employs four nodes to validate transactions.[a] This means that transactions cannot be seen by actors that are not a part of the authorized peer nodes. An additional benefit is that the cryptocurrency mining process is not needed to validate the transactions. This feature removes a key bottleneck to the processing speed and transaction capacity.[b] The system is designed to scale.

The WFP reported that by October 2017, it had distributed US$ 1.4 million in food vouchers to 10,500 Syrian refugees in Jordan.[c] As of early 2019, 106,000 refugees in Jordan's Azraq and Za'atari camps received cash transfers in cryptocurrencies. By that time, 1.1 million cryptocurrency transactions transferred more than US$ 23.5 million to refugees.[d]

When the applications reach a more advanced development stage in the future, more benefits can be realized. For instance, the WFP expects that refugees may be able to access their funds by controlling their own cryptographic keys. This would also allow them to incorporate and integrate personal data from diverse sources. For instance, their medical records could be with the World Health Organization (WHO), academic credentials with the United Nations Children's Fund (UNICEF), and nutritional data with the WFP.[e] In this way, they can build their economic identity.

Processing speed and efficiency can be increased with cryptocurrencies. For instance, once refugees are registered, the WFP's blockchain system encrypts their data and vouchers are transferred almost instantaneously. In this regard, a key attractiveness of blockchain-based FinTechs and cryptocurrencies is the ability to intervene in a fast and efficient way in societies that face the most difficult environments. For example, when vulnerable places that lack financial infrastructures such as ATM machines and banks face disasters such as earthquakes or storms, blockchain can help humanitarian organizations provide life-saving cash assistance faster than other available means. Cryptocash (crypto tokens) can represent local currencies such as Pakistani Rupees and Jordanian Dinar that can be traded outside of the banking realm. The recipients can use the cryptocash[f] to buy goods and services in participating shops. Cryptocurrencies can even replace scarce local cash, allowing aid organizations, residents, and merchants to exchange money quickly and electronically.

Blockchain increases the ability to get a secure and authentic identity at a low cost. Since ID cards in many countries are paper-based, which can be easily forged, blockchain solutions have significant potential to reduce fraudulent activities. In the WFP programme, an iris scan is used to verify refugee's identities.[g] Each user's account is linked to their iris. It is extremely difficult if not impossible for nefarious actors to falsify information or make up fake profiles to disburse the funds. Likewise future plans for the WFP's Building Blocks are to allow refugees and displaced people to control their own cryptographic keys and integrate personal data sources such as the WHO, the UNICEF, and the WFP[h] in order to build their economic identity and creditworthiness.

Notes:

[a] A Stanley (2017) 'Microlending Startups Look to Blockchain for Loans' *Coindesk*, https://www.coindesk.com/microlending-trends-startups-look-blockchain-loans.

[b] J Wong (2017) 'The UN Is Using Ethereum's Technology to Fund Food for Thousands of Refugees' *Quartz*, https://qz.com/1118743/world-food-programmes-ethereum-based-blockchain-for-syrian-refugees-in-jordan.

[c] N Kshetri and J Voas (2018) 'Blockchain in Developing Countries' *IEEE IT Professional* Vol 20(2) 11–14.

[d] M Seibert (2019) 'The World Food Program: Fighting Hunger with Blockchain' https://foodtank.com/news/2019/01/the-world-food-program-fighting-hunger-with-blockchain/.

[e] Wong (n [b]).

[f] wfp.org (2017) 'What Is "Blockchain" and How Is It Connected to Fighting Hunger' *World Food Programme*, https://insight.wfp.org/what-is-blockchain-and-how-is-it-connected-to-fighting-hunger-7f1b42da9fe.

[g] themerkle.com (2019) 'Using the Blockchain to Crackdown on Healthcare Fraud, One Iris-scan at a Time' *The Merkle Hash*, https://themerkle.com/using-the-blockchain-to-crackdown-on-healthcare-fraud-one-iris-scan-at-a-time/.

[h] Wong (n [b]).

Similar benefits can be achieved in the systems used to distribute donations and aids. For instance, the WFP (see In Focus 6.2: The world food programme's building blocks) expects that blockchain-based solutions would reduce its overhead costs from 3.5 per cent to less than 1 per cent.[16] What is even more important is that an estimated 30 per cent of development funds do not reach the intended recipients due to problems such as third-party theft and mismanagement.[17] Blockchain holds a great potential and promise to reduce such practices.

Second, blockchain-based systems can increase the speed of settlement in a transaction. As an example, Ripple's On-Demand Liquidity leverages XRP (the payment network's cryptocurrency) to send money faster at a lower

[16] N Kshetri and J Voas (2018) 'Blockchain in Developing Countries' *IEEE IT Professional* Vol 20(2) 11–14

[17] B Paynter (2017) 'How Blockchain Could Transform the Way International Aid Is Distributed' *Fast Company*, www.fastcompany.com/40457354/how-blockchain-could-transform-the-way-international-aid-is-distributed.

fee. Some users of RippleNet include Vietnam's TPBank, Pakistan's Faysal Bank,[18] the National Bank of Egypt[19] and Thailand's Siam Commercial Bank.[20] The Siam Commercial Bank has teamed up with the digital money transfer service provider Azimo to use RippleNet. Using non-blockchain solutions, sending remittances from Europe to Thailand takes more than one business day to settle. With RippleNet, Siam Commercial Bank clears pounds and euros into Thai baht in less than a minute.[21] Using On-Demand Liquidity, banks can avoid pre-funding[22] and thus settle remittances quickly.[23] On-Demand Liquidity is especially attractive to payment companies and non-banking institutions that are required to open overseas accounts to pre-fund their transfers. Many such institutions face difficulties opening overseas bank accounts due to concerns related to money laundering.[24]

Likewise, Stellar Lumens (XLM), which is the native cryptocurrency of blockchain-based payment network Stellar, provides a faster and cheaper way of sending money internationally. In order to send the money from the US to the UK, for instance, US dollars would be converted into XLM, which is sent to the destination, and then converted to British pounds. It is reported to take about five seconds to complete a transaction with the average transaction fee of 0.00001 XLM[25] or US$ 0.000002928 based on the price of US$ 0.2928 per Lumen on January 3, 2022 (https://coinmarketcap.com/currencies/stellar/).

---

[18]   Ledger Insights (2019) 'Ripple's Blockchain Cross-border Payments Network Grows to 300' www.ledgerinsights.com/ripple-blockchain-300-customers/.
[19]   M Huillet (2020) 'Egyptian National Bank Turns to Blockchain to Boost Remittance Business' *Cointelegraph*, https://cointelegraph.com/news/egyptian-national-bank-turns-to-blockchain-to-boost-remittance-business.
[20]   Ripple (2020a) 'Azimo and SCB Runs on Ripple for Instant Payments into Thailand' https://ripple.com/insights/azimo-and-scb-runs-on-ripple-for-instant-payments-into-thailand/.
[21]   Ibid.
[22]   prefunding involves taking money from the sender and 'pushing' the money to a beneficiary partner bank or a beneficiary money transfer operator. (Khan, 2020) 'What Is Pre-Funding and How Does It Work?' https://faisalkhan.com/video/how-to-start-a-money-transfer-business-video-series/what-is-pre-funding-and-how-does-it-work/.
[23]   Ripple (2020b) 'On-demand Liquidity' https://ripple.com/ripplenet/on-demand-liquidity/.
[24]   Ledger Insights (2019) 'Ripple's Blockchain Cross-border Payments Network Grows to 300' www.ledgerinsights.com/ripple-blockchain-300-customers/.
[25]   Sean Williams (Jan 1, 2022) '7 Cryptocurrencies that Can Triple Your Money in 2022' https://www.fool.com/investing/2022/01/01/7-cryptocurrencies-can-triple-your-money-in-2022/?source=eptyholnk0000202&utm_source=yahoo-host&utm_medium=feed&utm_campaign=article.

Third, blockchain-based systems are more effective to deal with fraudulent practices. Especially due to the ease with which trade transactions can be falsified in the non-blockchain world, the use of fake export invoices to disguise cross-border capital flows has been pervasive in many developing economies. Such challenges can be addressed with blockchain-based systems.

A further benefit of blockchain-based payment and settlement systems concerns a lower counterparty risk, which is the risk that the other party in an investment, credit, or trading transaction may fail to fulfil its part of the deal or default on the contractual obligations. It is argued that decentralized, open blockchains such as Bitcoin eliminate counterparty risks.[26]

Finally, despite some challenges,[27] blockchain-based payment and settlement systems perform better than most other systems in terms of the settlement finality. In a digital currency transaction, just like in an exchange of banknotes, as soon as the possession changes, a final settlement is reached between the parties. Due to the 'immediate finality' feature of CBDCs, no clogging will occur in the payment system unlike in the clearing and settlement systems involving bank-to-merchant transactions.[28] With transactions such as cashless payments by card, wire, cheque and digital apps, a deal is not fully settled when one party makes a payment to another. That is, until the banks have recorded, reconciled, and settled their respective debits and credits, there is a possibility that the transaction could be reversed.[29] In China, for instance, Alipay and WeChat Pay rely on commercial banks to settle payments.[30] Parties that rely on private companies such as Alipay and WeChat pay face risks such as business failure and bankruptcy of various companies in a payment ecosystem.

---

[26] Exodus (n.d.)'What Is Counterparty Risk? – Exodus Support.' [online] support. exodus.com. Available at: https://support.exodus.com/article/794-what-is-counterparty -risk#:~:text=Please%20note%3A%20Counterparty%20risk%20is.

[27] D Liebau and A Mohammed (Oct 1, 2020) 'Finality: A Necessary Condition for Blockchain Applications in Finance' https://blockchain.news/wiki/instant-finality -necessary-condition-blockchain-applications-finance.

[28] M. Casey (2020) 'Why the U.S. Shouldn't Let China Dominate the Digital Currency Race' *Fortune*, https://fortune.com/2020/04/07/china-us-digital-currency -coronavirus/.

[29] D. Nelson (2021) 'BIS: CBDC Research Gaining Steam but Widespread Issuance Years Away' *Coindesk*, https://www.coindesk.com/cbdc-central-bank-digital -currency-survey-2020.

[30] A. Kharpal (2021) 'China Has Given Away Millions in Its Digital Yuan Trials. This Is How It Works' *CNBC*, https://www.cnbc.com/2021/03/05/chinas-digital-yuan -what-is-it-and-how-does-it-work.html.

6.3   KEY PAYMENT AND SETTLEMENT APPLICATION AREAS BENEFITTING FROM BLOCKCHAIN

In this section, we discuss some key payment and settlement application areas that can greatly benefit from blockchain deployment.

6.3.1   DeFi

DeFi (decentralized finance) is a term used to refer to blockchain projects that focus on eliminating any human involvement from financial services. DeFi relies on decentralized networks such as blockchain to create financial products utilizing trustless and transparent protocols, which run without intermediaries (https://defiprime.com/). Proponents of DeFi, have argued that such an approach would provide faster and more inclusive financial services in a transparent manner.[31]

In December 2019, the DeFi ecosystem was valued at US$ 700 million.[32] It increased to more than US$ 7.8 billion by August 30, 2020 (https://defipulse.com/) and US$ 13 billion by December 2020.[33]

Starting in 2018, DeFi began to have success. Blockchain-based smart contracts have led to the emergence of many innovative financial products such as flash loans (See In Focus 6.3: What is a flash loan?). As of November 19, 2021, the DeFi crypto market capitalization was US$ 154.16 billion (https://coinmarketcap.com/view/defi/). All the top five DeFi tokens by market capitalization on this date had been launched in January 2019 or later. For instance, Avalanche's native AVAX token (ranked #1) was launched in 2020,[34] and Terra's Luna (ranked #2) was launched in April 2019.[35] The DeFi tokens with

---

[31]   *The Financial Times* (Dec 29, 2019) '"DeFi" Movement Promises High Interest but High Risk.' [online] Available at: https://www.ft.com/content/16db565a-25a1-11ea-9305-4234e74b0ef3.
[32]   R Ma (2020) 'How DeFi Is Reinventing the World's Financial System' *Forbes*, https://www.forbes.com/sites/forbestechcouncil/2020/08/28/how-defi-is-reinventing-the-worlds-financial-system/#509bc4fdbc14.
[33]   Kenneth Rapoza (March 21, 2021) 'What's the Big Deal about DeFi and How Do You Invest in It?' https://www.forbes.com/sites/kenrapoza/2021/03/21/whats-the-big-deal-about-defi-and-how-do-you-invest-in-it/?sh=629ad4e89ceb.
[34]   yahoo.com (2021) 'Avalanche's AVAX Token Surges to All-time High after Deloitte Deal, Defying Crypto Trend.' [online] Available at: https://www.yahoo.com/now/avalanche-avax-token-surges-time-160614818.html.
[35]   Proactiveinvestors NA (2021) 'Terra (Luna): Everything You Need to Know about the Alt-coin' [online] Available at: https://www.proactiveinvestors.com/companies/news/965446/terra-luna-everything-you-need-to-know-about-the-alt-coin-965446.html.

the next three biggest market capitalization – Wrapped Bitcoin's WBTC, Chainlink's LINK and Uniswap's Uni were launched in January 2019,[36] May 2019[37] and September 2020 respectively.[38]

IN FOCUS 6.3 WHAT IS A FLASH LOAN?

A flash loan is uncollateralized lending that several decentralized finance (DeFi) protocols based on the Ethereum network offer. Flash loans have the following unique properties:

a. Smart contracts ensure that the borrower pays back the loan before the transaction ends. If the borrower fails to pay back, the smart contract reverses the transaction. It is thus like a loan that never happened;
b. Unsecured: no collateral is required but the lender will get their money back in a different way. The borrower needs to pay back the money right away;
c. Instant: the smart contract for the loan needs to be fulfilled in the same transaction in which the loan is lent out. For instance, the smart contract for the loan interacts with other smart contracts that perform instant trades with the capital that has been loaned before the transaction ends.[a] The contract checks whether the borrower paid back the loan. If it has not been paid back, the transaction will be reversed.[b]

For instance, one can buy a US$ 1 million house using a flash loan if there is already another buyer lined up, who would pay higher so that the borrower can make a profit. As an example, a Cryptopunk NFT (non-fungible token) was sold for US$ 532 million in October 2021, which was the most expensive NFT until then. However, it was suspected that the buyer and the seller were the same person. The person transferred the NFT from Wallet A to Wallet B. Wallet C then bought the NFT from Wallet B. After that transaction, the NFT was transferred back to Wallet A. The three wallets were needed because the buyer needed to get a flash loan from others.[c] The participants voice over Internet protocol (VoIP), instant messaging and digital distribution platform Discord, and Twitter noticed the sale. As to the

---

[36] SoFi (2021) 'What is The Wrapped Bitcoin' (WBTC)? [online] Available at: https://www.sofi.com/learn/content/what-is-the-wrapped-bitcoin/#:~:text=Launched %20in%20January%202019%2C%20the.
[37] Ibid.
[38] The Motley Fool (2021) 'What Is Uniswap (UNI), and Should You Buy It?' [online] Available at: https://www.fool.com/the-ascent/cryptocurrency/articles/what-is -uniswap-uni-and-should-you-buy-it/.

motives, it is speculated that the transaction was the owner's publicity stunt to drive up the price of their CryptoPunk.

In traditional finance, this type of transaction is viewed as 'wash trading',[d] in which one person sets up what looks like a legitimate purchase-and-sale deal, but actually does the deal with themselves. That makes it look like there is more activity in the market than there actually is, artificially increasing demand and value.

Notes:
[a] A Hertig (2021) 'DeFi What Is a Flash Loan?' https://www.coindesk.com/learn/2021/02/17/what-is-a-flash -loan/.
[b] A Castor (Nov 1, 2021) 'Did a CryptoPunk NFT Just Sell for $500 Million? Sort of, in a Transaction that Illuminates How the NFT Market Differs from the Art Market' https://news.artnet.com/art-world/crypto -punk-500-million-sale-2028470.
[c] D Van Boom (Dec 19, 2021) 'Why This CryptoPunk NFT Sold for $532 Million. Sort of' https://www.cnet .com/news/the-cryptopunk-nft-that-sold-for-532-million-sort-of/.
[d] Bloomberg (May 24, 2018) 'Justice Department Opens Criminal Probe into Price Manipulation of Bitcoin, Other Digital Currencies' https://www.latimes.com/business/la-fi-bitcoin-investigation-20180524-story.html.

Most of the DeFi protocols run on Ethereum.[39] However, other blockchains are rapidly replacing Ethereum. Ethereum's share in TVL (total value locked) within DeFi declined from 98 per cent in January 2021 to 68.5 per cent in October 2021.[40] According to DefiLlama, which is a website and newsletter focusing on DeFi projects and their metrics, the TVL or the value of the tokens held in smart contracts in lending or trading within DeFi protocols platforms exceeded US$ 200 billion in October 2021. About US$ 140 billion of that amount was on the Ethereum.[41]

To be effective, most smart contracts require the use of a trusted third party, referred to as an oracle. Oracles need to be free from censorship and corruption and resistant to government regulation and cyberattacks.[42] In most cases, no satisfactory solution for an oracle currently exists. DeFi thus currently lacks a solid foundation. With the availability of relevant oracles in the future, DeFi has a potential to transform the financial landscape.

[39] S Li (2020) 'Ethereum Crypto Crashes to $340 after SushiSwap's Alleged Exit Scam' *Blockchain News*, https://blockchain.news/news/ethereum-crypto-crashes-340 -sushiswap-alleged-exit-scam.
[40] *The Fintech Times* (Oct 31, 2021) 'Hardbacon: 5 Fintech Trends that Will Reshape the Financial Services Landscape.' [online] *The Fintech Times*. Available at: https://thefintechtimes.com/hardbacon-5-fintech-trends-that-will-reshape-the-financial -services-landscape/.
[41] Ibid.
[42] K Torpey (2020) 'DeFi's Oracle Problem May Not Be Solvable' *Long Hash*, https://www.longhash.com/en/news/3324/DeFi%E2%80%99s-Oracle-Problem-May -Not-Be-Solvable.

6.3.2   Blockchain and International Remittances

In 2019, 200 million migrant workers sent money home to support over 800 million family members.[43] In 2020Q4, the cost of remittance averaged 10.96 per cent globally.[44] The transaction costs are especially higher for smaller remittances. Using MoneyGram, for example, a worker in the US, who wants to send US$ 50 to Ghana might have to pay US$ 10 in fees, meaning their family would receive only US$ 40.[45] Likewise, in order to transfer 300 Rand from South Africa to neighbouring countries, transfer fees varied from 35 to 68.2 Rand by bank draft to 19.2 to 62.5 Rand by electronic transfer, 25.3 Rand by Moneygram and 6.2 Rand by iKobo's services.[46]

As of April 2021, BitPesa, which provides cryptocurrency-based remittances for five currencies across Africa, had transacted US$ 235 million Bitcoin. By that time, it had served more than 26,000 customers, compared to 6,000 in 2017. Western Union teamed up with Coins.ph in the Philippines to offer mobile wallets to consumers, which allow them to hold and spend with both local and cryptocurrencies. The partnership is designed to make it easier for consumers in the country to receive cash remittances.[47]

It is reported that Kenya's Safaricom is considering adopting blockchain for remittance. Blockchain is expected to expand the M-Pesa service outside Kenya.[48] Note that M-Pesa allows consumers to make person-to-person transfers, receive mobile phone credits, pay school fees and electricity bills and save money. M-Pesa customers can pay off or collect on their loans with a text message.

Crypto remittances are being used to address challenges related to high costs and inefficiency in the international remittances market. In August 2021,

---

[43]   un.org (2021) Recovery and resilience through digital and financial inclusion https://www.un.org/en/observances/remittances-day.

[44]   The World Bank Group (2020) Remittance Prices Worldwide - Issue 36, December 2020 https://remittanceprices.worldbank.org/sites/default/files/rpw_main _report_and_annex_q42020.pdf.

[45]   News Ghana (Apr 10, 2017) 'Report Puts Ghana Amongst Countries With High Cost of Remittance' https://newsghana.com.gh/report-puts-ghana-amongst-countries -with-high-cost-of-remittance/.

[46]   N Kshetri (2017) 'Will Blockchain Emerge as a Tool to Break the Poverty Chain in the Global South?' *Third World Quarterly* Vol 38(8) 1710–32.

[47]   D Webber (Apr 21, 2021) 'Cryptocurrency In Cross-Border Payments: After Coinbase's Success, Can Crypto Flourish Beyond Assets?' https://www.forbes .com/sites/danielwebber/2021/04/21/cryptocurrency-in-cross-border-payments-after -coinbases-success-can-crypto-flourish-beyond-assets/?sh=7a02b53d416f.

[48]   CryptoGuru (2020) 'Safaricom Moves to Enable Bonga Point Digital Tokens for Payment Across Kenya' April 13, https://bitcoinke.io/2020/04/bonga-points-for -payment/.

Bitcoin exchange LocalBitcoins announced that there would be no deposit fees and transaction fees between wallets in the platform. The platform does not deal with fiat currency itself. Users can use the platform to transact with each other.[49] For instance, in order to send money from Venezuela to family members in Colombia, the sender buys Bitcoin with Venezuelan bolivars using a bank transfer in LocalBitcoins. The sender then can search sell offers of Bitcoin in Colombia and choose the offer with the best exchange rate. After the seller of Bitcoin in Colombia transfers Colombian peso to the family member's bank account, the sender transfers the Bitcoin. A user reported that the whole process takes less than an hour. The platform charges a 1 per cent fee to the user who offered to sell Bitcoins.[50] Other platforms such as Binance P2P and LocalCryptos offer similar services.[51]

New regulations related to cryptocurrency assets are also being put in place in some countries, which can reduce remittance costs. One example is the UAE. It is first worth noting that in 2020, migrant workers in the Gulf region sent US$ 43 billion in remittances to their home countries.[52] The high cost of remittance transfer fees has been a concern. In the third quarter of 2020, the global average cost of sending US$ 200 was 6.75 per cent of the amount.[53]

In 2020, the UAE's Securities and Commodities Authority specified conditions for offering crypto assets in the Emirates. Any entity providing such services must be formally licensed and comply with a number of laws related to anti-money laundering, cybersecurity and data protection. As of August 2021, six companies had satisfied the requirements of the regulations to create crypto exchanges. Two of them had reached the first stages of going live. One of them is crypto asset trading platform MidChains, which will be open to anyone. In order to use the services of crypto assets providers in UAE, clients are required

---

[49]   Namcios (2021) 'LocalBitcoins Cuts Deposit, Transaction Fees between Wallets in Platform to Zero.' [online] *Bitcoin Magazine*: Bitcoin News, Articles, Charts, and Guides. Available at: https://bitcoinmagazine.com/business/localbitcoins-reduce-fees -to-zero.

[50]   localbitcoins.com (n.d.) 'LocalBitcoins.com: Fastest and Easiest Way to Buy and Sell Bitcoins – LocalBitcoins.' [online] Available at: https://localbitcoins.com/fees.

[51]   CoinDesk (2020) 'Crypto Remittances Prove Their Worth in Latin America.' [online] Available at: https://www.coindesk.com/crypto-remittances-latin-america -geopolitical-tension.

[52]   S Essaid (Aug 3, 2021) 'Cryptocurrency Promise for UAE's Unbanked Migrants – But Not Yet' *Reuters*, Available at: https://www.reuters.com/article/emirates-tech -migrants/update-1-cryptocurrency-promise-for-uaes-unbanked-migrants-but-not-yet -idUSL8N2PA7UG.

[53]   *The National* (2020) 'How Covid-19 Transformed the UAE's Remittance Sector in 2020.' [online] Available at: https://www.thenationalnews.com/business/money/ how-covid-19-transformed-the-uae-s-remittance-sector-in-2020-1.1131325.

to provide a number of documents such as proof of residence, income and secure assets. Such requirements may prevent migrant workers from using the services. In the future, remittances are expected to be a regular feature of the UAE's cryptocurrency services.[54]

6.3.3 Crypto-denominated International Commerce

In recent years, crypto-denominated international commerce has become increasingly common.[55] Small businesses in developing economies are improving speed and efficiency by making payments in cryptocurrencies rather than in major international currencies, such as the US dollar and euro. To take an example, a Nigerian vendor of handsets and accessories, who sourced their products from China and the United Arab Emirates, reported that his suppliers prefer payments in cryptocurrencies. Paying with cryptocurrencies also increased his profits since he did not have to buy US dollars using the Nigerian naira or pay expensive fees to money-transfer agencies.[56]

The use of cryptocurrencies has been reported to grow in developing economies, such as those in Africa. According to US blockchain research firm Chainalysis, monthly cryptocurrency transfers of under US$ 10,000, which are typically made by individuals and small businesses, to and from Africa increased by more than 55 percent between June 2019 and June 2020 to reach US$ 316 million.[57]

Likewise, from June 2019 to June 2020, Latin America sent US$ 25 billion worth of cryptocurrency and received US$ 24 billion.[58] The Chainalysis data showed that East Asia was Latin America's significant counterparty.[59] The blockchain research firm's interviews with Latin America-based cryptocurrency operators indicated that many of the payments were commercial transactions between East Asia-based exporters and Latin American importers. A Paraguay-based cryptocurrency exchange explained that businesses in

---

[54] Essaid (n 52).

[55] N Kshetri (2021) *Blockchain and Supply Chain Management* (Elsevier, Amsterdam, Netherlands, Oxford, UK, New York, USA).

[56] M Orcutt (2020) 'Cryptocurrency May Be Supercharging Trade between Latin America and Eastern Asia' *The Block*, https://www.theblockcrypto.com/post/76839/cryptocurrency-eastern-asia-latin-america-trade-chainalysis.

[57] A Akwagyiram and T Wilson (2020) 'How Bitcoin Met the Real World in Africa' *Reuters*, https://www.reuters.com/article/us-crypto-currencies-africa-insight/how-bitcoin-met-the-real-world-in-africa-idUSKBN25Z0Q8.

[58] Orcutt (n 56).

[59] Chainalysis (2020) 'How Latin America Mitigates Economic Turbulence with Cryptocurrency' *Cahinalysis*, https://blog.chainalysis.com/reports/latin-america-cryptocurrency-market-2020.

Paraguay import significant amounts of goods from China. Some of them are then exported to other countries, such as Brazil. Many of the importers make payments using Bitcoin because of the speed and ease with which they can settle the payments. Due to concerns related to money laundering, banks in Paraguay are reluctant to do businesses with most companies. The banking application process is complex, which requires many supporting documents and takes a long time. Moreover, even if a business's application to make a payment in international currencies is approved, wire transfers are costly. Moreover, by making payments in cryptocurrencies, they avoid import taxes.[60]

6.3.4   Supply Chain Finance and Trade Finance

Supply chain finance (SCF) involves financial tools that are used to improve payments between companies and their suppliers. Upstream supply chain members such as manufacturers and raw material suppliers are not paid immediately after shipping products. In international trades, there is a time lag between an exporter's shipping of goods and an importer paying for them. SCF bridges this gap. SCF solutions represent technology solutions and financial services to connect various supply chain partners. The goal is to improve the effectiveness of financial supply chains by decreasing or even preventing the cost-shifting practices, which entail shifting inventory or other operating costs to supply chain partners. Such tactics can reduce a company's internal costs in the short term but not the total supply chain costs in the long run.[61] In order to improve the effectiveness of financial supply chains, downstream supply chain partners need to improve the visibility, availability, as well as costs of cash for upstream participants.[62]

In order to cover their working capital needs, suppliers borrow money at a higher cost than paid by the buyer.[63] For instance, manufacturers rely on intermediaries that pay immediately, but do not pay in full. In the above example, for instance, a US$ 100 invoice to a hospital might be worth US$ 90

---

[60]   Ibid.
[61]   scdigest.com (2013) 'Supply Chain News: What Are the Barriers to Lean Success?' *Scdigest*, http://www.scdigest.com/ontarget/13-01-30-2.php?cid=6680.
[62]   J Lamoureux.and T Evans (2011) 'Supply Chain Finance: A New Means to Support the Competitiveness and Resilience of Global Value Chains' *SSRN*, https://papers.ssrn.com/sol3/papers.cfm?abstract_id=2179944.
[63]   S George (2019) 'Blockchain-enabled Supply Chain Sustainability Scheme Hailed "successful" by Business Giants' *Edie Newsroom*, https://www.edie.net/news/8/Blockchain-enabled-supply-chain-sustainability-scheme-hailed--successful--by-business-giants/.

right away – and the intermediary would collect the US\$ 100 when it is finally paid.[64]

Trade finance is a broader term that encompasses financing to suppliers in order to help them manufacture goods and as well to buyers to help them buy those goods. Trade-related supplier financing is made available through bank loans, which are backed by insured foreign accounts receivable by selling accounts receivable to a factoring company.[65] Trade credit insurers provide protection to banks. However, they cover 50–90 per cent of loan amount.[66]

A current challenge is that there is a big gap between the demand and supply of trade finance. According to the Asian Development Bank (ADB), the global trade finance gap was US\$ 1.5 trillion, or 10 per cent of merchandise trade volume in 2018. This gap is expected to increase to US\$ 2.4 trillion by 2025.[67]

A challenge is that banks are not willing to lend money in places where fraudulent invoices are common, or where manufacturers and their customers might have inconsistent and error-ridden records. A blockchain system reduces those concerns because these records must be authenticated before being added to the ledger, and due to the distributed nature, they cannot be manipulated and changed.

Some studies have suggested that the global trade finance gap can be reduced by US\$ 1 trillion if blockchain is more widely used.[68] Blockchain-based smart contracts and single digital records for customs clearance are among the important mechanisms that enable SMEs' (small and medium-sized enterprises) access to trade finance by reducing credit risks, lowering fees and removing barriers to trade. Indeed, it is argued that SMEs in emerging markets can benefit more from the implementation of blockchain-based solutions than from the removal of tariffs or negotiation of trade deals.[69]

Currently high costs of financing prohibit the participation of many developing world-based small firms in international trade activities. These can be often attributed to high costs of due diligence. For instance, due primarily to

---

[64]   Kshetri (n 46).

[65]   Lamoureux and Evans (n 62).

[66]   P Tan (2020) 'Coronavirus Hastens Trade Finance's Blockchain Moment' *BBN Times*, https://www.bbntimes.com/technology/coronavirus-hastens-trade-finance -s-blockchain-moment.

[67]   P Vanham (2018) 'Blockchain Could Enable \$1 Trillion in Trade, Mostly for SMEs and Emerging Markets' *World Economic Forum*, https://www.weforum .org/press/2018/09/blockchain-could-enable-1-trillion-in-trade-mostly-for-smes-and -emerging-markets/.

[68]   Ibid.

[69]   Ibid.

frauds, bad loans account for about 20 per cent of bank loans in India.[70] Loan frauds in the country amount to about US$ 2 billion annually, which results in high interest rates due to low trust.[71]

Part of the problem also lies in the fact that many developing economies are characterized by the lack, or poor performance, of credit rating agencies to provide information about the creditworthiness of SMEs.[72] A national credit bureau would collect and distribute reliable credit information and hence increase transparency and minimize the banks' lending risks. Many emerging economies lack such an agency and some have a poorly functioning one. This situation puts SMEs in a disadvantaged position in the credit market. This is because SMEs tend to be more informationally opaque than large corporations because the former often lack certified audited financial statements, and thus it is difficult for banks to assess or monitor the financial conditions.[73]

In supply chain relationships, it is a common practice for buyers to evaluate the operational performance of suppliers. The process is referred to as vendor rating.[74] Information required to perform vendor rating is thus unavailable for small vendors from developing countries.

The above gap between the demand and supply of SCF can be partly attributed to the complexity of the traditional SCF models. For instance, the first-level suppliers (the suppliers to the buyer) need to contact lenders for a loan. They use the loan money to make payment to second-level suppliers (suppliers to the first-level suppliers) or to third-level suppliers. In some cases, the number of suppliers in an advanced global supply chain can be as deep as 13 layers. The funds thus may take many days or weeks to reach the actual manufacturer, which needs the money.[75]

[70]   W Suberg (2017) 'Indian Bank Wants Joint Effort to Share Data on Blockchain' *The Coin Telegraph*, https://cointelegraph.com/news/indian-bank-wants-joint-effort-to-sha///re-data-on-blockchain.
[71]   A Pitti (2018) 'Why India Can Become the Global Center for Blockchain Innovation' *Nasdaq*, https://www.nasdaq.com/article/why-india-can-become-the-global-center-for-blockchain-innovation-cm992358.
[72]   JE Stiglitz and A Weiss (1981) 'Credit Rationing in Markets with Imperfect Information' *American Economic Review* Vol 71(3), 393–410.
[73]   N Kshetri (2019) *Global Entrepreneurship: Environment and Strategy* (2nd edn, Routledge: New York).
[74]   D Luzzini, F Caniato and G Spina (2014) 'Designing Vendor Evaluation Systems: An Empirical Analysis' *Journal of Purchasing & Supply Management* Vol 20(2) 113–29.
[75]   M Del Castillo (2017) 'Legally Binding Smart Contracts? 10 Law Firms Join Enterprise Ethereum Alliance' *Coindesk*, https://www.coindesk.com/legally-binding-smart-contracts-9-law-firms-join-enterprise-ethereum-alliance/.

A typical cross-border transaction involves many parties. A letter of credit (LC), which is a promise to pay for the goods if certain conditions are fulfilled – is sent to the exporter by the bank of the importer. After receiving the LC, the exporter ships the goods. The risk that the bank faces is that the importer may be unable or unwilling to pay. The exporter then presents proof of shipping to get financing from its bank. The exporter's bank is paid directly by the importer's bank. Estimates suggest that, on the average, a single cross-border trade transaction involves the exchange of 36[76] to 40 different documents.[77] As many as 240 copies of such documents need to be exchanged among various parties such as financiers, logistics providers. customs officers and warehouse managers.[78]

Blockchain offers tremendous potential to address the various challenges noted above. A JP Morgan report published in early 2020 on enterprise blockchain and digital currencies identified trade finance, especially LC, as the most promising application.[79] In May 2020, China's National Internet Finance Association (NIFA) published a report about blockchain. Among all financial applications, SCF, trade finance and insurance accounted for 32.6 per cent, 11.2 per cent and 11.2 per cent of all applications respectively.[80]

The US computer technology corporation Oracle has claimed that in general, by automating trade finance processes such as LC issuance, processing times can be cut by 60 per cent, and time required to enter and scrutinize data can be shortened by 70 per cent.[81] With blockchain, it is also possible for all parties to see instantly all data related to transactions. Such data can have dramatic impact on the cost and availability of trade finance. Organizations using a common digital platform to track trade finance can also access data pools about potential clients as well as their transaction histories. New entrants such as institutional investors and technology firms that are interested in offering financing or refinancing also have access to such data. For these players, trade finance may yield higher returns than other options available to them such as public bonds. An upshot of competition is that the cost of basic trade financing

---

[76]   L Fletcher (2019) 'Forget The Paper Trail – Blockchain Set to Shake Up Trade Finance' *The Financial Times*, https://www.ft.com/content/04a4fcde-dfb5-11e9-b8e0 -026e07cbe5b4.

[77]   Lamoureux and Evans (n 62).

[78]   Fletcher (n 76).

[79]   Ledger Insights (2020) 'JP Morgan Blockchain Report Picks Trade Finance as Winner, Says Libra's Release "Failed"' *Ledger Insights*, https://www.ledgerinsights .com/jp-morgan-blockchain-trade-finance-libra-release-failed/.

[80]   Ibid.

[81]   Oracle (2020) 'Transform the Future of Trade Finance' *Oracle Corporation*, https://www.oracle.com/a/ocom/docs/industries/financial-services/trade-finance -process-management-br.pdf.

may fall close to zero. Banks may find it more attractive to make money by selling data about exporters or importers.

Some solutions currently aim to increase the availability of trade finance for domestic trade transactions. The technology and experience gained from this situation can transfer to facilitate international trade in the future. As discussed in Chapter 2, India's consumer electrical equipment manufacturing company, Bajaj Electricals, digitized vendor financing using blockchain.[82] As of mid-2018, 14 Indian banks had signed up to use the services of the blockchain platform India Trade Connect consortium, which was developed by the local software firm Infosys. The platform facilitates the issuance of loans that are backed by trade transactions.[83] The banks account for about half of India's internal trade. The solution is expected to speed up processes for approving new loans.

6.4   BLOCKCHAIN AND FINANCIAL INCLUSION

Blockchain can address various challenges associated with low-income people's lack of access to financial services. A notable feature of some blockchain-based solutions is the ability to aggregate information from many sources to build economic history. This aspect is especially important for developing economies because most of them lack reliable credit information on most people and companies, which is needed to minimize bank lending risks. Limited credit information can be attributed to the fact that Global South economies either lack a national credit bureau or have a poorly functioning one. For this reason, reliable credit information is not being collected and distributed to increase transparency and minimize bank lending risks.[84] In China, only 20 per cent of the adult population has a credit score.[85] Sierra Leone has one credit bureau with information on only 2,000 of the country's

---

[82]   R Kasteleln (2017) 'China Poised to Dominate Fintech and Blockchain Markets in 2017' *BlockchainNews*, http://www.the-blockchain.com/2017/01/04/indias-yes-bank-enlists-ibm-help-build-blockchain-solutions/.

[83]   R Satija and A Antony (2018) 'Banks Turn to Blockchain to Speed Up Indian Internal Trade Deals' *Bloomberg*, https://www.bloomberg.com/news/articles/2018-06-06/banks-turn-to-blockchain-to-speed-up-indian-internal-trade-deals.

[84]   N Kshetri (2019a) *Global Entrepreneurship: Environment and Strategy* (2nd edn, Routledge, New York); N Kshetri (2019b) 'Cybercrime and Cybersecurity in Africa' *Journal of Global Information Technology Management* Vol 22(2), 77–81.

[85]   S Lohr (2015) 'ZestFinance Takes Its Big Data Credit Scoring to China' *ZestFinance*, http://bits.blogs.nytimes.com/2015/06/26/zestfinance-takes-its-big-data-credit-scoring-to-china/ (Accessed 18 February 2016).

seven million people.[86] To overcome this challenge, theoretically, borrowers can show blockchain-based credit information to lenders and receive loans more easily.[87]

To take an example, the US-based blockchain company BanQu utilizes blockchain to establish economic identities and proof of record (which it calls 'economic passports') for unbanked persons.[88] A blockchain-based verifiable digital identity is expected to help disadvantaged groups establish ownership, business assets and production values and help them engage in economic transactions. It aggregates information from a number of sources, such as those related to financial history, land records, trust networks documenting trust-relationships with others, business registrations, vaccination records and remittance income. ID-related information sources include selfies, biometrics and key physical attributes. Blockchain's decentralized, secure ledger also provides Know Your Customer and other information to partners that can potentially offer products and services to these disadvantaged individuals.[89]

Another problem that blockchain might address is related to the lack of formal identity documents. Potential borrowers in many Global South economies cannot prove who they are, which is among the main reasons why many low-income people lack access to financial services. According to the World Bank's Identification for Development (ID4D) database, one billion people lack any form of identification. An additional 3.4 billion people have some type of identification, but lack the ability to use it in the digital world.[90] Sierra Leone addressed the above problem by launching in August 2019 a blockchain-based National Digital Identity Platform developed by Kiva.[91]

---

[86] A Hudli (2018) 'Sierra Leone to Develop Blockchain-based ID Platform with UN Partnership' https://www.coindesk.com/sierra-leone-to-develop-blockchain-based-identity-platform-with-un-partnership.

[87] A Stanley (2017) 'Microlending Startups Look to Blockchain for Loans' *Coindesk*, https://www.coindesk.com/microlending-trends-startups-look-blockchain-loans.

[88] Ibid.

[89] G White (2018) 'BanQu Seeks to Transform the Lives of Millions by Empowering Them with an Economic Identity' *Social Fintech*, https://socialfintech.org/banqu-seeks-to-transform-the-lives-of-millions-by-empowering-them-with-an-economic-identity/.

[90] O White, A Madgavkar, J Manyika, D Mahajan, J Bughin, M McCarthy and O Sperling (April, 2019) 'Digital Identification: A Key to Inclusive Growth' *McKinsey. com*, https://www.mckinsey.com/business-functions/digital-mckinsey/our-insights/ Digital-identification-A-key-to-inclusive-growth?cid=other-eml-alt-mgi-mck&hlkid= ecd8822bafc44de78b1f2670c2979652&hctky=2259579&hdpid=0945f28e-3aa8-4f73 -a111-6ba86e377b51.

[91] C Inveen (2019) 'San Francisco Crowdfunder Kiva Sets Up Sierra Leone Credit Database' *Reuters*, https://www.reuters.com/article/us-leone-kiva/san-francisco -crowdfunder-kiva-sets-up-.

(See In Focus 6.4: Kiva's solution to address the lack of formal identification and credit history, below).

IN FOCUS 6.4 KIVA'S SOLUTION TO ADDRESS THE LACK OF FORMAL IDENTIFICATION AND CREDIT HISTORY

Kiva's blockchain protocol aims to address two major barriers that hinders poor people's access to financial services: formal identification and verifiable credit history.[a] Kiva worked with the UN Capital Development Fund (UNCDF) and the UN Development Programme (UNDP) to develop a blockchain-based ID system in Sierra Leone. In August 2019, the government of Sierra Leone launched a blockchain-based National Digital Identity Platform (NDIP), which was developed by Kiva. Sierra Leone's government wants all banks and MFIs to use the system.[b]

Transactions are recorded in blockchain. A borrower will be assigned with a digital wallet, which will be accessible through an app. Individuals can access their wallets on cellphones. They can also work with an MFI or other agents that are already working in their community. The agents can also use the application offline[c] Lenders can view borrower's credit histories in the NDIP platform.[d]

When a lender provides a loan, the borrower gets a verifiable claim with all details. The borrower accepts the claim. The loan is then posted to the borrower's private credit ledger in the Kiva wallet. The same process is repeated when the borrower makes a loan repayment. The borrower approves a verifiable claim sent by the lender, which is then posted to the ledger. All credit-related events are thus captured in a single ledger connected to the wallet controlled by an individual. Financial institutions, government agencies and third-party agencies can access the information only with the owner's consent.

If a potential borrower's credit history has been verified by a local lender or Kiva Field Partner, the information can be accessed by other lenders. For instance, the borrower can apply for a loan from a national bank using the verified information. The new lender can get one-time access to the credit history of the borrower. The cost to operate the Kiva system is low. It eliminates fees that might prevent poor people or institutions from using other credit reports.

Kiva Protocol is built on Hyperledger Fabric. A member organization (e.g., Kiva) is responsible for setting up its peers to participate in the network. Kiva administers access to the nodes. Partners such as banks and government agencies act as peers. The users can share information that only the members can see. Once entered into the blockchain, the information cannot be altered. With this system people get secure and complete ownership of their personal information.

Notes:

[a] Cheney (2019) 'In Sierra Leone, New Kiva Protocol Uses Blockchain to Benefit Unbanked' *Devex*, https://www.devex.com/news/in-sierra-leone-new-kiva-protocol-uses-blockchain-to-benefit-unbanked-95490.
[b] C Inveen (2019) 'San Francisco Crowdfunder Kiva Sets Up Sierra Leone Credit Database' *Reuters*, https://www.reuters.com/article/us-leone-kiva/san-francisco-crowdfunder-kiva-sets-up-.
[c] Kiva (2019) 'Kiva Protocol FAQ' *Kiva*, https://pages.kiva.org/kiva-protocol-faq.
[d] tokenpost.com (2019) 'Sierra Leone Launches Blockchain-based National Digital Identity Platform' *Tokenpost*, https://www.tokenpost.com/Sierra-Leone-launches-blockchain-based-National-Digital-Identity-Platform-3139.

Blockchain-based solutions make peer-to-peer lending possible by directly connecting lenders and borrowers thereby eliminating the need for intermediaries. Doing this, the costs of financial services can be reduced. As an example, consider Kiva (see In Focus 6.4). The company does not make direct loans. While some investors mistakenly think that Kiva offers direct person-to-person connections, it actually works with local MFIs (microfinance institutions) as middlemen.[92] Kiva says that it conducts audits of its Field Partners to ensure that poor people are not exploited.[93] However, due to high overhead costs and other sources of inefficiency, Kiva Field Partners charge exorbitantly high interest rates. For instance, a Kiva Field Partner in Senegal was reported to charge an interest rate of 40 per cent.[94]

Such loans could be made more affordable by eliminating the middlemen such as Kiva Field Partners. In this regard, programs such as Kiva's blockchain-based IDs are a first step towards improving access to finance for the poor. True decentralization will be complete when impact investors and philanthropic funders can directly reach the poor with cryptocurrencies.

6.5   CHAPTER SUMMARY AND CONCLUSION

One of the biggest value propositions of blockchain is its ability to make payments and settlement more efficient. Especially there is a great need to increase efficiency and reduce costs in cross-border payments and settlement. For instance, many families living in refugee camps in Africa rely on remittances from friends and relatives overseas to survive. Blockchain is bringing a funda-

[92] S Strom (Nov 8, 2009) 'Confusion on Where Money Lent via Kiva Goes' *New York Times*, 12–13.
[93] J Barry (2012) 'Microfinance, the Market and Political Development in the Internet Age' *Third World Quarterly* Vol 33(1) 125–41.
[94] femalefounderstories.com (2019) *Julia Kurnia, Female Founder Stories*, http://www.femalefounderstories.com/julia-kurnia.html.

mental transformation to the way the international remittance market is functioning. A further encouraging development is the dramatic reduction in costs and increase in efficiency of South–South trade, thanks to recent developments in blockchain-based FinTechs and cryptocurrencies. Cryptocurrencies also can prove attractive to consumers and businesses in economies suffering from high inflation, high interest rates and unstable currency exchange rates.

Thanks to blockchain, new categories of financial instruments are also emerging. For instance, DeFi aims to replace the legacy financial system with smart contracts, which removes the need for trusted third parties.

The current trend of central bank activities clearly shows that CBDC is likely to be the future of banking and payments. The arrival of CBDC is set to transform the way payment and settlement systems function.

PART III

Opportunities, challenges, implications and the way forward

7. Opportunities, barriers and enablers of blockchain adoption in organizations

7.1   INTRODUCTION

As noted in Chapter 1, blockchain has been viewed as being among the biggest innovations and a computing mega-trend with a potential to bring economic, political, and social transformations. However, that promise has been far from realized. The diffusion and adoption of blockchain also vary widely across economies, industries and organizations. For instance, a number of successful uses of blockchain deployment have been reported in supply chains. As discussed in this book, companies such as Walmart, Carrefour and Maersk have used blockchain as a tool to reduce costs, increase the quality of products and enhance brand image. In the B2C (Business-to-Customer) setting, the video game industry is the most promising that is likely to drive the growth of blockchain[1] (see In Focus 7.1 below).

IN FOCUS 7.1 VIDEO GAMES SUPPORTING THE MASS ADOPTION OF BLOCKCHAINS AND CRYPTOCURRENCIES

Video games, especially multiplayer, online games such as Axie Infinity, Splinterlands, Roblox, Fortnite, Minecraft and Animal Crossing are supporting the mass adoption of blockchains and cryptocurrencies. According to DappRadar, more than 1 million digital wallets were connected to decentralized gaming applications every day in October 2021. These accounted for 55 per cent of the blockchain industry's overall activity in that month. The global gaming market is expected to reach US$ 178.4 billion in 2021 and US$ 268.8 billion in 2025.[a] As points of comparison, in terms of annual revenues, the global film industry is valued at US$ 100 billion and North American sports are US$ 73 billion.[b]

---

[1]   L Jiang (April 26, 2019) 'The Last Mile Problem: Understanding the Economics Affecting the Future of Blockchain' https://www.datadriveninvestor.com/2019/04/26/the-last-mile-problem-understanding-the-economics-affecting-the-future-of-blockchain/.

In the non-blockchain world of online gaming, which takes place in walled off networks of private gaming companies, users do not own their in-game assets such as avatar characters, virtual lands and weapons. The gaming platform owns them. New players such as Axie Infinity are disrupting this model by making it possible for users to own their assets, such as NFTs (non-fungible tokens). They can sell these assets in a free-market gaming economy for profit.[c] Thus, blockchain can help deliver the surplus value that ownership of a game asset is supposed to produce to gamers.

Incorporation of NFTs in games allow players to claim ownership of game assets in three main ways: creating or breeding new characters, purchasing digital items on native or third-party marketplaces, and earning new items. NFT-based online video game Axie Infinity, for instance, uses Ethereum-based cryptocurrency AXS (Axie Infinity Shards) and SL. Axie Infinity players breed and gather digital creatures called Axies, whose goal is to combat other players. Each Axie has a unique genetic fingerprint. The strengths and shortcomings of Axies are passed to their descendants. Axies are tradable on Ethereum NFT markets. The price of a given digital creature depends on its rarity and distinctive characteristics.[d]

In a survey conducted among 197 video game developers in the US and UK by blockchain platform Stratis, which was released in November 2021, 58 per cent of the respondents had begun using blockchain and 47 per cent had begun incorporating NFTs in their games; 72 per cent of the respondents participating in the survey said that they would consider using blockchain and NFTs for new games and 56 per cent were planning to do so in the next 12 months; 64 per cent of the respondents believed that blockchain would become prevalent in video gaming within the next two years and 53 per cent thought that NFTs would be more common by then. As to the benefits of blockchain in video games, 61 per cent of respondents said that blockchain makes games innovative and more interesting and 55 per cent believed that blockchain can help secure value for players. Other benefits of blockchain that respondents thought included rewarding players with real-word value (54 per cent) and network effects that incentivize the adoption of games (45 per cent).[e]

Notes:
[a] cryptelicious.com (2021) 'Why Video Games Will Boost Blockchain and Crypto Adoption.' [online] *Cryptelicious*, Available at: https://www.cryptelicious.com/2021/11/14/why-video-games-will-boost -blockchain-and-crypto-adoption/.
[b] Cointelegraph (2021) '5 Reasons Why Blockchain-based Gaming Economies Are the Future.' [online] Available at: https://cointelegraph.com/news/5-reasons-why-blockchain-based-gaming-economies-are-the -future.
[c] Ibid.
[d] thecanadian (2021) 'Top NFT Games in 2021: Ranked.' [online] *The Canadian*, Available at: https:// thecanadian.news/2021/10/21/top-nft-games-in-2021-ranked/.
[e] stratisplatform.com (n.d.) 'Video Game Developers Reveal Overwhelming Appetite for Blockchain and NFT Technology in a New Research Study from Stratis.' [online] *www.prnewswire.com*, Available at: https://www.prnewswire.com/news-releases/video-game-developers-reveal-overwhelming-appetite-for -blockchain-and-nft-technology-in-a-new-research-study-from-stratis-301420448.html.

The government sector, on the other hand, has been among the low performing sectors in terms of the adoption of blockchain. A 2019 report of the European Commission noted that blockchain 'has not yet demonstrated to be either transformative or even disruptive innovation for governments as it is sometimes portrayed'.[2] The report further suggested that ongoing blockchain projects have brought only incremental rather than fundamental changes to governments' operational capacities.

Even for a given application such as supply chain traceability, the difficulty of applying blockchain varies depending on the product being traced. A key challenge lies in mapping minerals and metals in one state to the successive stages of a supply chain. For instance, Tracr reported that matching a polished piece with the rough piece it came from involves a high degree of complexity.[3] The tasks of mapping and matching materials in successive stages are even more challenging for metals and minerals such as cobalt, zinc, gold, copper and silver. These products undergo physical and chemical transformations with the utilization of thermal treatment in the pyrometallurgy process and application of aqueous solutions in the hydrometallurgy process.

There are also high cross-country differences in the adoption of different applications of blockchain. For instance, a 2020 Statista Global Consumer Survey conducted in 74 countries found that 32 per cent of Nigerians used or owned cryptocurrency compared to 4 per cent in Japan. The survey found that Vietnam (21 per cent) and the Philippines (20 per cent) ranked second and third in the adoption of cryptocurrency. The Statista survey attributed the

[2]   D Allessie, M Sobolewski and L Vaccari (2019) *Blockchain for Digital Government*, F Pignatelli (ed), EUR 29677 EN, Publications Office of the European Union, Luxembourg, ISBN 978-92-76-00582-7, doi:10.2760/93808, JRC115049.
[3]   R Bates (2018) 'Inside Tracr, the De Beers-developed Blockchain Platform' *JCK*, https://www.jckonline.com/editorial-article/tracr-de-beers-blockchain-platform/.

high rates of cryptocurrency use in countries such as Nigeria, Vietnam and the Philippines to remittance payments.[4]

In order to get more insights into the above discussion, in this chapter, we focus on *key enablers* of the adoption of blockchain applications by organizations and individuals. We also offer an overview of opportunities and barriers in implementing blockchain and for this technology to act as an effective governance mechanism.

7.2   KEY ENABLERS

A number of factors and actors that have facilitated the adoption of blockchain.

7.2.1   Availability of Quick and Easy Options to Use Blockchain

An increasing competition in the area of enterprise blockchain has facilitated the adoption of this technology. There are several quick and easy options for enterprises to build blockchain projects. For instance, Hyperledger Fabric has become a popular enterprise blockchain platform for SCM (supply chain management). Several technology companies such as IBM, AWS (Amazon Web Service), SAP, Oracle and Microsoft offer enterprise blockchain solutions based on Hyperledger Fabric. For instance, SAP provides Hyperledger Fabric on its cloud platform. Likewise, Microsoft offers Hyperledger Fabric on Azure.[5]

In order to set up a blockchain based on Hyperledger Fabric, two components of costs are involved: infrastructure-related costs and the development cost. Most companies provide Hyperledger Fabric infrastructure. This means that companies do not need to worry about infrastructure, storage, and networking costs. A ready-made blockchain platform also has sharing, encryption, consensus algorithm, and P2P (Peer-to-Peer) network.[6]

Some blockchain platforms require only minimal IT skills. Toronto, Canada-based digital company Convergence.tech launched a blockchain pilot to trace the Mongolian Cashmere supply chains. The solution tracks the journey of these bales from the herders to a processing factory in Ulaanbaatar. The firm's two executives went to Mongolia to train the herders to use the blockchain. An Android app enables farmers to register their Cashmere bales

---

[4]   Katharina Buchholz (March 17, 2021) 'How Common Is Crypto?' https://www .statista.com/chart/18345/crypto-currency-adoption/.

[5]   devteam.space (2020) 'How Much Does It Cost to Build a Blockchain Project?' *DevTeam.Space*,   https://www.devteam.space/blog/how-much-does-it-cost-to-build-a -blockchain-project/.

[6]   Ibid.

with location tagging. These bales, along with the packing slips, are attached with high-frequency RFID (radio frequency identification) tags.[7]

7.2.2   Efforts of Civil Society Actors, Development and Multilateral Organizations and Other Powerful Actors

Various civil society actors, development and multilateral organizations and other powerful actors are taking a number of initiatives that are likely to intensify pressures on MNCs (multi-national companies) to demonstrate transparency in their supply chains using blockchain. Non-governmental organizations (NGOs) are trying to promote corporate social responsibility by naming and shaming companies knowingly and unknowingly responsible for human-rights abuse and child abuse in the DRC (Democratic Republic of Congo). In a 2016 article 'Is my phone powered by child labour?',[8] Amnesty International forcefully argued that global cellphone brands such as Apple and Samsung 'won't tell us if their cobalt supply chains are tainted by child labour. They have a responsibility to do so – to check for and address child labour in their supply chains, setting an example for the rest of the industry to follow'.

In October 2018, Amnesty International wrote to major carmakers – Daimler, Renault, Volkswagen, General Motors, Tesla, BMW and Fiat Chrysler – telling them that their supply chains potentially violate human rights. While all except Tesla were reported to respond, only three of them took essential first steps to address human rights abuse in their supply chains. Renault identified its cobalt suppliers. BMW and Daimler published details of smelters and refiners.[9]

Blockchain in mineral supply chains also have support of global actors such as the World Economic Forum. In October 2019, seven big mining companies – Antofagasta Minerals, Eurasian Resources Group Sàrl, Glencore, Klöckner & Co, Minsur SA, Tata Steel Ltd, Anglo American/De Beers – joined the World Economic Forum's Mining and Metals Blockchain Initiative.[10] The

---

[7]   Ledger Insights (2019) 'Glencore Joins IBM, Ford Blockchain Consortium for Cobalt Provenance' *Ledger Insights*, https://www.ledgerinsights.com/un-blockchain -cashmere-traceability-mongolia-convergence/.

[8]   Amnesty International (2016) 'Is My Phone Powered by Child Labour?' *Amnesty*, https://www.amnesty.org/en/latest/campaigns/2016/06/drc-cobalt-child-labour/.

[9]   J Gordon (2019) 'Cobalt: The Dark Side of a Clean Future' *Raconteur*, https:// www.raconteur.net/business-innovation/responsible-business-2019/cobalt-mining -human-rights.

[10]   A Russo (2019) 'Seven Mining, Metals Companies Partner on Responsible Sourcing with World Economic Forum' *World Economic Forum*, https://www .weforum.org/press/2019/10/seven-mining-metals-companies-partner-on-responsible -sourcing-with-world-economic-forum.

companies plan to create a blockchain platform to store information such as the tracing of materials and carbon emissions. They also want to address issues related to the lack of standardization. The intention is to send out a signal of inclusivity and collaboration across the industry. The initiative is expected to expand to small operations.[11]

7.2.3 Fast Developing Blockchain Ecosystem

As discussed in this book, a rich blockchain ecosystem is developing to facilitate smart contracts and other applications. In October 2021, the Associated Press (AP) announced that it would make its trusted economic, sports and race call data sets available to leading blockchains via Chainlink. This makes it possible for smart contracts on any blockchain to securely interact with the AP's real-world data. The data will be cryptographically signed to verify that it is from AP. By launching a Chainlink node, AP data is sold directly to and can be used by applications running across various blockchains.[12] Likewise, in December 2021, cryptocurrency exchange KuCoin announced a plan to adopt Chainlink Price Feeds to bring price reference data to Over-the-Counter (OTC) markets, which are decentralized markets for market participants to trade stocks, commodities, currencies and other instruments directly between two parties without relying on central exchanges or brokers. As of December 2021, KuCoin's OTC market supported 21 fiat currencies and allowed users to trade cryptocurrencies and fiat currencies at prices that are agreed upon by both parties.[13]

The success of blockchain depends on how effectively organizations can create an ecosystem. A 2018 study by Deloitte found 61 blockchain consortia worldwide across a dozen industries.[14] Blockdata's research published in November 2021 found 53 active consortia in operation. They included well-known consortia such as R3 and Hyperledger, as well as newer ones

---

[11] G Abdul (2019) 'Is Blockchain the New Ethical Gold Rush? Maybe' *New York Times*, https://www.nytimes.com/2019/12/06/fashion/jewelry-blockchain-gold-mining -world-economic-forum.html.

[12] Associated Press (2021) 'AP, Chainlink to Bring Trusted Data onto Leading Blockchains.' [online] Available at: https://www.ap.org/press-releases/2021/ap -chainlink-to-bring-trusted-data-onto-leading-blockchains.

[13] Business Wire (Dec 14, 2021) 'KuCoin Partnered with Chainlink to Bring Chainlink Price Feeds to Its OTC Market' https://muscatinejournal.com/lifestyles/ technology/kucoin-partnered-with-chainlink-to-bring-chainlink-price-feeds-to-its-otc -market/article_5809da43-f642-5741-b819-eb557166d970.html.

[14] deloitte.com (n.d.) 'Reaping Value from Blockchain Applications | Deloitte Insights.' [online] Available at: https://www2.deloitte.com/us/en/insights/focus/signals -for-strategists/value-of-blockchain-applications-interoperability.html.

such as Hong Kong's Global Shipping Business Network (GSBN), and insurance-based B3i. Likewise, several consortia have been operating in trade finance areas such as Contour, Marco Polo, we.trade, Spunta, and RiskStream Collaborative.[15]

7.2.4   Interoperability in Blockchain Networks

In order to benefit from the network effect in the multi-chain environment, where many blockchain networks are present, it is important for different blockchains to work together. This means that industry collaboration and common standards for interoperability[16] play a critical role to realize the full potential of blockchain.[17] In the context of blockchain, interoperability can be defined as the ability of different networks to exchange data among themselves and to thus move digital assets between their blockchains. An interoperable system can make it possible to create innovative new products and services by leveraging the benefits provided by multiple blockchain networks.[18]

Two main blockchain interoperability approaches can be suggested: APIs (application programming interface) and network-of-networks models.[19] Many APIs can be coordinated with an API Mashup, which categorizes and reveals all APIs as one API for the user.[20] 'Mashup' APIs can bring blockchain networks and solutions together using a 'mashup' application. Organizations interact with one API rather than an API for every network. Capabilities included are defined in data models and smart contracts. The API serves as 'the glue that joins various networks together'.[21] A drawback is that they

---

[15]   Lucas Schweiger (Nov 2, 2021) 'The State of Blockchain Consortiums in 2021'   https://www.blockdata.tech/blog/general/the-state-of-blockchain-consortiums-in-2021.
[16]   *The Oxford English Dictionary*, interoperability as 'the ability of computer systems or software to exchange and make use of information' (https://www.lexico.com/definition/interoperability).
[17]   International Finance Corporation (Jan 2019) *Blockchain: Opportunities for Private Enterprises in Emerging Markets* (2nd and Expanded Edition, International Finance Corporation, Washington D.C.).
[18]   Gemini. (n.d.) 'Why Is Interoperability Important for Blockchain?' [online] Available at: https://www.gemini.com/cryptopedia/why-is-interoperability-important-for-blockchain.
[19]   CRW de Meijer (2020) 'Blockchain and Interoperability: Key to Mass Adoption' *Finextra*, https://www.finextra.com/blogposting/18972/blockchain-and-interoperability-key-to-mass-adoption.
[20]   C Siegel (2019) 'What Is an API Mashup?' *API Friends*, https://apifriends.com/api-security/api-mashup/.
[21]   de Meijer (n 19).

cannot organize interoperability in the long run.[22] To take an example, China's Blockchain Service Network (BSN) project aims to integrate six public blockchains: Chainlink, Ethereum, Nervos Network, Iris Network, NEO, and Tezos.[23] The state-backed[24] BSN provides APIs to websites. It aims to build an ecosystem of decentralized applications (DApps) on public blockchains, which will be managed, launched and operated with blockchains that are available on BSN. Using BSN tools, developers can develop interoperable DApps.[25] The developers can run nodes and applications with BSN's resources such as data storage and bandwidth.[26] Benefits for users include BSN's cheap services and interoperability with other Chinese enterprise blockchains. They can also access financial data from China UnionPay, which is normally not accessible to foreign-based blockchain firms.[27]

Network-of-networks models involve finding a blockchain solution that many blockchain networks can use so that the industry networks to converge around the solutions.[28] It is the most efficient and scalable way to build interoperability.[29] Some companies have made efforts in this area. Circulor is working with blockchain start-up Everledger in order to make data interchange interoperable. The goal is to ensure that different solutions in a multi provider environment can 'talk' to each other.[30] Both Circulor and Everledger utilize the Oracle's blockchain platform (OBP). Circulor, Everledger and Oracle were reported to be working on interoperability involving a series of standards for a number of applications including the battery supply chain.[31] Oracle is a BaaS

[22] Ibid.
[23] Reynaldo (2020) 'China's Blockchain Initiative BSN First Integrates Chainlink, Ethereum, Tezos, NEO' *Crypto News Flash*, https://www.crypto-news-flash.com/chinas-blockchain-initiative-bsn-first-integrates-chainlink-ethereum-tezos-neo/.
[24] D Pan (2020) 'China's Blockchain Infrastructure to Extend Global Reach with Six Public Chains' *Coindesk*, https://www.coindesk.com/chinas-blockchain-infrastructure-to-extend-global-reach-with-six-public-chains.
[25] Reynaldo (n 23).
[26] Pan (n 24).
[27] Ibid.
[28] IBM Supply Chain and Blockchain Blog (2018) 'Network of Networks: Enabling the Blockchain Economy IBM Supply Chain and Blockchain Blog.' [online] Available at: https://www.ibm.com/blogs/blockchain/2018/12/network-of-networks-enabling-the-blockchain-economy/.
[29] de Meijer (n 19).
[30] ledgerinsights.com (2020) 'Volvo Invests in Blockchain Startup Circulor for Battery Supply Chain Traceability' *Ledger Insights*, https://www.ledgerinsights.com/volvo-invests-in-blockchain-startup-circulor-battery-supply-chain-traceability/
[31] ledgerinsights.com (2020) 'OECD Highlights Need for Blockchain Interoperability for Supply Chains, Including Recycling' *Ledger Insights*, https://www.ledgerinsights.com/oecd-blockchain-interoperability-supply-chains-recycling/.

(blockchain-as-a-service) provider and the OBP is based on Hyperledger Fabric. OBP sets up, manages, and maintains the blockchain platform for enterprises.[32]

7.3   MAJOR OPPORTUNITIES

Blockchain offers a number of opportunities for individuals and organizations. Some major opportunities are discussed in this section.

7.3.1   Blockchain-based Identity

The lack of formal identity documents to prove who they are is among the main reasons why many poor people do not get access to financial services. As noted earlier, one billion people lack any form of identification to prove who they are. An additional 3.4 billion people have some types of identification but lack the ability to use them in the digital world.[33] Worse still, in many countries, banks demand a variety of other documents in addition to identification cards to open an account. According to a McKinsey study conducted in five developing countries and two developed countries, in 2030, with full digital ID coverage countries could create economic value equivalent to 3 per cent to 13 per cent of GDP (Gross Domestic Product). Over half of this value is likely to go to individuals.[34] In light of these observations, an encouraging development is that a key component of some blockchain start-ups' initiatives has been to build blockchain-based identity solutions for the poor.

Kiva's blockchain protocol aims to address two major barriers that hinder poor people's access to financial services: formal identification and verifiable credit history.[35] Kiva worked with the UN Capital Development Fund (UNCDF) and the UN Development Programme (UNDP) to develop a blockchain-based ID system in Sierra Leone. In August 2019, the govern-

---

[32]   V Acharya (2019) 'Oracle Blockchain Platform (OBP) – A Driver in Proliferating Blockchain Adoption' *Government Blockchain Association*, https://www.gbaglobal .org/oracle-blockchain-platform-obp-a-driver-in-proliferating-blockchain-adoption/.
[33]   O White, A Madgavkar, J Manyika, D Mahajan, J Bughin, M McCarthy and O Sperling (April 2019) 'Digital Identification: A Key to Inclusive Growth' *McKinsey. com*, https://www.mckinsey.com/business-functions/digital-mckinsey/our-insights/ Digital-identification-A-key-to-inclusive-growth?cid=other-eml-alt-mgi-mck&hlkid= ecd8822bafc44de78b1f2670c2979652&hctky=2259579&hdpid=0945f28e-3aa8-4f73 -a111-6ba86e377b51.
[34]   Ibid.
[35]   C Cheney (Aug 21, 2019) 'In Sierra Leone, New Kiva Protocol Uses Blockchain to Benefit Unbanked' *Devex*, https://www.devex.com/news/in-sierra-leone-new-kiva -protocol-uses-blockchain-to-benefit-unbanked-95490.

ment of Sierra Leone launched a blockchain-based National Digital Identity Platform (NDIP), which was developed by Kiva. Sierra Leone's government wants all banks and microfinance institutions (MFIs) in the country to use the system by the end of 2019.[36]

All the transactions will be recorded in a blockchain. A borrower will be assigned a digital wallet, which will be accessible through an app. Individuals can access their wallets on cellphones. They can also work with an MFI or other agents that are already working in their community. The agents can also use the application offline.[37] Lenders can view borrower's credit histories in the NDIP platform.[38]

7.3.2   Property Registry

Across the world, land registries are inefficient and unreliable. One estimate suggests that over 20 million rural families in India do not own land and millions more lack legal ownership to the land where they have built houses and worked. Landlessness is arguably a more powerful predictor of poverty in India than caste or illiteracy.[39] A study conducted by the civil society organization Daksh indicated that property-related disputes in India account for a 66 per cent of all civil cases and cost the country 0.5 per cent of the GDP.[40] About US$ 700 million is paid annually in bribes related to land registrars in the country.[41] There are some encouraging initiatives to address this problem. For instance, blockchain's use in land registry in India's Andhra Pradesh state is expected to create many opportunities for landowners (see In Focus 7.2 below).

---

[36]   C Inveen (Aug 21, 2019) 'San Francisco Crowdfunder Kiva Sets Up Sierra Leone Credit Database' *Reuters*, https://www.reuters.com/article/us-leone-kiva/san -francisco-crowdfunder-kiva-sets-up-sierra-leone-credit-database-idUSKCN1VB262.

[37]   Kiva (2019) 'Kiva Protocol FAQ' https://pages.kiva.org/kiva-protocol-faq.

[38]   Tokenpost (Aug 22, 2019) 'Sierra Leone Launches Blockchain-based National Digital Identity Platform' https://www.tokenpost.com/Sierra-Leone-launches -blockchain-based-National-Digital-Identity-Platform-3139.

[39]   T Hanstad (2013) 'The Case for Land Reform in India' https://www.foreignaffairs .com/articles/india/2013-02- 19/untitled?cid=soc-twitter-in-snapshots-untitled-022013.

[40]   D Haridas (2018) 'This Indian City Is Embracing BlockChain Technology – Here's Why' https://www.forbes.com/sites/outofasia/2018/03/05/this-indian-city-is -embracing-blockchain-technology-heres-why/#73e2a58f562e.

[41]   A Bhattacharya (2018) 'Blockchain Is Helping Build Andhra Pradesh's New Capital – But Can It Cut Through the Red Tape?' https://scroll.in/article/887045/ blockchain-is-helping-build-andhra-pradeshs-new-capital-but-can-it-cut-through-the -red-tape.

IN FOCUS 7.2 BLOCKCHAIN'S USE IN LAND REGISTRY IN INDIA'S ANDHRA PRADESH STATE IS EXPECTED TO CREATE MANY OPPORTUNITIES FOR LANDOWNERS

In 2017, the government of India's Andhra Pradesh state announced plans to use blockchain for land registry. It was the first Indian state to do so. In October 2017, the Andhra Pradesh government collaborated with the Swedish start-up ChromaWay to implement a blockchain-based land recording project in the capital city Amaravati. Regarding the involvement of ChromaWay, it is worth noting that a complaint raised against the company is that it has merely proven the concept of blockchain-based land records again and again, while failing to show traction and scalability.[a] In this regard, the Andhra Pradesh project has attained some degree of scalability that was missing previously.

PRIVATE BLOCKCHAIN USED

Just like the Swedish system, the Andhra Pradesh project uses permissioned blockchains. In the Swedish system, relevant data such as the authenticity of land transactions related processes, signatures, files confirming ownership, mortgage deeds are secured in the Swedish land authority Lantmäteriet's blockchain. The copies of the records are also stored and validated by other participants (e.g., banks). Authorized third parties can verify information. These third parties are part of the process such as banks, buyers, sellers and real estate agents.[b] When a land title changes hands, each step of the process is verified and recorded. While this system provides a highly secure and transparent verification and storage service for property transactions, it does not function as a full-blown cryptocurrency in which land can be bought and sold in the same manner as a Bitcoin transaction.[c] The nodes in AP's land records include the Revenue Department, Chief Commissioner of Land Administration and other officials.

IMPLEMENTING BLOCKCHAIN IN AP

The director of land laws and policy at advocacy group Landesa noted that community involvement would be important to verify ownership, resolve disputes and get 'clean' land records, especially in rural areas.[d] Some landowners expressed suspicion and distrust toward the blockchain-based system. The stages before the land records are moved to blockchain are especially prone to fraud.[e] The CRDA (Capital Region Development Authority) officials visited villages to address these concerns, educate landowners and explain the benefits of using blockchain in land registry before starting the project.[f]

A typical land record in blockchain includes 58 attributes.[g] They include static attributes that describe the property, such as unique ID, plot code, geo-coordinates (latitude and longitude), survey number, boundary information (e.g., information about neighbouring plots, location in relation to roads or other landmarks) classification of land as well as dynamic attributes that are subject to change such as owner (e.g., Aadhaar number) and mortgage information, right of first refusal (ROFR) and litigation status. Events such as mutation, court case filing, stay issued by the court, sale, approval of buildings, conversion of lands (e.g., from agricultural to commercial), mortgage, and the owner's death are also recorded. The system also provides flexibility to add new attributes if such needs arise in the future.[h]

BENEFITS OF BLOCKCHAIN-BASED LAND REGISTRY

The case of Andhra Pradesh sheds light on various potential benefits of blockchain-based land registry systems. First, they are expected to reduce administrative and bureaucratic inefficiency and corruption. According to the civil society organization, Daksh, property-related disputes in India account for 66 per cent of all civil cases and cost the country 0.5 per cent of GDP. About US$ 700 million in bribes related to land transactions is paid every year.[i] A blockchain-based system in which many agencies act as nodes or validators of transactions could serve as a check and balance to assure that no agency can manipulate the system without being noticed by others. Blockchain-based land recording systems may use various types of consensus algorithms such as proof of work and proof of stake, in which all or some nodes verify transactions such as a change in the landowner's name for a plot.[j] Following this a new block of data involving land transactions is added to the ledger.

While bribes are not impossible, such activities face considerable challenges in blockchain-based records. In the centralized model, powerful and influential actors can pressure the individuals managing centralized databases to change records. Indeed, this was exactly what happened in the Bhoomi program in the neighbouring Karnataka state,[k] which was reported to increase corruption and bribes as well as time taken for land transactions.[l] The digitization was carried out by the centralization of land records and the management moved away from villages to district-level taluk offices. In a blockchain-based system, records cannot be tampered without this being noticed by other nodes. Moreover, in the Andhra Pradesh system, if any node tries to change the record, the landowner will receive a text message.[m]

Currently after a land transaction is finalized, the officer in charge of the collection of land revenues (*tehsildar*) needs to submit a land demarcation to register the deed. The process takes one to three months.[n] With blockchain, properties can be transferred in a day without paying bribes. The system would also be integrated with the property tax system,[o] which can lead to further efficiency improvements.

Blockchain can also lead to important cost-saving opportunities. Before the implementation of blockchain, farmers needed to pay at least US$ 68 to prepare registration papers in the Andhra Pradesh state. They can get system-generated digital documents for free in the blockchain system. A digital document with a quick response (QR) code can be sent directly to the land registrar for transactions.[p]

Second, a blockchain-based land registry system is expected to stimulate entrepreneurial activities and productivity.[q] The lack of land ownership, as well as documents to prove land ownership, remains among the most important barriers to entrepreneurship and economic development in India.[r] The Andhra Pradesh state hoped that the blockchain-based land registry system would allow people to collateralize property, receive loans from financial institutions, and make investments using that asset.[s] Detailed (with dozens of static, dynamic and event-related attributes) and verifiable information on land transactions would increase landowner access to financial information. Furthermore, the integration of the blockchain system with data related to soil and climatic conditions, availability of water, and other environmental conditions would benefit land owners. Such information would help take actions to increase productivity.

Third, the blockchain-based land registry system is expected to strengthen cybersecurity. Centralized databases are also susceptible to hacking. In 2018, the Bhoomi system experienced a security breach in which nefarious actors transferred 19 acres of government wasteland in the Devanahalli taluk to a private individual. Some of the largest owners of land, known as land sharks, were suspected of manipulating the records. The Bhoomi software had been breached twice before, when hackers made attempts to transfer government properties to private persons.[t] While nefarious actors can also exploit loopholes in blockchain systems, such systems are still more secure than centralized systems.[u] For instance, even if a hacker penetrates a network and changes records, multiple redundant and identical copies of the same records are stored in multiple computers, which serve as backups.[v]

Notes:

[a] Fintech (2020) 'Using Blockchain for Commercial Real Estate.' *Nanalyze*, https://www.nanalyze.com/2020/01/blockchain-commercial-real-estate/.

[b] chromaway.com (2017) 'The Land Registry in the Blockchain – Testbed' https://chromaway.com/papers/Blockchain_Landregistry_Report_2017.pdf.

[c] J Wong (Nov 3, 2017) 'The UN Is Using Ethereum's Technology to Fund Food for Thousands of Refugees' *Quartz*, https://qz.com/1118743/world-food-programmes-ethereum-based-blockchain-for-syrian-refugees-in-jordan/.

[d] R Chandran (2017) 'Indian States Look to Digitize Land Deals with Blockchain' https://www.reuters.com/article/us-india-landrights-tech/indian-states-look-to-digitize-land-deals-with-blockchain-idUSKBN1AQ1T3.

[e] A Bhattacharya (2018) 'Blockchain Is Helping Build Andhra Pradesh's New Capital – But Can it Cut Through the Red Tape?' https://scroll.in/article/887045/blockchain-is-helping-build-andhra-pradeshs-new-capital-but-can-it-cut-through-the-red-tape.

[f] Ibid.

[g] Ibid.

[h] NS Sai Baba (Feb 2, 2020) 'Securing Land Records through Blockchain' *Andhra Pradesh Human Resource Development Institute*, http://www.aphrdi.ap.gov.in/documents/Trainings@APHRDI/2020/feb_2/Citizen%20Centric%20Services/Block%20Chain%20Technology.pdf.

[i] Bhattacharya (n [e]).

[j] J Vos, C Lemmen and B Beentjes (2017) 'Blockchain-based Land Administration: Feasible, Illusory or Panacae?' in Paper Prepared for Presentation at the Annual World Bank Conference on Land and Poverty, 2017 (Washington, DC: The World Bank).

[k] S Benjamin, R. Bhuvaneswari and P. Rajan (2007) 'Bhoomi: "E-governance", or, an Anti-politics Machine Necessary to Globalize Bangalore?' CASUM–m Working Paper, https://www.semanticscholar.org/paper/Bhoomi-%3A-%E2%80%98-E-Governance-%E2%80%99-%2C-Or-%2C-An-Anti-Politics-Benjamin-Bhuvaneswari/f07edf3436b77a7888558ba95e37d3951875703e.

[l] Ibid.

[m] ENS (2019) 'Andhra Government to Adopt Blockchain Tech to End Land Record Tampering' *The New Indian Express*, https://www.newindianexpress.com/states/andhra-pradesh/2019/dec/15/andhra-government-to-adopt-blockchain-tech-to-end-land-record-tampering-2076359.html.

[n] V Ramnani (2018) 'Transfer of Property Title Likely on Same Day through Blockchain' https://www.moneycontrol.com/news/business/real-estate/transfer-of-property-title-likely-on-same-day-through-blockchain-2449981.html.

[o] Sai Baba (n [h]).

[p] Bhattacharya (n [e])

[q] N Kshetri (2019) *Global Entrepreneurship: Environment and Strategy* (2nd edn, Routledge, New York).

[r] N Kshetri (2016) 'Fostering Startup Ecosystems in India' *Asian Research Policy* Vol 7(1) 94–103.

[s] A Battacharya (2018) 'India's Government Wants to Kill Bitcoin, But It Loves Blockchain' *Quartz*, https://qz.com/1148361/budget-2018-indias-government-wants-to-kill-bitcoin-but-it-loves-blockchain/.

[t] M Akshatha (Sept 10, 2018) 'Karnataka's Gamed Land Record Database Bhoomi Faces Another Security Breach' *The Economic Times*, https://tech.economictimes.indiatimes.com/news/corporate/karnatakasfamed-land-record-database-bhoomi-faces-another-security-breach/65748534

[u] N Kshetri (2017) 'Blockchain's Roles in Strengthening Cybersecurity and Protecting Privacy' Telecommunications Policy Vol 41(10) 1027–38, https://doi.org/10.1016/j.telpol.2017.09.003.

[v] Ibid.

Source: N Kshetri (2022), 'Blockchain As a Tool to Facilitate Property Rights Protection in the Global South: Lessons from India's Andhra Pradesh State' *Third World Quarterly*, https://doi.org/10.1080/01436597.2021.2013116.

7.3.3 Demonstrating Sustainability

A number of forces have also contributed to the use of blockchain in facilitating the development of sustainable supply chains in developing countries.

Firms are facing increasing pressures especially from regulators, activists and consumers to develop sustainable supply chains.[42]

Partly in response to such pressures, firms are implementing blockchains in their supply chains. For instance, in 2016, Provenance conducted a pilot project to track fish caught in Indonesia using cellphones and RFID tags. When a product changes hands, it is automatically added to the blockchain system. The end customers can verify the product's origins through a mobile app. The system thus provides complete and verifiable records of the fishing industry's supply chains, which is likely to stop IUU (illegal, unreported and unregulated) fishing and human rights abuses.

By doing so, blockchain can also help provide product information to consumers to increase their confidence about the quality of products.[43] Blockchain-based product traceability is thus key in bringing supply chain transparency,[44] which can enhance consumers' perception of a firm's sustainability practices. For instance, Provenance's platform allows end customers to verify a product's origins through a mobile app.

7.4   SALIENT BARRIERS

While blockchain exhibits great potential, its deployment entails several practical challenges. This section outlines these barriers.

7.4.1   The Lack of Institutional and Absorptive Capacity

The lack of capabilities such as technical knowledge and skills also affect the deployment of blockchain. For instance, as of 2018, there were about 20 million software developers in the world but only 0.1 per cent of them knew about blockchain codes. No more than 6,000 coders were estimated to have the levels of skill and experience needed to develop high-quality blockchain solutions.[45] The Blockchain Academy's 'The Global Blockchain Employment

[42]   European Union (EU) (2020) 'Study on Due Diligence Requirements through the Supply Chain, Final Report' https://www.business-humanrights.org/sites/default/files/documents/DS0120017ENN.en_.pdf

[43]   W Nikolakis, L John and H Krishnan (2018) 'How Blockchain Can Shape Sustainable Global Value Chains: An Evidence, Verifiability, And Enforceability (EVE) Framework' *Sustainability* Vol 10(11) 3926.

[44]   K Hald and A Kinra (2019) 'How the Blockchain Enables and Constrains Supply Chain Performance' *International Journal of Physical Distribution & Logistics Management* Vol 49(4) 376–97.

[45]   P Suprunov (2018) 'How Much Does It Cost to Hire a Blockchain Developer?' *Medium,* https://medium.com/practical-blockchain/how-much-does-it-cost-to-hire-a-blockchain-developer-16b4ffb372e5.

Report 2021' found that the global demand for blockchain developers was increasing by 300–500 per cent yearly.[46]

Out of India's 2 million software developers, only 5,000 were estimated to have blockchain skills. Some speculated that about 80 per cent of these developers may pursue job opportunities outside the country.[47] Other developing countries are in an even more unfavourable situation.

A related point is that although many companies describe themselves as 'blockchain companies', few real-use cases have emerged. For instance, among China's 262 public companies that self-categorized themselves as 'blockchain companies', as of September 2020, only 23 had mentioned blockchain use cases that had gone live.[48]

Many countries thus lack adequate institutional and absorptive capacity to benefit from blockchain due to the lack of competences and skills. For instance, Walmart needed to train about 100,000 employees and suppliers to use its blockchain platform in China to make sure that enterprises or consumers can use it without additional costs.[49]

Building and maintaining an advanced system such as an IoT (Internet of Things) platform (e.g., required by Bext360) would typically require large investments in software infrastructure and local skill development. It is unreasonable to expect that blockchain solutions can be sent into rural Africa for artisanal miners to use them.[50] Even if such systems are set up with outside help, small farmers cannot perform technical tasks such as troubleshooting and maintenance.

The lack of user-friendliness of many blockchain apps further adds to the complexity. A *Financial Times* journalist covering cryptocurrency reported that it took over an hour for her to figure out how she could gain access to her

---

[46] The Blockchain Academy (2021) 'The Global Blockchain Employment Report' https://theblockchainacademy.com/wp-content/uploads/sites/6/2021/04/2021-Global-Blockchain-Employment-Report.pdf.

[47] M Agarwal (2018) 'Blockchain: India Likely to See Brain Drain as 80% Developers May Move Abroad' *Inc42*, https://inc42.com/buzz/blockchain-india-likely-to-suffer-brain-drain-as-80-developers-prepare-to-move-abroad/.

[48] S Kong (2020) 'Blockchain's Been a Bust for China's "Blockchain 50" Public Companies' *Decrypt*, https://decrypt.co/41657/blockchains-been-a-bust-for-chinas-blockchain-50-public-companies.

[49] W Zhuoqiong (2019) 'Walmart China Launches Blockchain Platform to Help Shoppers Track Products' *China Daily*, http://www.chinadaily.com.cn/a/201906/26/WS5d130a01a3103dbf1432a5e3.html.

[50] C Early (2019) 'Can High-tech Solutions Take the Risk out of Artisanal Mining?' *Reuters*, https://www.ethicalcorp.com/can-high-tech-solutions-take-risk-out-artisanal-mining.

wallet. This was the case although she had used the same wallet before, which had migrated to a new app[51]

Similarly, despite blockchain's potential to handle privacy issues in the healthcare sector, not all individuals are in a position to handle their medical data themselves. For instance, older persons or patients with mental illness and dementia may not be able to utilize blockchain to hold ownership and ultimate control over their information.

7.4.2   Lack of Connectivity

Another challenge is the lack of connectivity. For instance, in least developed countries (LDCs), which are low-income countries that perform poorly in human assets and face high economic vulnerability (https://www.un.org/development/desa/dpad/least-developed-country-category/ldc-criteria.html), 24.4 per cent of the population did not have cellphones and 73 per cent lacked Internet access in 2021 (see Figure 7.1 below). This population is far from ready to adopt blockchain. As noted earlier, it will be extremely challenging to use blockchain systems to capture supply chain activities of smallholder farmers that are not connected to the Internet.

7.4.3   Data Control- and Ownership-related Factors

There are also control- and ownership-related factors. For instance, healthcare providers may encounter barriers that prevent them from moving to blockchain. The psychological challenges that healthcare organizations face must be recognized and dealt with in order to address concerns related to privacy, security, and integrity of healthcare data. The current mindset among many healthcare providers is that they are the only 'steward' of patient healthcare data that is in their organizations.[52] It might be difficult to change this culture, but evidence says it is necessary.

7.4.4   Thin Markets

Low levels of economic activities in the agricultural sector are associated with thin markets, in which there are few buyers and sellers and few transactions

---

[51] I Kaminska (2019b) 'Here's How Much Izzy Paid to Move $19.1 Worth of Bitcoin' *Financial Times*: Alphaville, https://ftalphaville.ft.com/2019/06/13/1560398428000/Here-s-how-much-Izzy-paid-to-move--19-1-worth-of-Bitcoin/.
[52] L. Silverman, 'How Bitcoin Technology Could Securely Share Medical Records Among Your Doctors', Kera News, March 8, 2017, http://keranews.org/post/how-bitcoin-technology-could-securely-share-medical-records-among-your-doctors

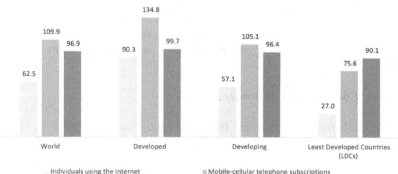

Source: ITU, Statistics (https://www.itu.int/en/ITU-D/Statistics/Pages/stat/default.aspx.

Figure 7.1   *Key indicators related to ICT access in economies with various levels of economic development (2021, percentage of the population)*

in which blockchain-based applications can be used. Additional challenges include high transaction costs and risks, and high unit costs in the development of technological and physical infrastructures.[53] Due to these factors, being a part of blockchain systems set up by large organizations would involve significant costs and efforts for smallholder farmers. These farmers often need to travel long distances to take advantage of blockchain systems such as Bext360's kiosks and Nile Breweries' buying centres. For instance, farmers in Eastern Uganda are required to transport their crops to Nile Breweries' buying centres, which are located 10 kms or farther from their towns.

An upshot of think markets is that there has been a lack of systems to accurately and fairly measure indicators such as the quality of crops before such data are entered into blockchain systems. For instance, to use the BanQu system Nile Breweries' officials check for quality and other details before recording the data in blockchain.[54] One stated benefit of blockchain is that aggregators can no longer exploit farmers. However, the possibility of

---

[53]   A Dorward, N Poole, J Morrison, J Kydd and I Urey (2003) 'Markets, Institutions and Technology: Missing Links in Livelihoods Analysis' *Development Policy Review* Vol 21(3) 319–32.

[54]   Equator News (2019) 'How Blockchain Technology Is Changing Lives of Farmers in Eastern Uganda' *Equator News*, https://equatornews.today/business/how -blockchain-technology-changing-lives-farmers-eastern-uganda.

exploitation by large industrial buyers such as Nile Breweries cannot be ruled out. Machines can classify products and measure quality indicators based on objective characteristics. However, the low levels of economic activities and thin markets can make investments in technologies unattractive. In the absence of supporting technologies, potential benefits of blockchain cannot be fully realized.

7.4.5   Educational Challenges

The main barriers to introduce blockchain may not necessarily be technical.[55] A main barrier to introduce blockchain in the country has often been educational rather than technical.[56] The lack of awareness, education and information of blockchain among key stakeholders has been a concern. In the context of blockchain-based trade finance, regulators in Europe were reported to be knowledgeable on blockchain and they were interested in innovation,[57] but there has been a lack of awareness of blockchain among key stakeholders in developing economies. For instance, the Georgian Minister of Justice Thea Tsulukiani and other officials noted that the main barrier to introducing blockchain in the country has been educational rather than technical.[58]

7.4.6   Regulatory Challenges

In the healthcare industry for instance, there are EHR (Electronic Health Record) privacy laws such as the Health Insurance Portability and Accountability Act (HIPPA) that must be enforced.[59] As mentioned earlier, blockchain's transparency is not always conducive to privacy. We believe however that so long as appropriate encryption is employed to the actual hard patient data, and proper control to a specific patient's chain occurs, these two competing forms of trust can occur simultaneously.

---

[55]   economist.com (2017) 'Governments May Be Big Backers of the Blockchain' http://www.economist.com/news/business/21722869-anti-establishment-technology -faces-ironic-turn-fortune-governments-may-be-big-backers.http://www.economist .com/news/business/21722869-anti-establishment-technology-faces-ironic-turn -fortune-governments-may-be-big-backers

[56]   Ibid.

[57]   N Acheson (2018) 'How Blockchain Trade Finance Is Breaking Proof-of-concept Gridlock'   https://www.coindesk.com/blockchain-trade-finance-breaking-proof -concept-gridlock/'

[58]   economist.com (n 55).

[59]   https://tinyurl.com/ydcllwzz'.

7.4.7   Scalability Challenges

There are also scalability challenges associated with blockchains. For instance, Ethereum can handle only 20 transactions per second (TPS).[60] This is extremely slow compared to Visa's average of 1,700 TPS, which can handle more at peak load. For instance, as the size of medical records increases, healthcare providers may find it difficult to handle them with blockchains. Using blockchain, complete medical records of a patient need to be stored at each node participating in the network. This may create data-storage and bandwidth problems.[61]

7.5   LIMITATIONS OF THE TECHNOLOGY

Various limitations of the technology need to be considered. As of October 2021, 60–70 per cent of public blockchains were estimated to run on the Ethereum platform.[62] Ethereum's high transaction costs and extremely slow speed are of concern. For instance, the average transaction or 'gas' fee on the Ethereum network was US$ 63 in November 2021, which was as high as US$ 70 in May 2021.[63] The *Financial Times* journalist mentioned above reported that she transferred US$ 19 equivalent of Bitcoin from one wallet to another. The fee to process the transaction was 109,773 satoshis (US$ 3.10 based on Bitcoin's price for the day).[64]

There are unique problems at every stage when minerals move along a supply chain. As discussed in Chapter 3, blockchain cannot effectively address the 'first mile' problem, which is arguably the most crucial step in assuring the ore's quality.[65] To address the challenges related to possible trust-

---

[60]   L. Mearian (2020) 'MIT's Blockchain-based "Spider" Offers 4X Faster Cryptocurrency Processing' *ComputerWorld*, https://www.computerworld.com/article/3518893/mits-blockchain-based-spider-offers-4x-faster-cryptocurrency-processing.html.

[61]   LA Linn and MB Koo (2016) 'Blockchain for Health Data and Its Potential Use in Health IT and Health Care Related Research' https://www.healthit.gov/sites/default/files/11-74-ablockchainforhealthcare.pdf.

[62]   M Vincent (Oct 20, 2021). 'What Are Digital Assets and How Are They Held?' [online] *Financial Times* Available at: https://www.ft.com/content/2691366f-d381-40cd-a769-6559779151c2.

[63]   Harry Robertson (Dec 9, 2021) 'Ethereum Transaction Fees Are Running Sky-high. That's Infuriating Users and Boosting Rivals like Solana and Avalanche' https://markets.businessinsider.com/news/currencies/ethereum-transaction-gas-fees-high-solana-avalanche-cardano-crypto-blockchain-2021-12.

[64]   Kaminska (n 51).

[65]   F Brugger (2019) 'Blockchain Is Great, but It Can't Solve Everything. Take Conflict Minerals' *African Arguments*, https://africanarguments.org/2019/04/23/blockchain-is-great-but-it-cant-solve-everything-take-conflict-minerals/.

worthy behaviours, in the tantalum blockchain system used in Rwanda, participants that have been identified and trusted perform their allocated roles when the mineral passes through various stages of supply chains. A key weakness of the system lies in 'the gate' when the ore is first registered to enter the ledger's 'safe space'. A facial recognition system provides a guarantee that the participants entering the data at this initial point are known and verified. However, this system by itself is far from enough to guarantee that the ore registered by the verified persons originated from legitimate sources. For instance, individuals from a mine controlled by armed groups may use illegal kickbacks and bribes to influence the persons registering the ore into colluding and entering false data. In this way, mutual illegal gains occur to both parties and a batch of tantalum produced by an armed group could be tagged as a legitimate ore by the verified participants. Thus, the recording of facial scanning or GPS (global positioning system) cannot guarantee the source from which the authenticated seller got the tantalum.[66]

Different types of problems are faced when the minerals move along the supply chain. A main challenge is that during smelting and refining ores from multiple sources are often mixed and amalgamated into single batches of metal. This cannot be addressed by current blockchain-based solutions.[67] Global risk analysis firm Verisk Maplecroft's vice president Gus MacFarlane put the issue this way:

> 'The fact that a whole batch of metal could be made up of multiple ore sources (some traceable and some not) and could be "contaminated" by ore from any single source linked to human rights abuses, potentially presents its own challenges in terms of maintaining the unbroken integrity of the blockchain process.'

We also discussed the last-mile problem in Chapter 3. Appropriate intermediaries can play a critical role in bridging 'the last mile' between a digital record and physical assets represented by the record. When it comes to dealing with physical assets, blockchain is not about eliminating intermediaries. The issue here is about reshaping how business transactions are managed.[68]

---

[66]   Ibid.
[67]   B Kilbey and F Warwick (2020) 'Blockchain Not Silver Bullet for Mine Operations: Verisk Maplecroft VP' *S&P Global Platts*, https://www.spglobal.com/ platts/en/market-insights/latest-news/metals/012920-blockchain-not-silver-bullet-for -mine-operations-verisk-maplecroft-vp.
[68]   Leo Jiang (Apr 26, 2019) 'The Last Mile Problem: Understanding the Economics Affecting the Future of Blockchain' https://www.datadriveninvestor.com/2019/04/ 26/the-last-mile-problem-understanding-the-economics-affecting-the-future-of -blockchain/.

As discussed in Chapter 3, a limitation thus is that blockchain solutions often cannot protect a supply chain against attacks such as physical tampering and modification. For this reason, some critics say that blockchain can be easily gamed. Manual entries may lead to human error or intentional manipulation. For instance, products in the FBSCs (food and beverage supply chains) can be easily adulterated and it may not be possible to know who did it, when and how.[69] Bloomberg columnist Matt Levine notes:

> if you drill a hole in the container, take out all the teddy bears, and replace them with cocaine, the blockchain won't catch that. The blockchain is about taming all of the virtual attributes of the container, all of the paperwork that accompanies it. But the boundary between the physical and virtual worlds will always be a bit more lawless.[70]

Finally, some technologists who like completely decentralized networks such as Bitcoin think that the newer, corporate-designed blockchains lack one of the main elements that made Bitcoin a success: the decentralized structure. For instance, anyone in the world is able to join Bitcoin and study the ledgers. On the other hand, only a limited set of participants can have access to blockchain system like that of IBM. This feature can make such a system more vulnerable to attack. For instance, a hacker can target a few of the participants. Despite a higher degree of decentralization of IBM's blockchain-based technology for tracking shipments compared to previous methods, it arguably 'concentrates power in a handful of entities'.[71]

7.6   CHAPTER SUMMARY AND CONCLUSION

In this chapter, we attempted to develop an understanding of enablers, limitations and barriers for the adoption and diffusion of a blockchain ecosystem. Among the major limitations of blockchain systems, while they are secure, their data, as is the case of other databases, are only as accurate as what is entered. For instance, in Walmart's case, details about products such as mangos and pork are entered by the farmers that grow or raise such products.

---

[69]   J Luzi-Ann (2018) 'Farm to Table? Check the Blockchain' *Bloomberg Businessweek*, 00077135, 4/16/2018, Issue 4565.

[70]   M Levine (2017) 'Cargo Blockchains and Deutsche Bank' *Bloomberg*, https://www.bloomberg.com/view/articles/2017-03-06/cargo-blockchains-and-deutsche-bank.

[71]   N Popper and S Lohr (2017) 'Blockchain: A Better Way to Track Pork Chops, Bonds, Bad Peanut Butter?' https://www.nytimes.com/2017/03/04/business/dealbook/blockchain-ibm-bitcoin.html.

There is always the possibility of data manipulation before entering into the blockchain system.

Blockchains still have technical challenges such as scalability, which are likely to be addressed. For instance, as noted above, Ethereum's low through-put has been concerning. However, Ethereum 2.0, which is slated for launch in 2022, is expected to handle 100,000 TPS.

Due to development costs and complexity, it is not currently practical to implement blockchain systems for low-cost products. Firms such as Carrefour and Walmart have limited blockchain deployment to products with high value or high information costs. The problem is worsened by the fact that developing countries lack local talent to develop blockchain applications. However, these challenges are expected to be gradually addressed.

8. Discussion, conclusion, and recommendations

8.1   INTRODUCTION

Blockchain undoubtedly is among the biggest technological innovations that affect people, organizations, nations and societies. Blockchain especially can add value when high trust is needed between parties to engage in transactions. Blockchain-based solutions can reduce the costs of verification, costs of measurement and costs of enforcement. For instance, this technology makes it possible to verify information about past transactions and attributes of the transactions as well as the current ownership in a digital asset. American entrepreneur, television personality, and media proprietor Mark Cuban said that blockchain and crypto 'will have the same impact on business and consumers as the internet did, if not more'.[1]

However, blockchain's value creation potential and trust-producing roles vary across different areas of economic activities and types of transactions. A McKinsey.com article asserted that blockchain's potential lies mainly in three areas.[2] First, in some niche applications such as supply chains, blockchain can address problems related to inefficiency, opacity, and fraud. Second, in some sectors, blockchain can help modernize value by helping the digitization process, simplifying value creation process and facilitating collaboration. Some specific areas include smart contracts in the global shipping industry, trade finance, and payments applications. Third, blockchain is being used by some firms to enhance reputational value by demonstrating their ability to innovate.

---

[1]   CoinDesk (Dec 7, 2021) 'Most Influential 2021: Mark Cuban: "It Will Have the Same Impact on Business and Consumers as the Internet Did, if Not More."' https://www.coindesk.com/business/2021/12/07/most-influential-40-mark-cuban/.

[2]   Matt Higginson, Marie-Claude Nadeau and K Rajgopal (Jan, 2019) 'Blockchain's Occam Problem' https://www.mckinsey.com/industries/financial-services/our-insights/blockchains-occam-problem?cid=other-eml-alt-mip-mck&hlkid=f1ff7216a70e4041951d60293978a0ea&hctky=2762145&hdpid=95e9bdfa-0709-4b4d-8252-f401bcaac86d.

As to the importance of trust, some consumers may know that businesses may misuse their information but are still willing to give up their privacy in order to receive benefits. These consumers may not necessarily value the trust that blockchain can create compared to costs and experience. This might be the reason behind the success of big social media companies such as Facebook.[3] Organizations, on the other hand, value trust and user privacy.

As to blockchain's effect on reducing the cost of networking, various parties can start a self-sustaining process and operate a marketplace. It is not necessary to assign control to a centralized intermediary. This is possible because blockchain can verify the state at a low cost. Economic incentives can be targeted to reward valuable activities from a network perspective. They include contribution of resources needed to operate and scale the network and secure a decentralized stage. The digital marketplaces that result from such collaborations allow the participants to make joint investments to create shared digital assets.[4] Building the initial network, however, may be resource- and time-consuming. Once a network is established, blockchain can lower the cost of maintaining and operating the network.

Due primarily to the above-mentioned features of blockchain, a key feature of Web3 protocols is that most of the funding in this sector has not come from established companies. For instance, Bitcoin was created by a pseudonymous founder without any venture capital investment. A college dropout started Ethereum, who crowdfunded the start-up capital.[5]

Among the biggest criticisms of blockchain networks is the fact that they consume substantial amounts of energy to operate. According to a Bloomberg report the Bitcoin network was estimated to use 67 terawatt-hours (TWh) of electricity in 2020, which was expected to increase to 91 TWh in 2021.[6] This is about the same amount of electricity as consumed by the Philippines.[7]

---

[3]   Leo Jiang (Apr 26, 2019) 'The Last Mile Problem: Understanding the Economics Affecting the Future of Blockchain' https://www.datadriveninvestor.com/2019/04/26/the-last-mile-problem-understanding-the-economics-affecting-the-future-of-blockchain/.
[4]   C Catalini and J Gans (2019) *Some Simple Economics of the Blockchain*. Rotman School of Management Working Paper 2874598.
[5]   Parag Khanna and Balaji S Srinivasan (Dec 11, 2021) 'Great Protocol Politics' https://foreignpolicy.com/2021/12/11/bitcoin-ethereum-cryptocurrency-web3-great-protocol-politics/.
[6]   Amanda Ahl (Sept 13, 2021) 'Bitcoin's 2021 Energy Use Has Already Surpassed 2020' https://www.bloomberg.com/news/articles/2021-09-13/bitcoin-s-2021-energy-use-has-already-surpassed-2020-bnef-chart?sref=323RPL5z.
[7]   Martin Young (Sept 15, 2021) 'Bitcoin's Power Consumption This Year Has Already Surpassed All of 2020's' https://cointelegraph.com/news/2021-s-btc-energy-use-passes-2020-s-new-study-suggests-each-tx-produces-272g-of-e-waste.

Blockchain's proponents, however, have pointed out that electricity consumed by blockchain networks comprises only a small proportion of the electricity waste from other sources. Quoting a study of Cambridge Centre for Alternative Finance (CCAF), a cointelegraph.com article noted that electricity losses in transmission and distribution in the US could power the Bitcoin network 2.2 times.[8] Galaxy Digital Mining's study found that the amount of electricity lost in transmission and distribution is about 2,205 TWh/yr, which is 19.4 times that of the Bitcoin network. Likewise, 'always-on' electrical devices in US households consume about 1,375 TWh/yr, which is 12.1 times that of the Bitcoin network.[9]

8.2   THE FUTURE OF BLOCKCHAIN

Blockchain technology has a bright future. The investment in this technology is increasing rapidly. For instance, according to Seattle, the US-based financial data and software company PitchBook, in the first 11 months of 2021, venture capitalists invested more than US$ 27 billion globally in crypto start-ups. This investment was more than the investments in the previous ten years combined.[10]

Global software development efforts in blockchain have also increased in recent years. As of early 2022, over 4,000 developers were actively working on the Ethereum blockchain platform. By that time, more than 40 of the top 100 cryptocurrencies based on market capitalization had been built using the Ethereum platform.[11]

Thanks to these massive investments and development efforts, the ease of use has been improving rapidly. In the context of supply chains, for instance,

---

[8]   Matthew Van Niekerk (Dec 11, 2021) 'Enterprise Blockchain to Play a Pivotal Role in Creating a Sustainable Future'
https://cointelegraph.com/news/enterprise-blockchain-to-play-a-pivotal-role-in-creating-a-sustainable-future.
[9]   Rachel Rybarczyk, Drew Armstrong and Amanda Fabiano (May 2021) 'On Bitcoin's Energy Consumption: A Quantitative Approach to a Subjective Question' *Galaxy Digital Mining*, https://www.lopp.net/pdf/On_Bitcoin_Energy_Consumption .pdf.
[10]   Ephrat Livni (Dec 1, 2021) 'Venture Capital Funding for Crypto Companies Is Surging' https://www.nytimes.com/2021/12/01/business/dealbook/crypto-venture -capital.html.
[11]   K Speights (Jan 24, 2022) '1 Cryptocurrency I'd Buy Right Now Without Any Hesitation: It Has Staying Power' https://www.fool.com/investing/2022/01/24/1 -cryptocurrency-id-buy-right-now-without-any-hesi/?source=eptyholnk0000202&utm _source=yahoo-host&utm_medium=feed&utm_campaign=article.

companies that want to use blockchain can just plug in applications such as VeChain's ToolChain and start using the technology.

Significant progresses have also been made over the past few years in block-chain standardizations. For instance, in 2018, Maersk and IBM announced that the two companies jointly developed a blockchain-powered shipping solution TradeLens (https://www.tradelens.com/), which has brought various parties involved in international trade together, supports information sharing among them and enhances transparency. The main purpose of TradeLens is arguably to promote interoperability between various players in the ecosystem. For TradeLens to work, the most important prerequisite is that the systems used by carriers, freight forwarders, custom offices, ports and other participants must be able to communicate with each other. That is happening by connecting with their legacy systems using APIs (application programming interfaces) that support industry standards.[12] As of June 2021, the TradeLens ecosystem consisted of more than 300 organizations that included more than ten ocean carriers and 600 ports and terminals.[13]

A further encouraging development is that more diverse categories of participants are now entering this ecosystem. EY and Guardtime established Insurwave, which is arguable the world's first blockchain-enabled insurance platform. They collaborated with software corporation Microsoft, shipping company AP Møller-Maersk and many companies in the insurance industry. Insurwave started its commercial operations in June 2018. Insurwave integrates and secures data from a large number of sources. It uses blockchain and distributed ledger technologies based on Microsoft Azure infrastructure. The Association for Cooperative Operations Research and Development (ACORD) data standards are followed.[14] The project took about one year to complete following a 12-week proof-of-concept phase.[15] By September 2019, the Insurwave platform processed about 30,000 transactions and insured more

---

[12] N Morris (2019) 'Hapag-Lloyd, ONE Join IBM Maersk TradeLens Shipping Blockchain' *Ledger Insights*, https://www.ledgerinsights.com/hapag-lloyd-one-ibm -maersk-tradelens-shipping-blockchain/.

[13] *Supply Chain Quarterly* (June 17, 2021) 'Maersk and IBM's Tradelens Container Shipping Data Platform Expands in China' [online] Available at: https:// www.supplychainquarterly.com/articles/4948-maersk-and-ibms-tradelens-container -shipping-data-platform-expands-in-china.

[14] M Wingrove (2019) 'Blockchain's Impact on Shipping and Insurance' *Riviera*, https://www.rivieramm.com/news-content-hub/news-content-hub/blockchainrsquos -impact-on-shipping-and-insurance-56256.

[15] M Lerner (2019) '2019 Innovation Awards: Insurwave' *Business Insurance*, https://www.businessinsurance.com/article/00010101/NEWS06/912330544/2019 -Innovation-Awards-Insurwave.

than 1,000 vessels.[16] Insurwave's permissioned distributed ledger was built on the Corda platform, created by R3CEV, which developed Corda. It connects participants such as buyers, brokers, insurers and reinsurers in a secure, private network.[17]

It is envisioned that public blockchains in the future can function as a ubiquitous and decentralized, 'world computer', which will automate every aspect of human lives using data that are delivered through 5G or higher generation cellular networks. For instance, satellites can capture real-time road usage data, record in blockchain and send to autonomous vehicles. Weather stations can send data related to temperature, wind and rain in remote areas, which can be used to automatically price weather-based crop insurance contracts for farmers.[18] All these developments will be facilitated by super-fast data processing. For instance, in 2019, the most advanced systems used in the world were 300,000 times more powerful than those used in 2012 in terms of processing capacity.[19]

There have also been efforts to enhance integration and interoperability of various blockchain systems. For instance, IBM's VP of Blockchain Global Trade Todd Scott discussed the possibility of integration between Food Trust and TradeLens. IBM reportedly had detailed discussions with its clients about the potential integration.[20]

Blockchain-based tools are becoming more accessible to smaller players. In some cases, costs associated with using a system are covered by big corporations. For instance, as discussed earlier, Everledger and Swiss-based jewellery retailer Gübelin provide a no-cost solution to track coloured gems produced or manufactured by ASMs (artisanal and small-scale mining). ASM can use Everledger's blockchain platform to create traceability and document retention for free.[21] Likewise, as discussed in Chapter 6, the SCF (supply chain finance)

---

[16]   Ibid.
[17]   Ibid.
[18]   B Jesel (2020) 'Chainlink's New Acquisition from Cornell University Could Transform Blockchain for Good' *Forbes*, https://www.forbes.com/sites/benjessel/2020/08/29/chainlinks-new-acquisition-from-cornell-university-could-transform-blockchain-for-good/#da9a8c4162bb.
[19]   *Financial Times* (2019) 'The Billion-dollar Bet to Reach Human-level AI' *Financial Times*, https://www.ft.com/content/c96e43be-b4df-11e9-8cb2-799a3a8cf37b.
[20]   Morris (n 12).
[21]   Y Cholteeva (2019) 'Everledger Launches Blockchain Platform to Ensure Transparency in Diamond Sourcing' *Mining Technology*, https://www.mining-technology.com/news/everledger-launches-blockchain-platform-to-ensure-transparency-in-diamond-sourcing/.

platform Chained Finance charges P2P (peer-to-peer) lenders a fee to access the system instead of charging suppliers, which are often small.

Some technology companies have identified increasing opportunities in blockchain as a key priority area for action. They are growing the block-chain workforce. For instance, as of early 2020, Deloitte had 1,400 full-time employees working on blockchain. Likewise, the blockchain unit India's Tata employed 1,000 employees and 600 of them worked full time.[22]

Companies are also facing external pressures from regulators and consumers to ensure that their supply chains are free of conflict minerals. By focusing on the emotional issues of violence and children working under dangerous conditions, NGOs (non-governmental organisations) have established causal relationship between the consumption of products such as cellphones and cars with conflict minerals from the DRC (Democratic Republic of Congo) making consumers feel guilty. On the policy front, the 2010 Dodd–Frank Act has required companies to include conflict minerals reporting.[23] Some jurisdictions such as France and the EU (European Union) have passed more wide-ranging and even stricter regulations to protect disadvantaged workers from various abuses.

8.3   IMPLICATIONS FOR ORGANIZATIONS

Blockchain solutions provide various mechanisms to shape the way organizations operate. Innovative uses of this technology are continuously evolving that can act as a transformative force to influence the way organizations function. For instance, one of the main functions of NFTs (non-fungible tokens) currently is to authenticate digital artworks. There are, however, a number of largely unexploited uses. Some have predicted that the biggest market would be in the accreditation of assets. For instance, a system to authenticate car number plates, would give controlled access to relevant data to the car owner, government agencies, and the insurer (e.g., mileage, engine number and repair history).[24] This is likely to transform the way the insurance sector functions.

---

[22]   M Del Castillo (2019) 'Blockchain Goes to Work at Walmart, Amazon, JPMorgan, Cargill and 46 Other Enterprises' *Forbes*, https://www.forbes.com/sites/michaeldelcastillo/2019/04/16/blockchain-goes-to-work/#6be95052a408.
[23]   J Reinecke and S Ansari (2016) 'Taming Wicked Problems: The Role of Framing in the Construction of Corporate Social Responsibility' *Journal of Management Studies* Vol 53(3) 299–329.
[24]   C Feng (Jan 25, 2022) 'China Introduces State-backed NFT Platform Unlinked to Cryptocurrencies' https://www.scmp.com/tech/tech-trends/article/3164681/china-introduces-state-backed-nft-platform-unlinked.

Blockchain solutions can contribute to the corporate bottom line and market performance. For instance, as of early 2021, Carrefour was tracking more than 30 product lines on the blockchain. They included farm-raised eggs, Norwegian salmon and Rocamadour cheese. A QR (quick response) code is tagged with each product, which can be scanned by customers to find out details such as where their food comes from. Carrefour found that blockchain-based traceability has boosted sales. The company's goal is to expand the solution to 100 product lines by 2020.[25]

Companies are also under increasing pressure from consumers to be more sustainable. In a survey, 66 per cent of respondents were willing to pay more for sustainably and ethically sourced products. The proportion was 73 per cent for millennials.[26] Blockchain can help firms demonstrate the sustainability of their actions to consumers and other stakeholders. For instance, blockchain can help provide product information to consumers to increase their confidence about the quality of products. Blockchain-based product traceability is thus key in bringing supply chain transparency, which can enhance consumers' perception of a firm's sustainability practices.

The use of blockchain to provide detailed information about a product is especially valued by millennials. According to the Nielsen Company's survey three-quarters of millennials reported that they would alter their buying habits in order to reduce environmental impact compared to only 34 per cent of baby boomers.[27] This has an important implication for firms since millennials and Generation Z will account for about four-fifths of luxury industry growth in the near future.[28] Firms are realizing that blockchain can play a crucial role to increase consumer confidence and trust in their products.

Blockchain-based solutions can also make a wrongdoing visible, which could hurt a company's brand name, public image and reputation. To celebrate McDonald's McRib's official return to nationwide menus on November 1, 2021 and the sandwich's 40th anniversary, the company created a limited number of McRib NFTs to give away to a few lucky fans, who follow

---

[25] M del Castillo (Mar 5, 2021) 'Blockchain 50 2021.' [online] *Forbes*. Available at: https://www.forbes.com/sites/michaeldelcastillo/2021/02/02/blockchain-50/?sh=45a0832231cb.

[26] Forbes Africa (2018) 'Blood Diamonds to Blockchain Diamonds?' *Forbes Africa*, https://www.forbesafrica.com/technology/2018/09/03/blood-diamonds-to-blockchain-diamonds/.

[27] nielsen.com (2018) 'Was 2018 the Year of the Influential Sustainable Consumer?' *Neilsen*, https://www.nielsen.com/us/en/insights/article/2018/was-2018-the-year-of-the-influential-sustainable-consumer/.

[28] C Ballentine (2020) 'The Guilt-free Engagement Ring Is Here' *Bloomberg*, https://www.bloomberg.com/news/articles/2020-02-20/ethical-engagement-rings-that-are-truly-eco-friendly-guilt-free.

McDonald's on Twitter and retweet the Sweepstakes Invitation. This was a big marketing success for the company. More than 21,000 participated in the first few hours.[29] Social media management company Hootsuite's study found that McRib's 40th anniversary and NFT announcement were mentioned 20,532 times online.[30] In December 2021, a Twitter user noticed that an early transaction to the Ethereum address that appeared to be associated with the official McRib NFT collection had a racial slur. The slur was written directly on the Ethereum blockchain.[31]

8.4   IMPLICATIONS FOR POLICYMAKERS

Blockchain has been touted as a transparency-enhancing tool with a potential to fight unethical and corrupt practices linked to the lack of responsibility, accountability, integrity, and transparency. Some politicians have advocated using blockchain for fighting economic crimes such as corruption and embezzlement. Solomon Adaelu, a member of the House in Nigeria, argued that blockchain can help eradicate corrupt practices in both the public and private sectors of the country.[32]

Policymakers need to encourage the use of blockchain solutions to bring desired political and economic outcomes. For instance, blockchain-based land records can provide many benefits for developing economies. Tamper-proof property titles in a digital form provide many benefits. Thanks to 'super audit trails', and powerful checks and balances, blockchain-based land registries reduce predatory risks from government officials and other actors and streamline the process of buying and selling land. A typical property sale involves many stakeholders such as land registry, a buyer, a seller, lawyers, mortgage providers, mortgage surveyors, and estate agents. Blockchain can make the

[29]   adage.com (Nov 9, 2021) 'How NFTs Are Used by Marketers – a Continually Updated List.' [online] Available at: https://adage.com/article/digital-marketing-ad-tech-news/how-brands-are-using-nfts-continually-updated-list/2376086.

[30]   Alexandra Canal (Nov 4, 2021) 'McDonald's McRib NFTs Fuel Social Media Mentions, New Data Show' https://news.yahoo.com/mc-donalds-mc-rib-nf-ts-fuel-social-media-mentions-new-data-shows-195354186.html.

[31]   D Nelson, W Gottsegen, A Thurman (Dec 11, 2021) 'McDonald's McRib NFT Project Links to Racial Slur Recorded on Blockchain: A Company Needs to Weigh the Risks and Rewards when Deciding to Create NFTs' https://www.coindesk.com/business/2021/12/11/mcdonalds-mcrib-nft-project-links-to-racial-slur-recorded-on-blockchain/.

[32]   O Avan-Nomayo (2019) 'Africa Using Blockchain to Drive Change, Part One: Nigeria and Kenya' *CoinTelegraph*, https://cointelegraph.com/news/africa-using-blockchain-to-drive-change-nigeria-and-kenya-part-one.

entire process more transparent and cut bureaucratic red tape thus reducing the time and costs of property-related transactions.

Blockchain can also limit problems such as manipulation in public procurement processes.[33] The shared and immutable records cannot be censored or altered by government agencies. Records of bids and public comments cannot be deleted, and a vendor cannot be denied from bidding. Bids or tender offers cannot be altered once they are submitted.[34] These features make blockchain an effective tool to fight corruption in procurement. Such benefits are especially likely to accrue from permissionless blockchains like Ethereum.[35] Some international agencies have also advocated for the use of blockchain in fighting corruption in public procurement. The United Nations Office on Drugs and Crime (UNODC) has suggested the Kenyan government use blockchain to fight economic crimes. Government officials in Kenya allegedly manipulate procurement procedures and systems to inflate costs for their own gains. The country's highest offices including the vice president have been connected to scandals.[36] According to Kenya's Auditor General, the country loses US$ 10 billion annually to corruption.[37]

IN FOCUS 8.1   THE BLOCKCHAIN-BASED GAME AXIE INFINITY
MADE IT POSSIBLE FOR MANY FILIPINOS TO MAKE
A LIVING DURING THE COVID-19 PANDEMIC

The blockchain-based game Axie Infinity allows players to make real money by playing. Players buy digital pets called Axies, which fight with other Axies. Players that fight well can earn Axie's native token Smooth Love Potion (SLP), which is an ERC-20 token. With enough tokens, a player can

---

[33]   transparency.org (2018) 'Promise and Peril: Blockchain, Bitcoin and the Fight Against Corruption' *Transparency International*, https://www.transparency.org/en/news/promise-and-peril-blockchain-bitcoin-and-the-fight-against-corruption#.

[34]   R Davidson Raycraft and A Lannquist (2020) 'How Governments Can Leverage Policy and Blockchain Technology to Stunt Public Corruption' *World Economic Forum*, https://www.weforum.org/agenda/2020/06/governments-leverage-blockchain-public-procurement-corruption/.

[35]   I Allison (2020) 'Colombian Government and WEF Weigh Public Ethereum in Bid to Fight Corruption' *Coindesk*, https://www.coindesk.com/colombian-government-and-wef-weigh-public-ethereum-in-bid-to-fight-corruption.

[36]   S Kaaru (2020) 'UN Calls for Blockchain to Fight Rampant Corruption in Kenya' *CoinGeek*, https://coingeek.com/un-calls-for-blockchain-to-fight-rampant-corruption-in-kenya/.

[37]   K Isaac (2019) 'Kenya Loses Ksh.1 Trillion Every Year to Corruption – What Could 6 Trillion Stolen So Far in Jubilee Government Do?' *Soko Directory*, https://sokodirectory.com/2019/02/kenya-loses-1-trillion-every-year-corruption/.

breed their Axies and create new ones.

There is a marketplace within the game (https://marketplace.axieinfinity
.com/) which allows the trading of Axie NFTs. Tokens earned from playing
the game and the proceeds from selling Axies in the marketplace within the
game can also be taken to open marketplaces outside the game to convert
into traditional currency.[a]

In mid-2021, there were about half a million daily active users (DAU),
which increased to 2.5 million in December 2021.[b] About 60 per cent of users in mid-2021 were from the Philippines. The average player earned 4,500
SLP a month.[c] On August 26, 2020, the news site specializing in Bitcoin and
digital currencies, CoinDesk, published a story about an Axie player, Ijon
Inton from the Cabanatuan City of the Philippines, who was earning around
10,000 PHP (Philippine peso) (US$ 206) per week by playing the game.[d]

The all-time high price of SLP was US$ 0.399727 in July 2021 (https://
www.coingecko.com/en/coins/smooth-love-potion).   This   translated
to a monthly income of US$ 1,799 or an annual income of US$ 21,585
(0.399727*4500*12). In 2020, the average monthly salary in the Philippines
was about 45,000 PHP[e] (US$ 894). A 2020 survey conducted among repa-
triated Filipino overseas workers (OFWs) during the COVID-19 pandemic found that more than half of the respondents had a monthly income in
the 20,000–50,000 PHP (US$ 397–US$ 993) range.[f] This means that an
average Filipinos Axie Infinity player earned significantly higher than an
average Filipino working in the Philippines as well as an average OFW in
July 2021.

A criticism of the game concerns the volatility of cryptocurrencies. The
price of SLP declined following the all-time high level of July 2021. For instance, on December 11, 2021, 1 SLP was trading for around US$ 0.03751
(https://coinmarketcap.com/currencies/smooth-love-potion/). This trans-
lates to an annual income of US$ 2,026.

Notes:

a Mark Sullivan (Dec 9, 2021) '5 Surprising Ways NFTs Could Transcend the Hype and Become Seriously Useful, https://www.fastcompany.com/90704232/new-uses-for-nfts.

b cointelegraph.com (Dec 31, 2021) 'NFTs Find True Utility with the Advent of the Metaverse in 2021' https://cointelegraph.com/news/nfts-find-true-utility-with-the-advent-of-the-metaverse-in-2021.

c L Callon-Butler, (July 17, 2021) 'Leah How Axie Infinity Creates Work in the Metaverse. A Cute NFT Pet Game Called Axie Infinity Is Currently Raking in More Protocol Revenue than Ethereum and Bitcoin. Filipinos Are Benefitting' *CoinDesk Insights*, https://www.coindesk.com/markets/2021/07/17/how-axie-infinity-creates-work-in-the-metaverse/.

d L Callon-Butler (Aug 26, 2020) 'The NFT Game that Makes Cents for Filipinos during COVID: Axie Infinity, a NFT Trading Game Running on Ethereum, Has Proven a Pandemic Lifeline for a Small Community North of Manila' *CoinDesk Insights*, https://www.coindesk.com/markets/2020/08/26/the-nft-game-that-makes-cents-for-filipinos-during-covid/

e 'Average monthly salary in the Philippines from 2016 to 2020 (in 1,000 Philippine pesos)' (Jun 21, 2021) https://www.statista.com/statistics/1048636/philippines-monthly-average-salary/.

f 'Range of monthly income of returning overseas Filipino workers (OFW) while abroad in 2020 (in Philippine pesos) (Jun 30, 2021)' https://www.statista.com/statistics/1245088/repatriated-ofw-philippines-income-range/.

Web 3.0 and the metaverse are being heralded by industry analysts and media commentators as the next big things, which underscores the importance of increasing political and economic engagement with the metaverse. For instance, Barbados become the first country to acquire virtual land and create a 'metaverse embassy'.[38] The importance of initiatives such as this becomes clear if we look at the rapid growth of the metaverse economy. For instance, a study of digital currency investing services company Grayscale Investments noted that the metaverse can provide a US$ 1 trillion annual revenue opportunity in the near future.[39] Labour exporting countries also need to analyse the economic opportunities offered by the metaverse (See In Focus 8.1).

Finally, it is important for policymakers to understand the various risks associated with illegal transactions involving cryptocurrencies. For instance, a cryptocurrency tumbler (also referred to as a crypto mixer or crypto mixing) is a paid service in which potentially traceable coins are mixed with other clean coins in order to make it harder to trace them.[40] By doing so, a coin's potential

[38] Michael J Casey (Nov 19, 2021) 'Why Barbados' Metaverse Embassy Matters. Some Say It's a Gimmick for the Island Nation to Buy a Plot of Land in Decentraland. But They're Not Thinking Big Enough, Says CoinDesk's Chief Content Officer. The Metaverse Has Plenty of Promise for Governments'. *CoinDesk Insights*, https://www.coindesk.com/policy/2021/11/19/why-barbados-metaverse-embassy-matters/.

[39] Harry Robertson (Nov 25, 2021) 'The Metaverse Is a $1 Trillion Opportunity, Crypto Giant Grayscale Says as Virtual Land Sales Boom' https://markets.businessinsider.com/news/currencies/metaverse-1-trillion-opportunity-grayscale-virual-land-sales-decentraland-2021-11.

[40] Gizmodo Australia (2021) 'What the Heck Is a Crypto Tumbler and Is It Even Legal?' [online] Available at: https://www.gizmodo.com.au/2021/06/cryptocurrency-tumblers-mixers-explained/.

connection to suspicious wallets or transactions is 'washed'.[41] Such a practice poses various risks, especially related to the anti-money laundering (AML) category.[42] Development of national capabilities to tackle such illicit actions is critical to benefit from the transformative power of blockchain.

8.5   IMPLICATIONS FOR CONSUMERS AND INVESTORS

Consumers can play a huge role in promoting sustainable supply chains. This is especially important since the work of commodity producers and farmers in the Global South is undervalued. To take an example, on January 14, 2019, news website *Reuters* published a story about an Ethiopian coffee farmer, who received US$ 0.29 for a kilogram of coffee beans.[43] At that time, the average price of regular cappuccino in the US was US$ 4.02.[44] For the amount of coffee used to prepare a cappuccino, the Ethiopian coffee farmer's share translated to less than US$ 0.01 for every cup of cappuccino sold in the US.[45] Similarly, in an article published in NextBillion website, which explores the links between enterprise and development, the executive director of Uganda's National Union of Coffee Agribusinesses and Farm Enterprises (NUCAFE) noted that the country's coffee farmers receive less than 5 per cent of the retail value of coffee beans they grow. He also stated that many Ugandan coffee farmers make less than US$ 1/day.[46] Only consumers can force dominant players in the commodity supply chains, such as the global coffee supply chains, to change. An obvious way to force unjust supply chain participants to act more fairly would be to ask them to provide blockchain verified information regarding payments to different value chain partners. When there is the possibility of

---

[41]   Toshendra Kumar Sharma (July 10, 2018) 'How Is Blockchain Verifiable by Public and Yet Anonymous?' *Blockchain Council* (last visited May 2, 2021), available at: https://www.blockchain-council.org/blockchain/how-is-blockchain-verifiable -by-public-and-yet-anonymous/.

[42]   Gizmodo Australia (n 40).

[43]   A Maasho and N Hunt (Jan 14, 2019) 'Coffee Price Slump Leaves Farmers Earning Less than a Cent a Cup' https://www.reuters.com/article/coffee-farmers/coffee -price-slump-leaves-farmers-earning-less-than-a-cent-a-cup-idUSL8N1YJ4D2.

[44]   H Byrnes (2019). 'The Price You'll Pay for a Cup of Coffee around the World' https://www.usatoday.com/story/money/2019/03/02/coffee-price-cost-regular -cappuccino-around-world/38920143/.

[45]   N Kshetri (2021) 'Blockchain and Sustainable Supply Chain Management in Developing Countries' *International Journal of Information Management* Vol 60,   October   102376   https://www.sciencedirect.com/science/article/abs/pii/ S0268401221000694.

[46]   J Nkandu (May 31, 2018) 'Why Coffee Farmers Are Poor – And How an Innovative Ownership Model Can Help' https://nextbillion.net/why-coffee-farmers-are -poor-and-how-an-innovative-ownership-model-can-help/.

being punished by consumers, firms are less likely to engage in unfair behaviours. A challenge in the non-blockchain world, however, is that there is no data to assess the fairness of some participants' behaviours. Blockchain-based transparency makes it more difficult to hide unfair or unjust practices.

In the Web2.0 era, online gamers spend their money and time to play games just for having fun. Blockchain-based games allow consumers to make money, and have fun (see In Focus 8.2 below).

IN FOCUS 8.2 PLAY-TO-EARN (P2E) GAMES IN THE METAVERSE ALLOW PLAYERS TO OWN THEIR CREATIONS AS NFTS

Play-to-earn (P2E) games are among the most popular leisure activities in the metaverse. In such games, players are able to monetize the time and effort they have invested playing, in building digital assets in the metaverse.

P2E games are built on blockchain. In the metaverse, players can own their creations in the game in the form of an NFT. The NFTs they created can be traded within the game. They can also be sold for tokens, which can be exchanged for fiat currency.

To take an example, NFTcraft.game is a P2E NFT game metaverse, which is built on the Polygon blockchain. The game is centred around the goal of collecting as much of the game's governance token, Radiant ($RAD) as possible. The Radiant is used as fuel for a rocket that is used to capture a large asteroid that contains the neo-gold Ether (ETH), which is the most valuable substance in the universe.[a]

At the start, a player chooses the NFT dwarf and the islands that the dwarf will explore. A rarer dwarf has more powerful parameters. The game's characters can be upgraded in the secondary market. Different islands vary in terms of size and resource abundance. In addition to earning the Radiant, the players can extract various resources. For example, rubies can be used to temporarily increase a dwarf's parameters. The players can build NFT objects in the Main City using those resources. At the end of the main game cycle, ETH rewards are distributed to the player. The more Radiant a player owns, the larger the reward they receive at the end of the game.[b]

Notes:

[a] cointelegraph.com (Nov 11, 2021) 'NFTcraft: Gaming Platform and Metaverse' https://cointelegraph.com/press-releases/nftcraft-gaming-platform-and-metaverse

[b] R Wardrop (Nov 21, 2021) 'NFTCraft : The First Play-to-earn Game Combining the Metaverse with NFT Elements' https://nftevening.com/nftcraft-the-first-play-to-earn-game-combining-the-metaverse-with-nft-elements/.

Unsurprisingly P2E (play-to-earn) games are among the most notable trends in the blockchain industry. In 2021Q3, on average, the blockchain industry registered 1.54 million daily Unique Active Wallets (UAWs), 49 per cent of which interacted with blockchain-based games.[47] For instance, blockchain-based gaming platforms such as IQeon pay to play the game. Players are able to convert in-game currencies into IQN tokens, which can be exchanged into digital assets on crypto trading platforms such as EXMO, Exrates, BitForex, and HitBTC.[48]

IN FOCUS 8.3 CYBERSECURITY ISSUES IN CRYPTOCURRENCIES

Cybersecurity issues at various levels need to be considered in cryptocurrencies. First, the coins and tokens themselves could be vulnerable to hacking. For instance, as noted in Chapter 5, Ethereum was hacked in 2016 by exploiting vulnerability in the DAO's (decentralized autonomous organization) code.

At the next level, cryptocurrency exchanges which facilitate cryptocurrency transactions and help customers buy and sell cryptocurrencies, have their own vulnerabilities. Such exchanges function as centralized web services that are deployed in a cloud or a data centre. The custom codes in such web services are not built on blockchain.

There are several examples of such exchanges being hacked. In August 2021, Japanese cryptocurrency exchange Liquid was hacked.[a] According to blockchain analytics company Elliptic, cybercriminals stole US$ 97 million worth of Ethereum and other digital coins.[b]

Similar problems have been encountered in NFT marketplaces such as OpenSea and Rarible, which function in a centralized manner.[c] In September 2021, a bug in the OpenSea token market led to the disappearance of 42 NFTs that were valued at more than US$ 100,000.[d]

Finally, cybercriminals can also hack cryptocurrency wallets. There are two options for a cryptocurrency wallet: hot wallet (e.g., account in exchange/website-based wallet) and cold wallet (e.g., hardware or paper-based). The coins and tokens stored in a hot wallet are under the control of the wallet provider. For instance, custom protocols are used for accounts in crypto exchanges, which are often not based on a blockchain system.[e]

---

[47]   Pedro Herrera (Oct 14, 2021) 'BGA Blockchain Game Report Q3 2021' https://dappradar.com/blog/bga-blockchain-game-report-q3-2021.

[48]   Bitcoinist (2021) 'How Blockchain Technology Is Transforming Online Gaming Landscape' [online] Bitcoinist.com. Available at: https://bitcoinist.com/how-blockchain-technology-is-transforming--online-gaming-landscape/.

A large number of cryptocurrency users have become victims of digital wallet theft. The US-based pay television business news channel CNBC reported that thousands of Coinbase customers in the US had complained about such thefts. There were many instances of account takeovers, in which users' money disappears from their account.

An approach to hack cryptocurrency wallets is 'SIM swapping', in which a hacker dupes a wireless carrier to transfer a target's phone number to their own device. SIM swapping is reported to be associated with many of the cryptocurrency thefts.[f]

By taking over a wallet holder's phone number the hacker can intercept SMS-based two-factor authentication codes. The information is used to access and steal cryptocurrency accounts.[g] It is reported that skilled hackers can steal money in a wallet in less than 30 minutes after a successful SIM swapping.[h] In November 2021, a Canadian teen was arrested for allegedly engaging in such scam. The teen was accused of stealing US$ 36.5 million worth of cryptocurrency from a US victim.[i]

Notes:

[a] Chris Morris (Aug 19, 2021) 'Hackers Hit Japanese Crypto Exchange, Steal Nearly $100 Million' https://fortune.com/2021/08/19/hackers-liquid-crypto-exchange-japan-100-million-ethereum/.

[b] elliptic.co (Aug 19, 2021) 'Liquid Exchange Hacked: $97 Million Stolen' https://www.elliptic.co/blog/liquid-exchange-hacked-94-million-stolen.

[c] L Keller (Dec 17, 2021) 'Does Content Moderation on Platforms like OpenSea Amount to Censorship?' https://forkast.news/does-opensea-censor-nft-content/.

[d] '$100,000 worth of NFTs disappear forever, thanks to OpenSea bug Cryptocurrency' (Sept 9, 2021) https://www.investing.com/news/cryptocurrency-news/100000-worth-of-nfts-disappear-forever-thanks-to-opensea-bug-2611477.

[e] Ivan Novikov (May 3, 2018) 'The Three Layers of Cryptocurrency Security' https://www.forbes.com/sites/forbestechcouncil/2018/05/03/the-three-layers-of-cryptocurrency-security/?sh=12e0ec3e29aa.

[f] Scott Zamost, Eamon Javers, Jennifer Schlesinger, Stephen Council and Angélica Serrano-Román (Aug 24, 2021) 'Coinbase Slammed for What Users Say Is Terrible Customer Service after Hackers Drain Their Accounts' https://www.cnbc.com/2021/08/24/coinbase-slammed-for-terrible-customer-service-after-hackers-drain-user-accounts.html.

[g] Kate Rooney (Nov 21, 2018) 'Hacker Lifts $1 Million in Cryptocurrency Using San Francisco Man's Phone Number, Prosecutors Say' https://www.cnbc.com/2018/11/21/hacker-lifts-1-million-in-cryptocurrency-using-mans-phone-number.html.

[h] Zamost et al. (n [f]).

[i] Brian Barrett (Nov 20, 2021) 'Security News This Week: A Canadian Teen Was Arrested in a $36.5M SIM-swap Heist' https://www.wired.com/story/teen-sim-swap-theft-fbi-email-hack-stripchat-leak-security-news/.

The blockchain industry has become popular among investors, but they need to be aware that investment scams in cryptocurrency have proliferated in recent years. Millions of cryptocurrency investors have been scammed out of massive sums of real money. In 2018 alone, losses from cryptocurrency-related crimes amounted to US$ 1.7 billion.[49]

Likewise, the meteoric rise in frauds involving cryptocurrencies has been an issue of pressing concern to investors and consumers (see In Focus 8.3). According to Chainalysis, in 2021, investors lost US$ 2.8 billion in DeFi (decentralized finance) scams. The 'rug pull' scam, in which the founders of a project raise investment money and disappear, has been especially growing rapidly. In 2021, investors lost about US$ 3 billion to rug pull scams, which are mainly related to DeFi tokens.[50] In 2021, rug pulls accounted for 37 per cent of all incomes of DeFi scammers compared to 1 per cent in 2020.[51]

Even seasoned investors fall prey to such scams. It was reported that Mark Cuban suffered a loss of about $200,000 in a DeFi investment as he became a victim of a rug pull scam. The value of the DeFi token reduced from $60 to almost zero in a day due to panic selling when crypto whales dumped their holdings.[52]

In order to avoid falling victim to DeFi scams, Chainalysis has recommended users not to invest in new tokens that have not undergone a code audit. In a code audit, a third-party company analyses the smart contract code and confirms publicly that there are no mechanisms to allow developers to gain access to investor funds.[53]

More recently NFTs have been an attractive category for fraudsters. Fraudsters are reported to be selling NFTs of valuable artworks without the knowledge and permission of the artist. For instance, a scammer had listed the Chinese artist Qing Han's (known as Qinni) popular artwork titled *Bird Cage* on NFT social-marketplace, Twinci. Twinci subsequently deleted the NFT and banned the account, when the fraud was reported. However, other Twinci accounts had five other listings connected to NFTs of Qing's artworks. Some

---

[49]   Gertrude Chavez-Dreyfus (Jan 29, 2019) 'Cryptocurrency Thefts, Scams Hit $1.7 Billion in 2018: Report' https://www.reuters.com/article/us-crypto-currency-crime/cryptocurrency-thefts-scams-hit-1-7-billion-in-2018-report-idUSKCN1PN1SQ.

[50]   N Dailey (Jan 27, 2022) 'Mark Cuban Learned His Crypto Investing Lesson the Hard Way after Losing $200,000 on a Little-known Token' https://markets.businessinsider.com/news/currencies/mark-cuban-learned-crypto-lesson-after-losing-200000-coin-titan-2022-1.

[51]   Cvbj (Dec 17, 2021) 'Rug Pulls, a Prevalent Type of Cryptocurrency Scam on DeFi and Has Grown This Year' https://cvbj.biz/rug-pulls-a-prevalent-type-of-cryptocurrency-scam-on-defi-and-has-grown-this-year.html.

[52]   Dailey (n 50).

[53]   Cvbj (n 51).

NFTs were listed for as much 500 TWIN (Twinci's crypto-coin) (1 TWIN = US$ 0.54 on November 25, 2021).[54]

Many fraudulent investment schemes involving NFTs have also emerged. One example is the popular NFT project Evolved Apes, which is described on OpenSea as 'a collection of 10,000 unique NFTs trapped inside a lawless land' (https://opensea.io/collection/evolved-apes-inc). The scammers took 798 Ether out of the project's funds in multiple transfers. Proper vetting and analysis can help investors stay away from seemingly attractive but deceptive deals. Investors can use the VoIP (Voice over Internet Protocol), instant messaging and digital distribution platform Discord to understand the community behind the cryptocurrency project in order to get a feel for the project. It is also important to check if the project creator has an inflated social media following with a high proportion of fake Twitter followers. For instance, an analysis by crypto news media TrustNodes in 2019 of 50,000 new Twitter followers of Tron's founder found that about 20,000 of them had zero-day accounts created that month with almost no followers or tweets.[55] In cases such as this, Followeraudit.com (https://www.followeraudit.com/?ref=alternativeassets .club) can be used to track the number of active, inactive, and fake followers of a project.

While decentralized, open blockchains such as Bitcoin eliminate counterparty risks, which some crypto assets carry. Especially digital assets tied to real-world commodities or government-issued fiat currencies may carry counterparty risk. This is because the organization issuing the digital asset may not own or control the real-world asset to back the digital counterpart. Stablecoins are especially susceptible to counterparty risk since such coins achieve relative 'price stability' by holding the underlying asset in question as collateral. For instance, a company issuing stablecoins backed by US dollars may not actually have sufficient US dollars to back the digital assets.[56]

8.6   FUTURE RESEARCH IMPLICATIONS

In this section, we suggest several fruitful future research avenues. As discussed in Chapter 4, organizations have set a number of sustainability goals

---

[54] C Nast (July 28, 2021) 'An Artist Died. Then Thieves Made NFTs of Her Work.' [online] *Wired UK*. Available at: https://www.wired.co.uk/article/nft-fraud-qinni-art.

[55] trustnodes.com (Mar 24, 2019) 'Close to Half of Justin Sun's New Followers Revealed as Fake – Trustnodes.' [online] Available at: https://www.trustnodes.com/ 2019/03/24/close-to-half-of-justin-suns-new-followers-revealed-as-fake.

[56] Exodus (n.d.) 'What Is Counterparty Risk?' [online] Exodus support. Available at: https://support.exodus.com/article/794-what-is-counterparty-risk#:~:text=Please %20note%3A%20Counterparty%20risk%20is.

to be achieved using blockchain. Consumers' higher purchase intention and willingness to pay more for products that are tracked with blockchain are a precondition to achieve these goals. Prior research has suggested that companies can obtain a price premium by using blockchain as a means to verify product quality and provenance.[57] There is a need to extend such research to sustainability. Future research thus should look at whether consumers are willing to pay more for sustainably sourced products that can be traced with blockchain solutions.

Second, blockchain systems discussed in this book utilize diverse technologies such as machine vision, the IoT (Internet of Things) and RFID (radio frequency identification) tags. Other technologies incorporated in blockchain solutions include satellite imagery and digital twins.[58] Several categories of information collected and shared in such systems include environmental conditions (e.g., temperature and humidity), economic variables (e.g., earnings of supply chain participants), and personal information (e.g., identity). In order to provide a systematic understanding of these phenomena, future researchers might develop a typology of indicators and sources of information in various blockchain systems.

Finally, companies are combining two hot digital concepts – NFTs and the metaverse – in their product and marketing communications strategies. NFTs are emerging as an important tool to increase brand awareness.[59] Some companies are designing and developing products based on NFTs that are responsive to the need of the marketplace of the metaverse. In light of these observations, future research can examine how firms are using non-fungible tokens in product and marketing communications strategies.

8.7   FINAL THOUGHT

Blockchain is as disruptive and transformative as other revolutionary technologies such as the Internet. However, most of the potential of this technology to disrupt economies and transform societies can be materialized only by

---

[57]   S Cao, U Dulleck, W Powell, C Turner-Morris, V Natanelov and M Foth (2020) 'BeefLedger Blockchain-credentialed Beef Exports to China: Early Consumer Insights' Queensland University of Technology, Australia https://eprints.qut.edu.au/200267/15/BeefLedger_Survey_Results_Report_V7.pdf.

[58]   N Kshetri (2021) *Blockchain and Supply Chain Management* (Elsevier, Amsterdam, Netherlands, Oxford, UK and New York, USA).

[59]   eur-lex.europa.eu (2019) 'EUR-Lex - 52020PC0593 - EN - EUR-Lex.' [online] Available at: https://eurlex.europa.eu/legalcontent/EN/TXT/?uri=CELEX:52020PC0593.

combining with other new and emerging technologies such as AI (artificial intelligence), the IoT and satellite imagery.

Blockchain's transformative potential, however, varies widely depending on the contexts, industries, economic sectors, types of transactions and other aspects. For instance, blockchain solutions are more likely to be adopted in a B2B (business-to-business) setting since key value propositions of blockchain such as trust, security and privacy are more important in this setting. Likewise, blockchain has a higher value proposition in tracing and tracking digital assets compared to physical assets. The last-mile problem has been a key barrier that impedes the growth of blockchain's deployment in the transaction and management of physical assets. However, this problem is likely to be resolved over time with the development of third-party verification systems in the form of an oracle to verify events in the real world.

In closing, with the development of ecosystems around this technology, blockchain's potential to act as a 'trust machine' as noted in Chapter 1 is likely to be realized across more and more contexts and settings. While the real truth in any situation is not easy to verify directly, by combining blockchain with other emerging technologies, parties in a transaction can reach as close to the real truth as possible.

Index